ACRL Publications in Librarianship no. 47

Academic Libraries

Research Perspectives

MARY JO LYNCH
editor

ARTHUR YOUNG
associate editor

American Library Association
Chicago and London 1990

Text prepared by ALA Books, using a
BestInfo Wave 4 prepress system and
output to a Linotronic 500 by
Publications Association Typesetter

Display type prepared by RT Associates, Inc.

Printed on 50-pound Glatfelter, a pH-neutral
stock, and bound in 10-point Carolina
cover stock by Braun-Brumfield, Inc.

The paper used in this publication meets the minimum requirements of American National Standard for Information Sciences – Permanence of Paper for Printed Library Materials, ANSI Z39.48-1984. ∞

Library of Congress Cataloging-in-Publication Data

Academic libraries : research perspectives / edited by Mary Jo Lynch.
p. cm. – (ACRL publications in librarianship ; no. 47)
ISBN 0-8389-0532-3 (alk. paper)
1. Libraries, University and college. I. Lynch, Mary Jo.
II. Series.
Z674.A75 no. 47
[Z675.U5]
020 s – dc20
[027.7] 90-32120

94 93 92 91 90 5 4 3 2 1

Contents

Introduction

Academic libraries are changing rapidly and profoundly today as practitioners learn how to take advantage of the opportunities offered by new technologies for generating, storing, and transmitting information. Those developments have great potential to enhance the library's ability to fulfill its historic mission—to organize information and facilitate its use. The challenge of advancing technology, combined with related economic and social dynamics, makes this a very uncertain time for academic librarians. It seems a most opportune time to examine the research base of academic librarianship.

Some may argue that we have no time to look back or that research is a lofty, theoretical enterprise whereas the current need is for practical skills and political power. Others will recognize that the research of the past contributes to the knowledge base that informs the field today. We can move forward with greater certainty if we know what that knowledge base is and can think about the future in relation to it. ACADEMIC LIBRARIES: RESEARCH PERSPECTIVES is intended to provide that context and to provoke that thinking. Experts have been asked to examine recent research and current issues in major topic areas and consider the following questions: What have we learned from research that might help us deal with present and future issues in this area? If past research does not seem useful in addressing these issues, why is it irrelevant? In any case, what research questions should be addressed now and what methodologies seem useful?

The essays in this volume focus primarily on the last twenty years, but earlier work is mentioned if that seemed appropriate. Each author was asked to examine basic and applied research on the assigned topic and to select the most meaningful studies to describe and evaluate here. Doctoral research was considered along with action research, in-house studies, and consultant studies if the results or methodology were judged to be useful beyond a specific site.

Studies by researchers outside the field of library and information science were also included if they dealt with library issues.

The volume begins with a consideration of what has traditionally been considered the basic component of any library—the collection. Charles Osburn's "Collection Development and Management" points out, however, that the current perspectives on this topic which both flow from and give direction to research are essentially new in the last two decades. Next is "Bibliographical Control" by Elaine Svenonius. Although her essay is organized around three very traditional topics—descriptive cataloging, classification, and subject heading assignment—the focus throughout is on the research problems and possibilities that result from the use of computers to provide better or cheaper means of bibliographical control.

The next three essays deal with research on library use. Jo Bell Whitlatch surveys research in "Access Services"—an area of concern that was not even conceptualized until quite recently. The essay deals with three very broad topics: the role of accessibility in determining information source use, user interaction with library staff and bibliographic systems, and physical access to library buildings and to documents both within libraries and from remote locations. Mary George surveys the research in "Instructional Services." Although she is devoted to the topic as practitioner, editor, and researcher, George has no illusions about the quantity and quality of research within the vast literature devoted to it. Paul Metz's "Bibliometrics" reviews the library use and citation studies that make an important contribution to librarianship as well as to the emerging science of bibliometrics.

The next two essays differ from the others in that they do not review a large body of existing research. Instead, they present a perspective on what research is needed. William Gray Potter's "Insurmountable Opportunities: Advanced Technology and the Academic Library" uses Vannevar Bush's 1945 conception of the "memex" as a way of organizing his presentation. Most of the research that informed those developments was done outside the library world, but Potter describes what research is needed to turn his own vision of the memex into reality for library users. In "Analysis and Library Management," Malcolm Getz describes the research he believes is needed to assist library managers in making decisions. He points out that most existing work fails to define the causal connections between the actions library managers take and how library use changes as a consequence. Such connections are essential to good management.

Finally, Beverly Lynch's "Management Theory and Organizational Structure," reviews the small body of research on those topics as they relate to academic libraries and comments on two lists of research questions.

The editors are aware that numerous topics important to academic librarians are not covered by separate chapters in this volume. The index shows, however, that almost every important topic is covered somewhere. In selecting a group of topics for specific treatment here, we looked for areas where a large body of generalizable research existed and areas where research is not so abundant but where we could identify an author willing to deal with research aspects of the topic. History also is omitted in this book because it is not a component of the practice of librarianship but is, instead, an approach to it and deserves separate treatment.

Originally, the authors were asked to consider the two lists of research questions that follow Lynch's essay as they thought about future needs in their own area. Most authors indicated that this requirement could not be easily accommodated, and it was removed from the specifications for the essays. Readers of this volume may wish to consider these questions, as the lists come from agencies that have been and will continue to be influential forces in academic librarianship. The first list was sent to interested persons in August 1987 by the president at the time of the Association of Research Libraries, Herbert Johnson.The second list appeared in the Council of Library Resources (CLR) Annual Report for 1985, in which CLR announced "an expanded research program." Both of the lists are thoughtful summaries of issues that are of great concern to the most scholarly of academic libraries. The issues are of interest to all libraries, however, and provide a useful context for examining research on academic librarianship.

The editors believe that ACADEMIC LIBRARIES: RESEARCH PERSPECTIVES will be of interest to many groups in the library community. Academic librarians will find it helpful in expanding their understanding of the work they do every day. Researchers will find it useful in providing ideas and background for future work. Library school faculty and students will find it an indispensable aid to the study of a major component of librarianship. The volume has considerable value also for practitioners in other types of libraries and for researchers, teachers, and students interested in those libraries. Since libraries of all types share functions and problems, the research pertaining to academic libraries can illuminate functions and problems in the other types as well. All of us face a complex future and need to be armed with the knowledge that is produced by research.

Charles B. Osburn

Collection Development and Management

In 1987, following public hearings on a draft manual and a review of it by more than one hundred librarians, the Collection Management and Development Committee of the Resources and Technical Services Division of the American Library Association concluded that the meanings of the terms *collection development* and *collection management* "are not themselves uniformly perceived in the library profession."[1] Consequently, these terms remained undefined in the first number in the committee's "Collection Management and Development Guides" series. This hesitancy reflects the profession's reaction to the rapid evolution of an unnamed, dispersed, slipshod operation for which the responsibility was ambiguous into an activity that is perceived as inherently pervasive. For purposes of the present chapter, collection management is defined as a process of information gathering, communication, coordination, policy formulation, evaluation, and planning. These processes, in turn, influence decisions about the acquisition, retention, and provision of access to information sources in support of the intellectual needs of a given library community. Collection development is the part of collection management that primarily deals with decisions about the acquisition of materials.

Until two decades ago the literature of collection management was sparse. What literature existed had primarily to do with selection of materials, almost as an isolated phenomenon, but even that literature had mostly to do with public libraries, not academic libraries. Tinkering with data on size and growth of academic library collections was an attraction, as were attempts to quantify aspects of use and user behavior by discipline, and there were a few major studies that quickly achieved influence. But the more inclusive literature of collection management did not really assume a corpus until the early 1970s when it became evident to all but the most tenaciously conservative that the relationship between the mounting information explosion and diminishing fiscal resources had become severe and would surely remain so for a long time. Collections had to be developed that no longer would be ideal in their own terms but that would reflect as closely as possible the university's goals and priorities. The literature of collection management, therefore, issued from professional recognition of crisis and change.

In the 1970s, textbooks on the broader considerations of collection development began to appear, some of them having undergone several revisions by the late 1980s. Research and thinking in the field were summarized for the first time in 1980, with the publication of the two-volume set *Collection Development in Libraries: A Treatise.*[2] It was around that time that the literature was brought under rather good bibliographic control, although now it is becoming ever more entwined with other aspects of librarianship and information science, as well as with the more recently emerging field of scholarly communication. In 1978, Magrill published a review of the literature as it applied to university libraries, treating primarily the literature of the preceding twenty years.[3] With a few exceptions, each year since then the journal *Library Resources and Technical Services* has published in its summer or fall issue a review of the previous year's literature on collection management, authored by various scholars, while professional activities in the area of collection management are reviewed annually in the *ALA Yearbook* under the heading "Collection Development" or "Collection Management." Along with *Dissertation Abstracts International,* these sources provided the formal framework for the bibliographic searching required of the present chapter. Included in this chapter are works that have been influential in, or can be expected to become influential in, the practice of and the thinking related to collection management. (While most of the titles cited report research, others reflect original thinking of a different kind that also has advanced collection management.) Reference is made to works that are more than twenty years old when they are particularly valuable in understanding the significance of more recent contributions.

It is to be expected that the research supporting the profession of librarianship would be applied far more than basic, and that within collection management, which links the constrained functions of the library to the unconstrained universe of academic research and instruction the library serves, the approaches and methodologies would be diverse. A growing part of the recent literature seeks easy answers and solutions through the collection of data. What these studies provide are pieces of a puzzle, to which many more pieces need to be provided and then assembled properly to present an integral picture of the situation under study. But it should be noted that the convergence of computer applications with a heightened interest in achieving an understanding of issues in collection management has resulted in the breaking of ground on many fronts.

Much of the scholarship in collection management is the result of reflection based on experience, informed speculation that helps posit a new theory or perception, which then stimulates further research. Lacking in research in collection management is the cumulative product that makes possible the leap from theory to practice. Too many of our findings are, alone, highly inconclusive both statistically and logically.

Organization and Staffing

The central function of collection development and management is the selection of materials, a function whose organization and staffing are highly dependent upon the degree to which the library bears responsibility for selection decisions. It is primarily within the area of academic librarianship that the debate about whether librarians or teaching faculty should make these decisions has been waged and continues without clear resolution.

Nearly a century ago, at a time when selection was totally a responsibility of the university faculty, Potter described succinctly the imbalances that develop in collections that are built by faculty, and that then hinder future generations of scholars.[4] Several decades later, Waples and Lasswell conducted a survey that supported what had become by that time the firm consensus of a growing portion of the academic library profession. They established a list of 500 books in the social sciences, which were judged by faculty to be the most important titles, and compared it to the holdings of some of the largest university libraries and the New York Public Library. NYPL was found to hold 92 percent of the titles, while Harvard held the next greatest percent, 63, and other large university libraries held consistently lesser percentages of the titles.[5] In this study, the university library selection had been a responsibility of faculty, while librarians were responsible for that function at NYPL, which operated with a smaller acquisitions budget than the university libraries in the study.

The Waples and Lasswell study was limited to the social sciences and was dependent on a list that would likely be as challengeable as any other list of best books, but it does suggest strongly that, if long-term value to scholarship is a criterion for good selection, then library subject specialists can do the job better than faculty. With attention to the short-term value to scholarship of selections made by faculty versus those made by librarians, Evans also found greater success among librarians. In his study, success was determined by circulation activity during the first twelve months after acquisition of more than five hundred titles, studied randomly in four universities. Evans's assumption was that librarians would be more successful than faculty because of their contact with a greater number of patrons.[6]

Danton, working a quarter century later than Waples and Lasswell, reinforced their findings from a somewhat different and less objective perspective. In his highly influential analysis of book selection, Danton studied the use of subject specialists in university libraries in Germany, a nation whose scholarship had served as the model for the United States during the nineteenth century and first half of the twentieth. There he found the strongest aspect of the subject specialist system to be the area of collection development. Comparing the German approach to collection development with the American, he found them quite opposite. The American university library collection, according to Danton, was the result of "scores of thousands of individual, uncoordinated, usually isolated decisions, independently made by hundreds of faculty members," while the German university library collection was the result of "a planned, purposeful activity, having balance and coordination."[7]

The Subject Specialist Movement

At about the time Danton was establishing a rational basis for librarian responsibility for collection development rather than faculty responsibility for it, subject librarians, often called "bibliographers," began to be used more and more frequently in university libraries to engage in collection development. With the theoretical basis laid for this innovation in American academic librarianship, attention easily was drawn to its practical implementation. The experience at Indiana University was among the first to be described to the profession, and the 1966 report was quite positive.[8] Indiana had created ten subject specialist positions during the previous three years, reporting that the library's image had improved as a result, and that the library was viewed as more personalized and sensitive to the user. The report is highly subjective and impressionistic, and it ignores the many problems inherent in engaging subject specialists. But the contribution is important because it reports on a systematic, highly visible experiment, and because it describes expectations for the subject specialist that go consistently beyond the narrow function of selection during a critical period in the history of American university librarianship.

Subsequent literature on the debate over responsibility for selection and on the role of the subject specialist places the function more in the context of a social system than had been done before. Haro advocated expansion of the subject specialist role into reference, research, instruction, and liaison between library and faculty.[9] Tuttle argued against the pervasiveness of the position advocated by Haro, noting both the impossibility of carrying out all those functions and the arrogance of presuming to be able to do so.[10] Based on a series of interviews funded by the Council on Library Resources, Smith's research revealed that, while services seemed to have improved in university libraries employing subject specialists, new problems also were emerging as direct results of engaging subject specialists. These positions, for example, did not fit the bureaucracy or the hierarchy as it traditionally had been understood, thus leading to a variety of negative implications inside the library's social system.[11]

By the late 1970s and early 1980s the debate about who should select materials in academic libraries was pretty much determined de facto by the patterns of practice in those libraries. Based upon a series of interviews in nineteen academic research libraries, a report by Baatz revealed a common concern among librarians that the faculty did not manifest much interest in collection development. He also found that the faculty expressed interest only when they had lost confidence in the librarians' ability to discharge that responsibility satisfactorily and that faculty had otherwise relinquished the collection development responsibility, by and large, except in the science and engineering fields.[12] This series of interviews followed a standard format and was conducted by a seasoned collection development officer, in possession of the experience necessary to fully understand the content of the interviews and to pursue implications of the answers. It is reported in an informal tone that should not, however, detract from its value.

All academic libraries did not follow this path, as disclosed by Dudley in his analysis of the organizational implications of collection development.[13] Libraries serving academic institutions of smaller size and less complexity than comprehensive universities, and without a strong research mission, continue to rely heavily on faculty for selection decisions in all fields, and the organizational structure of the library has not been visibly affected. Dudley's findings are not drawn from an investigation that is in any way scientific, but rather from his informal exchange of thought and experience with many college librarians over a considerable number of years.

Perhaps the most eloquent arguments against the use of subject specialists in the library for purposes of selection were advanced by Dickenson, whose admonitions and recommendations are founded more on reason than observation. Central to his position on this issue are the unarguable thoughts that faculty possess a better understanding of the subject matter of their research as well as first-hand knowledge of their own needs. A forum that surrounds Dickenson's views with six responses from both librarians and faculty summarizes the debate at its zenith.[14] What emerges from this forum is a consensus that raises the issue to a new plateau, the plateau on which it now rests. And that is the increasingly widespread notion that library materials selection in an academic setting must result from the combined efforts of library and faculty, with librarians managing the business of gathering information from the faculty and transforming it into policy to guide selection decisions.

Broader Organizational Concerns

The chief reason behind this resolution of the debate about selection responsibility in academic libraries is to be found in the rapid evolution of collection development into an integral part of library operations and planning.

Sloan was perhaps the first to study in a systematic way the organizational patterns of collection development as they began to emerge in the early 1970s in university libraries. Based on examination of organization charts and other internal documents from twenty-four libraries in the northeastern United States, her study found three fundamental models for the organization of collection development: dispersed among larger functional units; a distinct activity in a separate administrative unit; a coordinated function carried on by specialists drawn from various units and other responsibilities for the purpose of collection development.[15] Although collection development had become clearly a library responsibility by that time, and subject specialists constituted an accepted part of the work force in libraries, no single organizational model for collection development had established itself. More than a decade after Sloan's analysis, Sohn's survey of ninety-three members of the Association of Research Libraries revealed little movement toward a standard model for collection development, but it did bring to light other considerations.[16] While there is no predominant organizational pattern for collection development among the seventy-three libraries that responded to the survey, an administrative officer of the library had oversight responsibility for the function, in most cases, signifying that collection development had been upgraded in importance. More significantly, however, is the demonstration that the collection development responsibility was becoming more complex as it became more involved in and integrated into other sets of library responsibilities and activities.

Analysis of Functions

Owing to the pervasiveness of collections in library functions, this trend toward formal interconnectedness was identifiable very shortly after the responsibility for collection development was absorbed by the library. But Lopez, writing in 1969, was ahead of his time in his assertion of the basic functions of collection development, for he drew from his own experience as bibliographer and middle manager a profound understanding of the full implications of what is now called collection management.[17] He incorporates into the bibliographer's responsibilities fiscal management, marketing, planning, evaluation, review, quality control, and resource sharing. When these considerations are taken into account, the notion of selecting the best books becomes highly complex and raises questions about the amount of time required to engage in an activity whose product traditionally has been expected to be simply the addition of volumes to the local collection. Those who have studied collection development in an attempt to determine a model of operation from which could be extracted production standards and other predictable elements of the function, such as time required, have not been successful. Having applied a structural-functional model of social science research to collection development, Ferguson concludes that it failed to yield useful results because "the human behavior that it dissects is not conducive to quantification."[18] Hazen's effort to discover a model applicable to collection development concludes with the thought that it "entails almost bewildering complexity. . . The model here advanced is not now quantifiable in all its parts. It may never be."[19]

Adequate staffing of collection management has long been a perceived problem, especially as it increasingly is expected to assume more responsibilities. Bryant attempts to establish a model for this purpose, dividing collection development into two components: microdecisions based on specific items and communications with the client.[20] Admittedly the data used are not verifiable, and much of the model is drawn from impression. But Bryant's discussion of the elements that should be incorporated in the model and their possible variations is quite useful, for it clarifies the issues that remain to be resolved.

Qualifications of Staff

Relatively little has been published about the specific qualifications of collection development librarians. Based on practical experience and observation, Osburn summarized the qualifications of the successful collection management librarian to include knowledge of the information and publication universe; ability to control that information bibliographically; knowledge of the community to be served related to publication of information; understanding of the likely causes of change in the information universe and in the community; ability to monitor the information universe of the community; knowledge of signs of change in each; ability to adjust policy and procedures; knowledge of quality control techniques; and ability to effectively integrate collection development policy and procedures into library operations.[21]

More recent descriptions of the desired qualifications of academic librarians, generally, and of research library directors, specifically, imply similar characteristics. For example, in describing desirable qualifications of the library director, Weber emphasizes "a broader understanding of the academic environment and of the teaching and research" along with managerial skills, options, and techniques, singling out interpersonal and supervisory skills.[22] In their separate assessments of the desirable attributes of current and future academic library professionals, Battin and Holley reinforce the importance of these qualifications.[23]

One could argue that as the pervasiveness or the essentiality of collection development in librarianship has become more and more evident, the qualifications of academic librarians generally have begun to emphasize environmentally conscious management abilities. A study based on such an hypothesis would be useful. Similarly, more could be explained about the increasing pervasiveness of collection development and management functions if we knew how the responsibilities of specific collection development positions changed over the period of the past twenty or twenty-five years.

Size and Growth of Collections

An interest in size and growth of library collections is not expressed generally throughout librarianship, but is limited to the areas of academic and research librarianship. Since these libraries tend naturally to increase in size, owing to their purposes of reflecting the continuity of cultural development, their growth began to emerge as a very visible phenomenon in the late nineteenth century. How large could a large university library become? Can we predict how large such libraries might be ten or twenty years hence? What is the relationship between size of a collection and its quality? These questions were raised partly out of intellectual and professional curiosity about a social phenomenon, partly out of the desire to plan future space, and partly to learn more about the fundamental nature of the relationship between scholarship and library management. The phenomenon of collection growth had all the appearances of facile quantifiability, while that feature in combination with the goal of prediction was a clear call for the application of statistical methodologies.

Growth Rates

Based on the hypothesis that the past is a good predictor of the future, a substantial corpus of literature has developed around the growth rates of academic research libraries during the past fifty years. The single most influential work in this area was contributed by Rider a half century ago.[24] Rider acknowledges the work of his predecessors in the study of growth and advances very forcefully several conclusions: that, indeed, the past is a model for the future; that growth is exponential; and that the pattern had been consistent for the three centuries preceding his study. Rider advanced theories that then were tested and found to be faulty by all those who followed. His work is the frame of reference in this area of research, and his axiom that research libraries double in size every sixteen years is still quoted by those who have not followed the debate.[25]

In the mid-1960s university libraries flourished as they never had before, attracting a heightened degree of attention to library growth. Thus prompted, a team at Purdue University began a long-term study of the growth phenomenon with the purpose of predicting levels of several growth variables through 1980, based on data gathered over a twenty-year period.[26] This study revealed that for part of the time the pattern was exponential, but that for the latter part it became more arithmetic. The use of regression analysis was an advance over earlier studies because it reflected more variables than had been taken into account until then.[27]

The landmark contributions to the study of growth rates of large academic library collections have been critiqued in terms of statistical methodology and consistency by Molyneux, who also carries the analysis of collection growth patterns in the Association of Research Libraries membership to 1982.[28]

Molyneux finds growth patterns similar to those revealed by the Purdue study, but he also lifts the debate about growth rate to a new level. He interprets the combination of arithmetic and exponential growth as a natural result of libraries' behavior in a changing environment. This combination he calls logistic growth.

If Molyneux is correct —and both reason and data suggest that he is —then collection growth cannot be predicted on the basis of past collection growth only. Perhaps predictability can be achieved if the most influential environmental forces can be identified and then studied historically in conjunction with past growth rates to determine the past patterns of relationships. Research of this scope would draw on expertise in many fields and surely would still not result directly in reliable predictability. But it would be a further step toward predictability, and certainly could shed considerable light on the library's interaction with its environment.

Standards

Because of the relative ease that quantification lends to comparison, the size and growth statistics that American university libraries have kept for many years have been put to use in establishing standards for the evaluation of libraries. Decades ago, when Downs distinguished four levels of a university library collection, his intention seems to have been to suggest qualitative measures for evaluation.[29] But it would not be for at least another quarter century until quantification began to yield place to qualification.

In 1965, Clapp and Jordan advanced a set of adequacy criteria that became highly influential.[30] Their criteria, referred to commonly as the Clapp-Jordan formula, were derived from a mixture of considerations and approaches, including best books in various fields, and weight factors such as relative value of older materials, programs served, and number of faculty and students. These data were then blended with the authors' experience and impressions into a formula that was tested against several select libraries. Theirs is a formula for the determination of liminal adequacy of collections. This work was intended by the authors to be only a rudimentary beginning, for they are quick to acknowledge its inconclusiveness and to point to further research that would improve the formula. The formula does not address journals nor does it consider the differing nature of research by field. But it is a significant contribution because it very quickly became a standard for evaluating collections (and designing budget requests), very quickly became a frame of reference for further development of standards, and gave considerable impetus to experimentation with formulas for other aspects of collection development.

First among the direct descendants of the Clapp-Jordan formula is the Voigt formula, published a decade later.[31] It presents a model for current acquisitions and does not depend on student count or size of collection, or even on a theory of exponential growth. Beginning with a basic number of volumes that should be added annually to meet the minimum needs of the undergraduate program, volumes are added or deducted on the basis of the existence of specified graduate or professional programs and other local conditions. For example, the distance separating the library from another research library is one condition; the number of volumes to be added for this condition may be 0, 10,000, or 20,000. The formula represents an attempt to quantify professional judgment and experience, and to rationalize and stabilize a process that otherwise is very unstable and very political. As subjective as it is, the Voigt formula has received fairly wide acceptance as a standard for planned growth, its strength residing in its adaptability to, or dependence upon, the local array of programs. Standards for collection size and growth that have been promulgated by the Association of College and Research Libraries have been influenced deeply by the Clapp-Jordan formula and the Voigt formula.[32] However, in light of other aspects of academic librarianship that are undergoing change, these formal standards also stress resource sharing and the goal of providing access. Much like current thinking that is applied to the general phenomenon of academic library collection size and growth, the formal standards are beginning to acknowledge the process considerations of a system in its environment.

Although the question of the relationship of size and growth of collections to the quality both of the collection and of the library is implicit in these quantitative studies, very little research has been devoted to this issue explicitly. Qualitative rankings of institutions and programs very often do refer to the library, the most important, if not the single, distinguishing feature of which is collection size. But this ranking is done without comment, evidently under the assumption that the larger the collection, the better the library. Rider made this assumption, noting that "there has always existed a direct correlation between the educational effectiveness of a college and the growth of its library, a correlation so close and so consistent that it cannot have been fortuitous."[33] So did Clapp and Jordan when they hypothesized the possibility of providing "a meaningful quantitative measure of adequacy in library collections," whereas Rider saw the correlation of quantity and quality as a function of growth rate.[34]

Axford tested Rider's correlation between collection growth and quality for the period 1946 to 1960 in the twenty-five largest academic members of the Association of Research Libraries and found Rider's emphasis on growth rate to be "essentially correct."[35] However, Piternick quickly took issue with Axford on this matter, pointing out the flaws and general unreliability of the data (primarily ARL statistics) that served as the basis for Axford's conclusions. Piternick carried the debate in a slightly different direction in his comparison of growth and size of libraries to comprehensive ratings of graduate programs, for his study concludes that "the magnitude of yearly gross additions, like the holdings themselves, are of more significance than growth rate in determining library quality."[36] Thus, the debate was widened, rather than closed.

Changing Environment, Changing Focus

In spite of a fair amount of research on the various implications of growth, growth rate, and size of collections, no conclusions have been reached that could be considered at once definitive and useful for planning. Anyone familiar with library statistics is aware of the variance with which they are kept and reported, even among contemporary, peer institutions. These data are bound to become less reliable as more and differing institutions are involved, and even less so over a period of decades.[37] Whatever their methodologies, the attempts heretofore to achieve a formula for the predictability of collection size have been based on data that flaw them seriously, leaving them open to much skepticism and even ridicule. More than that, the methodologies employed were fueled by simplistic notions and hypotheses. Academic library growth is not static, as Molyneux has made clear, but is likely to reflect the dynamism of its environment. Very concisely, Molyneux observes that past studies failed to distinguish between growth patterns and the processes of growth, processes that either were ignored or simply not understood by the researcher.[38] The area of growth processes and their relationship to growth patterns is rich for further investigation.

It is not surprising, then, that even less is understood about the relationship between quantitative aspects of the library collection and the qualitative aspects of the academic programs it supports. In the frequently cited assessment of quality in American graduate education conducted by Cartter, the author attempts to come to grips with this issue in his identification of discernible patterns among the twenty-nine disciplines included in the survey. One of the common patterns among the departments judged to be of highest quality was the presence of a large library collection or the close proximity of a very large collection in the field. About the institutions that are strong in all disciplines, he observes that they "invariably have major national research libraries."[39]

Do these institutions have strong collections because their stellar faculty require them or do the strong collections attract the best scholars and scientists? Probably both of these possibilities contribute considerably to the relationship of quantity and quality, but a good deal more research could shed useful light on the phenomenon. One very essential variable would be the relationship between quantity and quality within the collection. Little has been done in this area.

To what extent is the size—or even the quality—of the collection an indicator of the quality of the library? Is collection size as accurate a measure of a library's success today as it may have been thirty years ago? How valid a measure will it be thirty years from now? In just the past decade, materials selection and collection development have evolved into collection management, which continues its evolution into a more complex and dispersed function. At the same time, the provision of access has become as important a part of the library's mission as ownership of materials, and shows signs of becoming the dominant feature of the mission. How will this trend, or should this trend, affect standards? In assessing the quality of collection support to programs, is there and will there be a distinction between how the balance of ownership and access applies to undergraduate education and how it applies to graduate education and research? Can we distinguish levels of quality among collections of different institutions, regardless of collection size, and how could such knowledge inform planning? Size and growth of collections and their relationship to quality are an area that offers many avenues for further research.

The Core Concept

By the mid-1970s many American academic libraries had rapidly achieved very considerable size, but by that time it was beginning to become clear that the information universe was growing even faster and that funding for library collection growth would very likely not continue apace. New direction was needed. In 1975, research and thinking in several relevant areas were brought together in a national conference to suggest that new direction, one that would derive from a concept of a core collection. In a program called "Touching Bottom in the Bottomless Pit," the Associated Colleges of the Midwest Conference on Space, Growth, and Performance Problems of Academic Libraries examined the rationale and data that would support the notion of doing better with less in the management of library collections.[40] Several years earlier, Buckland had found, through experimentation, that when measures—such as shortening the loan period of high demand books—were taken to improve the availability of material, the per capita use rate more than doubled.[41] Gore used these and other findings to develop a formula for performance of libraries that works this way: whereas the holdings rate of a library is the percentage of desired titles recorded in the catalog, and the availability rate is the percentage of desired titles recorded in the catalog that are available on the shelves, the performance rate is the percentage of all desired titles available on the shelves, or holdings rate times availability rate.[42] Through a combination of simple mathematics and logic, Gore demonstrates that more volumes do not necessarily improve the performance rate as he calculates it, but that they do add great cost, demand for space, and complexity for the user. The research of Trueswell and of Fussler and Simon, discussed below, also figured prominently in this conference, which was pivotal because it brought sound research and thinking in several areas to focus on one major issue.

Use and User Studies

So much research has been done in the area of use and user studies, most on a small scale, that this chapter only summarizes the general value of such studies and focus as on the specific studies that have been most influential in collection management. Use and user studies are examined in much greater depth in the present volume in the "Bibliometrics" chapter by Paul Metz.

The general weakness of use and user studies resides in the large number of variables involved and the lack of control over them, so that findings are rarely if ever conclusive. They may suggest conclusions, but the findings of other relevant studies need to be compared. Long a critic of and participant in use and user studies, Broadus has determined the conclusions that he believes are valid about the worth of these studies and has discussed the research he judges to be the most important in reaching each conclusion. Fundamentally, his conclusions are that overall use is less than we would like it to be; in-house use and external circulation are correlated; use is concentrated over a small number of titles, and previous use is generally the best single predictor of subsequent use; interest in materials is subject to a process of obsolescence; and foreign language materials are significantly underutilized in proportion to holdings.[43] Each of these conclusions is challengeable since no definitive study exists in any of the categories just listed.[44]

There are a few research efforts in the area of use studies that have, nonetheless, been particularly influential, owing either to methodology or to focus. The work of Fussler and Simon at the University of Chicago is perhaps the most comprehensive research on user patterns, for it examines data for the entire collection at intervals of five and twenty years.[45] The study ranked all volumes by number of users per year and related that ranking to age of the volume, last date of use, language, accession date, and use in the last five years. Fussler and Simon then validated their study by comparing use patterns prior to 1954 with those of 1954 to 1958. The chief general findings of this study, whose methodology has stood up well to scrutiny, are that use distributes itself among distinguishable clusters and that past use is the best single predictor of future use.

The study that quickly became known as the "Pitt" study is important because it covers a large body of data and, especially, because it raised great controversy within the academic library profession. Funded by the National Science Foundation, this research analyzed circulation and acquisition records for a period of more than seven years with the purposes of determining the relationship between cost of materials acquired and the circulation of those materials, and of comparing those costs with the likely savings that could be achieved through resource sharing. The study found that 39.8 percent of the books acquired in 1969 never circulated during their first six years, that each year's acquisitions behave in that regard much like any other year's; that in-house use and circulation correlate; that 48.37 percent of the entire collection did not circulate in seven years; and that past use is a valid indicator of future use. Although the methodology of this study has been widely attacked, the most profound reservations held by the rest of the community seem to stem from the potential of casual conclusions that could be drawn in terms of the library's role in academic research and in terms of funding for the library. The general unreliability of large library data, owing to inconsistencies among libraries over time, is, of course, the Achilles' heel of any use study of this magnitude, and even the principal investigator acknowledged the continuing problem throughout the study "of obtaining agreement as to precise baseline data."[46]

While the studies discussed above are limited to conclusions about collection use, the study by Metz relies on the power of an automated circulation system to help gain insights into the users of the collections. Metz gathered circulation data over a two-day period, representing all books circulated to all patrons (58,457 books to 10,126 borrowers), except in a relatively small, discrete category. Metz verified his study in a test taken several months later at a different point in the academic term. His findings include the following: faculty and graduate students use the library more intensely than do others; social scientists and to a lesser degree humanists rely more on books outside their fields than do physical scientists; physical scientists use journals more than social scientists and humanists; all researchers make frequent use of outside literature; books are read principally by nonspecialists. Clearly, Metz's study brings strong confirmation to our understanding of the interdisciplinary activities of scholars, and in doing so presents the library in a new light: "The findings support a view of the library as a most unrestricted and unpredictable bazaar for the exchange of ideas and reflect a much more catholic and interdependent view of knowledge than citation studies have ever suggested."[47]

A substantial part of the professional career of Trueswell, an industrial engineer, was spent on refining a methodology to determine the core of a collection for the purpose of discard or removal to storage.[48] His approach is based on the use of the cumulative distribution function of last circulation date, whereby he analyzed books currently circulating in terms of book age and previous date of circulation, assuming the pattern of current circulation to be typical of future circulation. He then determined the books required to satisfy 99 percent of circulation demand. Trueswell's work began with his dissertation and continued for a dozen years or so with replication in several libraries, resulting in a half dozen publications. His methodology, too elaborate to be captured adequately here, has not been attacked so much as has been the presumed possible uses of it. Two basic findings repeated in his studies are that "there is a predictable optional number of volumes for a library's core collection that will satisfy a given percent of user circulation requirements," and that "the last circulation date may be an ideal statistic to define and measure circulation requirements and patterns." [49]

Bradford's Law

More than half a century ago, Bradford published the results of his study of journals, a study that examined neither their use nor their relative ranking of importance, but simply their contents. Bradford found that, in pursuing a given subject through the journal literature, there would be a few journals containing many articles on that subject, a larger number containing a moderate number of relevant articles, and many containing only a few articles on the subject.[50] This distribution by cluster or zone of subject literature through the journals became known as Bradford's law of scattering and has been influential in any discussion of a core collection and its formulation. Bradford's law has been tested countless times, most often has been found valid, and has stimulated the imagination of many scholars in applying its principles to related aspects of library use and library users. The law is simple and it reflects common sense, yet its discovery of distinct zones is of particular significance and has given it wide acceptance as one of the very few theories of social phenomena that can reliably be built upon and applied to the development of theory related to other phenomena.

Less close to definitive than the clustering aspect of Bradford's law is the question of quality or importance of articles in relation to their distribution among the journals. Bradford did not address this issue, which is highly significant in the selection phase of collection development, but Lamb has demonstrated a correlation between the high density zone of journals in the field of mathematics and importance of the articles they contain.[51] A corollary of Bradford's distribution of subject articles among journal titles may also be found in use patterns, as one would expect certainly that the journals carrying the largest number of items on a subject would be used most heavily by those pursuing the subject. Goffman and Morris determined this to be the case in studying 371 journals that circulated 876 times in a month.[52]

In terms of practical application of Bradford's law to collection management, it could be assumed that a distinct core of journals could be identified that would contain a relatively large number of articles in a given field, and that the list could be studied every few years to be certain that the greatest number of relevant articles are received through the smallest number of subscriptions. Cost of the journals is, however, another matter. Books, also, are another matter. Is the relationship among publishers, books, and their subjects analogous to the relationship among journals, articles, and subjects, as described by Bradford? Baughman concludes that it is, that a few publishers account for the bulk of monographs cited in journal articles, and that production is distributed by clusters or zones of publishers. His conclusions are drawn from a random sample of 495 books in sociology, representing 10 percent of the 4,954 titles identified through a citation count of 446 articles in 71 journals. Half of the monographs were published by 12.6 percent of the publishers.[53] More work along these lines needs to be done; but, although there very likely are a number of variables from one field to another, such as language, Baughman's findings seem to be solid enough to suggest the validity of applying Bradford's law to books. Approval plans, after all, are based on this premise. To what extent can the implications of Bradford's work be taken in implementing a selection policy to maintain a core collection? This question has not been explored fully.

The purpose in determining a core collection is to meet the greatest demand with the fewest materials, assuming that to some extent that also translates into the least expense. There are two kinds of core collections: the collection that represents the intellectual nucleus of each discipline, consisting of the classic, synoptic, and most influential texts, whether in articles, books, or other formats; and a nucleus of materials that is determined by heaviest use. Reason suggests that the two cores are one and the same in a collection that has been developed with extraordinary care. But it is important to bear in mind that a core that is determined solely by use will in any case emerge, de facto, owing simply to the presence of the materials, regardless of their quality.

A complete discussion of the core concept divides the topic in two parts: (1) establishment of the core and maintenance of the core through continued selection, and (2) continued refining of the core through deselection either for storage or discard. To the extent that deselection decisions are informed by data supplied by research on obsolescence, citation patterns, Bradford's law, circulation activity, and other reported observations of use, the latter is the less difficult function. Considerable guidance in the identification of highly pertinent criteria has been generated by the research cited here. But the establishment and maintenance of the core through continued selection are far more difficult, for it looks to the future and attempts to predict the greatest of variables, human behavior. To what extent, for example, might a core vary from one institution to another? It is primarily this variable in the core concept that now needs research.

Selection

Selection is the foundation of collection management. It is a process of judgment that applies principles and criteria to distinguish the most relevant from the less relevant in terms of purpose. The principles and criteria employed in selection inform most, if not all, other aspects of collection management. It is not surprising, therefore, that collection management as it is understood in the late twentieth century is but a complex ramification of the selection function. "The high purpose of book selection is to provide the right book for the right reader at the right time," observed Drury long ago in introducing his classic text on the subject.[54] Since then, we have interpreted "book" to mean "generic book," that is to say any information source, and "provide" to mean "make accessible." However, judging from the foregoing pages devoted to research in collection management, we have not yet achieved an understanding of Drury's adjective "right" that is satisfactory to our needs.

The explanation for this is that the selection function is uniquely intense, having been rendered so by a society that both creates and craves information at a bounding pace, a condition for which technology has supplied at once a potential cure and a further cause. Kraft contributed a well-framed inventory of the need for greater attention to selectivity in university libraries. It is quite applicable to the situation today if the reader can overlook some of the author's evident prejudices and can read this convincing argument in the context of concerns of the 1990s, for Kraft defines the selection function as a "serious attempt to distinguish between the explosion of knowledge and the explosion of the printing presses."[55] Her article is significant because it is a well-reasoned and well-articulated analysis of the need for renewed attention to the full meaning of selectivity at a critical juncture in the management of academic library collections.

Reflecting the strong trend toward specialization in all aspects of research, the few existing comprehensive treatments of selection, other than textbooks, are collections of scholarly papers prepared on a disciplinary basis by specialists. And it is noteworthy that the first of these works dedicated to the selection function in academic libraries was not published until late in this century. The collections edited by McClung and by Shapiro and Whaley bring together an unprecedented concise accumulation of research, analysis, and experience, dedicated to a broad range of fields.[56] These volumes probably constitute in our profession the current paradigm for thought and research on selection against which new theory will be tested.

The Process

Establishment of a methodology for the selection of current materials continues to pose the single greatest challenge in collection management. Increasing attention has been paid to attempts to describe or model the selection process presumably as a theoretical basis for subsequent prescription. The selection process involving microdecisions, that is, title-by-title selection, is described by Atkinson in terms borrowed from the theory of literary criticism.[57] Atkinson organizes the many complex considerations that enter into the selection of one title from among the many according to three frames of reference: the syntagmatic context, which is the citation; the contexts of supplementation, which are the selection sources; and the contexts of resolution, which constitute the selector's experience with the collection, the clientele, and the subject. One context will be more or less influential than the other, depending largely upon the magnitude of fiscal support. The importance of this contribution resides in its application of accepted theory to a highly complex phenomenon of conscious and subconscious decision making, such that the entire process can be analyzed in an objective and orderly fashion.

While Atkinson's model is an attempt to explain the complex selection phenomenon, the model presented by Rutledge and Swindler is an attempt to supply a means to rationalize the process.[58] Having studied general selection criteria that have been identified by other scholars over the years, Rutledge and Swindler arrange them visually in six categories to illustrate their interrelationship. They are also ranked by priority, so that the influence of the criteria can be adjusted by priority to conform with fiscal resources; this ranking also permits modification from one library to another. The value of this contribution is that it is a highly pragmatic mechanism that is also quite adaptable to varying conditions and is easily amenable to monitoring, reporting, and adjustment. But the scheme merits further work to determine how it could be applied on a daily basis to large numbers of selection microdecisions.

In his elaboration of the elements that would be contained in a model of the selection process, Edelman offers the following observation on macroselection: "Once a block of literature in a subject field has been identified, quantified, and priced, experience as well as efficiency and expediency suggest that the highest yield of bibliographical items per decision is the most economical decision in the long run."[59] It is on this theory of macroselection that a variety of business arrangements have been based, arrangements that include the Farmington Plan, the PL-480 Plan, LACAP, blanket order plans, and, most commonly, book approval plans. The literature of acquisitions contains many studies that demonstrate the economic advantages of macroselection. But a lingering question has surrounded the issue of economics versus quality in the collection, and it is on that issue that turns the debate of the value of the macrodecision in the selection process.

Working with a medium-sized academic library and a major book vendor, Leon Raney ran a test to compare the selections made through an approval plan with those made by library selectors.[60] The study was limited to U.S. and Canadian publishers, plus the Oxford and Cambridge university presses, and was focused on a half dozen representative disciplines. Raney found that of the 4,559 titles involved in the study, more than 82 percent had been preselected through the approval plan. This finding does not necessarily testify to the high value of the books acquired through macroselection, but it does suggest that macroselection can mirror the policy on collection development—for good or bad. Raney's study was fairly comprehensive and therefore is an important contribution; but it is dated and should be repeated in a larger library that functions with a comprehensive, written policy for selection. A survey of ARL membership in 1982 revealed that 85 percent of the libraries operated with approval plans, but that an average of less than 10 percent of the acquisition budget was spent in acquiring materials this way.[61] A survey of that group six years later showed the percentage of respondents with approval plans had increased to 93.6 percent, and that the percentage having both foreign and domestic plans had climbed from 64 percent in 1982 to 86.2 percent in 1988.[62] What seems to have remained the same, however, is great diversity of practice among these libraries, and the relatively small proportion of total expenditures (about 10 percent) that is accounted for by approval plans.

Policy

Guiding selection decisions, whether on the micro or macro scale, is the policy for the development of collections. Since the mid-1970s there has been considerable attention paid to this aspect of selection, for a written policy supplies the principles that underlie all functions of collection management in its broadest definition. In spite of the evident centrality of such policy to library operations generally, there is surprisingly little research that evaluates the influence of policy on the quality of collections or on the performance of the library. Nor is there research that measures the influence of the act of creating the policy on attitudes or behaviors both within and outside the library. That may be because comprehensive, written collection development policies are a relatively recent management tool in academic libraries and are not yet common. Scholarship focusing on policy tends to treat the ways it should be generated, what it should contain, and what can be expected of it.

The process of drafting a policy can be simple or complex, depending upon the range of purposes behind the process. Osburn emphasizes the values that can be derived from the process of drafting policy according to planning guidelines he recommends, but he does not indicate how success in achieving these process values can be measured.[63] That the process for drafting policy is becoming more complex is evidenced by the survey of collection development policies conducted by Futas in preparation of her anthology of policies.[64] She found in preparing the 1984 second edition that far more written policies were the product of committees than in the first 1977 edition. This change suggests that expectations for the policy also were more complex, and that subject is worthy of further investigation. In many respects, the drafting of policy is an experiment, but it is an experiment with so many variables and based on such weak theory that it is not yet replicable. In a preliminary effort to render this experiment more amenable to replicability, Koenig records the experience of drafting the first written policy at the University of California at Berkeley.[65] Her contribution recounts the strategies used in developing the methodology and the coordination of implementation.

Atkinson focuses on the policy not simply as a tool of communication, but as a system of communication that comprises "a complex and subtle network of relationships."[66] As an illustration of the significance of grasping the importance of the communications aspects of policy, he points to the implications for resource sharing of varying interpretations of collection levels among institutions and among individuals. Atkinson urges further study of the policy as a complex communications system that can be used to realize the inherent power of the policy.

Evaluation and Preservation

The evaluation of collections is an essential aspect of selection insofar as selection is influenced by a knowledge of collections. Traditionally, evaluation has concerned itself with the intellectual content of materials. But during the past decade increasing attention has been given to research in the physical condition of materials, with a view toward conserving either the physical artifact or its content, or both. While much of this work, which tends to be referred to in a generic sense as preservation, addresses methods of chemical treatment, it touches collection management at a critical point. And that is the point of selecting the intellectual entities to be preserved for future use and determining the format in which they should be preserved.

The variety of methods for evaluating collections is rich, including those treated above in the discussion of core concept, and the literature on that subject has been surveyed often.[67] Again, we are confronted with the inconclusiveness of research, even though collection evaluation is by its nature a research undertaking. Those who have analyzed research on collection evaluation methodology tend to agree with Mosher, who finds that "two or more types of studies are required before one can be confident of a set of conclusions."[68] Futas and Vidor present a list of questions that illustrate the great complexity of collection evaluation and the likelihood that precision may be unachieveable.[69] Their questions could be of value in structuring a solution to the problem of identifying a set of methodologies that might lead to usable conclusions when matched appropriately with purposes of the evaluation and type of collection being evaluated. Sorting out the most meaningful relationship among clusters of methodologies, clientele, and objectives should now prove to be a productive area for research, especially for the development of models.

Perhaps the most comprehensive evaluation ever undertaken is the study reported by Raney many decades ago.[70] This evaluation involved more than 200 University of Chicago faculty members in the establishment of over 400 special subject bibliographies and a list of 32,000 journals. Comparison of these lists against the catalogue yielded a desiderata file of 1,405,097 volumes and consequent success in securing added funding for the library. The study of needs varies in detail and quality from one department to another, but the direct involvement of the immediate academic community in establishment of the standards for comparison was an important methodological innovation. The overall evaluation is also historically important because it took into account five other large libraries in Chicago.

While the Raney methodology may be impractical in many academic settings in the latter part of the twentieth century, a frequently cited methodology described by Webb offers a satisfactory compromise.[71] This report is a fairly detailed description of library selectors and university faculty collaborating on a comprehensive sample evaluation of collections at the University of Colorado. The significance of the evaluation methodology reported is that it is about as replicable as anything this complex can be, and that it emphasizes the process values as suitable goals in themselves, thereby also broadening the scope for further research in evaluation methodology.

It is clear that there is no dearth of methodologies for the evaluation of library collections, but also that efforts to relate them and their conclusions to policy on collection development are rife with complexities and risks. What may be useful now is research on methodologies for the evaluation of collection management performance or, to state it another way, for the evaluation of the ongoing implementation of policy. Such research would be particularly timely as the general goal of acquiring locally owned materials gradually is replaced by the goal of providing access to information. This approach also would appear to have validity because existing methodologies for collection evaluation focus on locally owned physical materials and therefore have little to do with the reconceptualized collection of the future that will result from the great influx of electronic capabilities. In any case, collection evaluation methodologies will have to be revised to accommodate both new goals and new formats.

If collection evaluation is to assess more than the intellectual scope and depth of resources as they are represented bibliographically in the catalog, then the physical materials under evaluation must actually be in usable condition. Widespread concern about the physical condition of library materials was kindled within the profession over thirty years ago by Barrow's studies of the durability of the book. A chemist employed by the Virginia State Library, Barrow tested the physical properties of 500 books published in the United States from 1900 to 1949 and concluded his series of tests with the simple statement that "it seems probable that most library books printed in the first half of the twentieth century will be in unusable condition in the next century."[72] This study was followed by others in the Barrow laboratories, sponsored in part by the Council on Library Resources, and it led directly to the sponsorship by the Association of Research Libraries of a comprehensive analysis of the status of preservation in American research libraries. This analysis was the Williams report of 1965, which described the vast dimensions of the challenge of preservation and outlined a plan for the preservation of library resources nationwide.[73] It contains an early section on selection for preservation, and is important historically as the report that gave impetus to national planning for preservation.

The literature on preservation has been fairly well documented in the past decade, beginning with Darling and Ogden, who analyze the "major events and attributes that have contributed to the emergence of preservation as a vital specialty within librarianship in the United States."[74] Since 1979 the literature has been reviewed annually in *Library Resources and Technical Services,* first as part of the review of collection development and later as a separate area for review. That, alone, suggests the swiftness with which preservation became a significant dimension of academic librarianship. The part of that diverse dimension that pertains to the selection of materials to be preserved is quite small.

Tomer has related the work of Trueswell, discussed above, and of Barrow, mentioned above, in an effort to establish an objective basis for selection for preservation. Analysis of a random sample of 500 books in the Case Western Reserve University Library focused on specific bibliographic and physical characteristics of the materials, matched against their circulation record. Tomer's work suggests that "the date of publication is a generally reliable index of a book's present physical condition; and the frequency with which a book has been circulated corresponds significantly with its date of last circulation."[75] This formula needs further testing through replication in order to be validated, and it should be noted that it addresses only the issue of determining those volumes that are likely to be worn out through heavy use.

Fundamental work has also been contributed by Hazen, who establishes a model to illustrate the analogy between selection for acquisition and selection for preservation.[76] Hazen's model argues clearly and convincingly that both microdecisions and macrodecisions for preservation follow criteria that are very similar to those followed in the development of collections, and he considers these criteria in five categories: user demand; tradition; scope and cost of materials available; alternatives to purchase; and patterns of research by discipline.

Recognizing that by far the greatest part of preservation that will take place will be done cooperatively on a national scale, Atkinson observes that of the three classes of materials in existence, one of them may fall by the wayside and not, in the end, be preserved.[77] The three classes he identifies are those of great monetary value, those that are heavily used, and those of little monetary value and in little use. Owing to financial limitations the latter class will likely not be preserved in a national scheme unless given special attention, according to Atkinson, who advances the requirements of a program to do just that. His conceptualization of the national collection to be preserved provides a framework through which to organize future research and activity directed at preservation.

Most collaborative efforts at preservation, however, address the challenge on the basis of subject, rather than some other categorization. And few are recorded as research upon which to build. Funded by the National Endowment for the Humanities and the Mellon Foundation, a joint project of Columbia University and the American Philological Association undertook what may be the first major effort of a scholarly discipline to preserve its literature.[78] The purpose of the project was to preserve on microfiche the most important classical studies published between 1850 and 1918. From the universe of some 20,000 volumes, a board of seven specialists selected nearly 30 percent for preservation on a title-by-title basis. The significance of the report itself lies in its provision of a record of the advantages and disadvantages of selection by scholars, suggestions for improving the methodology, and other practical considerations.

Allocations

The allocation of fiscal resources establishes the practical parameters for the development of collections by determining the degree to which policy can be implemented, the degree to which judgment can be liberal or must be conservative in applying the policy. Therefore, the way in which allocations are determined is of fundamental importance in collection management. Yet, the volume of research in this area does not reflect its importance. This paradox may be explained by the complexity of unquantifiable considerations that enter into allocation and the inconclusiveness of any approach to allocation, since reliable means of testing for success have not yet been developed.

In efforts to become more scientific and also to behave proactively rather than reactively, the research dedicated to allocation has leaned most heavily on the quantifiable aspects of collection development and user activity. These efforts to establish formulas for allocation are a relatively recent phenomenon, although interest within the profession in the bases for allocation is as old as the perception of budget inadequacy. Schad examines the research historically, emphasizing the more recent experiments with formula allocations of the acquisitions budget among subjects.[79] Analyzing the strengths and weaknesses of a number of formulas, he finds them inconclusive, which is to say unreliable, and concludes that only a combination of detailed knowledge, objective data, and sound professional judgment can lead to a valid procedure for allocation.

Shirk challenges the notion that the materials budgeting formulas that have been devised thus far are at all scientific, following a critique of a few of the more frequently cited. He points out that they cannot predict the long-term effects on the library's goals for collection performance, that they are not based on tested theory, that their success depends upon their political acceptance, and, therefore, that the use of formula is justifiably limited.[80]

Several of the more influential models have focused on use patterns, either by subject classification or academic department, as determined through circulation statistics. McGrath, who has engaged in considerable quantitative work, has presented a model wherein the number of books circulated is multiplied by the average cost, the product of which is then converted to a percentage of the overall cost-use.[81] This percentage becomes the basic allocation value for the pertinent category, and is multiplied by the total dollar amount available for all categories. McGrath concedes that his model is only skeletal, for it ignores many variables, needs to be tested over a number of years, and depends on the untested assumption that unsatisfied demand is proportional to satisfied demand. The assumption underlying a model developed by Pierce is that the book budget should be spent on the basis of relative departmental use. Pierce conducted a survey of faculty at Notre Dame University and gathered circulation records, applying multiple regression analysis to help account for other relevant considerations, including existing collection, relative costs, departmental hard/soft index, and clientele demographics.[82] Pierce's model is intended only as a framework to provide a set of objective initial allotment figures, which would require further adjustment.

Circulation data are also the basis for the model advanced by Hodowanec, who uses them to weight each category of the library's subject classification.[83] He gives further dimension to the model by considering formal circulation activity as a part of total circulation and considering the number of departments served by each category of the classification. The net weighting is then represented as a percentage of the budget to be allocated to support that field.

More recent models or assessments of formulas for the allocation of the materials budget have moved away from heavy dependency on circulation data, perhaps because even though the data are clear, their meaning is not. McPheron and others shift the focus to a less ambiguous element, the size and nature of the information universe in each disciplinary category.[84] They relate to that focal point other elements, such as relative degree of monograph dependency, demographics, and previous library support in an effort to reconcile it with the other unambiguous element, the budget. Their model does not address program priorities and incorporates substantial judgment. Schad takes the investigation a step further with the elusive characteristics of the allocation process that are inherent in its human and social considerations.[85] He applies research and theory from social psychology and examines their role in understanding the environment surrounding the process of allocation. Schad convincingly uses tested theory and research to suggest principles for allocation that can be translated into procedures with measurable results, emphasizing the role of the process itself. Discussed earlier in this chapter is Voigt's work which provides a model for allocation as well as the basis for a standard for current acquisitions levels.[86]

Acceptable formulas for the allocation of the materials budget have not yet been devised, primarily because we have not yet identified the characteristics of the expectations or for the success for these formulas. Nor have we yet established meaningful connections between policy and allocation or between evaluation and allocation. How should these be related? Surely the environment in which collection management operates must be understood better and must find its way objectively into the principles of budget allocation. An area that has not been explored fruitfully is the relationship between citation studies and the size and configuration of the information universe. What has become very evident is that no set of data in and of itself is of much value in determining allocations, but that the discovery of meaningful connections between or among sets of information can provide useful direction. It is very likely that a great deal along these lines can be learned from studying the many values for academic administration, for faculty, and for the library that are gained through the process of discussing budget allocations. For that purpose, a formula offers what seems to be at this time its single most important contribution, which is a framework to incorporate, and perhaps even to organize, the many, many pieces of a difficult puzzle.

The Environment of Collection Management

In the history of collection management, two trends are evident in the manner in which it is regarded by the profession and, therefore, in the nature and scope of research applied to it. The trend toward an increasing pervasiveness of collection management into formerly distinct areas of responsibility has been addressed at several points in this chapter. The other major trend, which only now is beginning to manifest itself clearly, is the importance of the interrelationship between collection management and its environment, especially the influence of the latter upon the former.

The immediate environment of collection management in an academic setting has several distinguishable elements, all of which are interrelated, and each of which will tend to predominate in its own time in influencing collection management. These environmental forces are: scholarly activity at the national level; the publishing industry; technological innovation and adoption; higher education policy; federal and foundation funding policy; the general economy; the academic and research library world; and the local community to be served. There are many other elements of the environment, of course, but these forces have affected collection management most directly. Research and thinking devoted to these environmental considerations can further be conceptualized in two categories from the perspective of collection management: the scholarly communication system and interlibrary cooperation.

Scholarly Communication System

The scholarly communication system refers to the interactions of a number of agents in a functional system who create, distribute, collect, preserve, make retrievable, and use the product of scholars and scientists. Study of scholarly and scientific communication as a system is a relatively recent undertaking, although study of its various elements is certainly not. Perhaps the earliest attempt to apply the systems concept to this social phenomenon is the economist Machlup's study in 1962, which amassed a variety of data to develop a conceptual framework for the analysis of "knowledge production." Machlup emphasizes education, which he concludes is the largest of the knowledge industries, and analyzes the growth rate of all relevant media as well as the growing and changing work force related to the production and distribution of knowledge. He makes no distinction between information and knowledge, considering the function of both to be "instrumental in increasing the efficiency of the economy."[87]

The economics of the scholarly communication system is driven in large part by the publishing industry, and it is the cost of materials that most directly affects collection management, in both the short and long terms. Costs of materials have been monitored, reported, and analyzed by librarians and others for decades, having been a particular expression of concern in the literature through the 1970s and 1980s, but Fry and White were the first to analyze in depth the relationship of publishers and librarians via the activity of scholarly journal publishing.[88] The purpose of their work was not just to study costs, but rather to examine the kinds of decisions made and the context surrounding them in publishing and in academic librarianship in an effort to assess the viability of the journal system for communicating scholarly and research information. The Fry and White report gathered data for the years 1969 through 1973 using questionnaires and follow-up telephone conversations with publishers and librarians and examining published sources. They bring to bear on the subject considerable information on production, costs, growth, holdings, cancellations, and borrowing and lending.

The picture presented by Fry and White is one of actions, reactions, and further actions between publishers and librarians that lead consistently to higher prices and cancelled subscriptions. But the picture is not complete without a similar examination of books and, now, electronic publishing, for library decisions in each of these areas affects decisions and planning in the others. The Fry and White report could supply a useful model for a broad scale study of the nature of interrelated decisions in publishing and academic librarianship.

What brought wide attention to the total system of scholarly communication, in which libraries play so large a role, was the survey and report conducted by the American Council of Learned Societies (ACLS) and funded by the Ford, Mellon, and Rockefeller foundations, and NEH.[89] The study conceptualized scholarly communication as a system, and this accomplishment, alone, was even more significant to future research in the area than the report's many recommendations. The ACLS study was based on a comprehensive questionnaire distributed broadly and upon published sources of information, such as the work by Machlup discussed above. Many flaws have been found in the methodology of the ACLS survey and report, but the validity of its conclusions, in terms of recommendations, seems to have been borne out, and its emphasis on a system perspective paved the way for what is becoming a discipline in its own right.

Published at about the same time as the ACLS national enquiry, Osburn's study of the environment surrounding collection management analyzes changes in the forces that affect scholarly communication and their relationship to collections and collection management.[90] He concludes that although scholarly communication is not a static phenomenon, the policy of collection management in university libraries had not, through the 1960s and 1970s, reflected the transformations of the rest of the system. The study concludes that de facto policy in collection management, brought about by the independence of academic libraries and librarianship, was diminishing the potential of library service to scholarship, and that this trend could be reversed only through the advancement of collection management as a cooperative enterprise of scholars and librarians.

With focus on a particularly crucial moment in academic library history, the Association of Research Libraries issued a statement in 1986 summarizing the thinking of a large number of academic research library directors on the then-current status of the rapidly evolving system of scholarly communication.[91] This report describes the emerging potential for both opportunities and problems in the system, posed primarily by the introduction of a range of new technologies, and calls for close cooperation not just of librarians and scholars, but also of publishers and other key agents in the system.

By the latter half of the 1980s the concept of a system of scholarly communication was beginning to be appreciated by librarians, publishers, and learned societies. Concurrently, a much needed guide to the field was produced by Morton and others.[92] An annotated bibliography, this comprehensive guide suggests the full range of involvement of the scholarly communication system. It is well organized and annotated thoroughly enough to serve as an introduction to the subject, primarily from the scholar's perspective. Some of both the selections and omissions may be challengeable, and the science and engineering fields are purposely not covered as well as are other areas, but *Writings in Scholarly Communication* clearly moves the potential of research in this field to a new plateau.[93]

Cooperative Collection Development

Resource sharing and cooperative collection development may constitute the most distinguishing feature of North American academic librarianship. Many of the national and regional programs, projects, and experiments have been described well elsewhere, so they will not be reviewed here.[94] In this chapter, the focus is specifically on research on the present status of cooperative collection development.

Hewitt and Shipman have produced the most comprehensive survey to date of cooperative collection development programs among U.S. academic research libraries, a survey that is also thorough enough to permit inferences about the general status of this aspect of the environment that increasingly is influencing collection management. They tested their questionnaire in six libraries, then sent them to the 93 U.S. members of the Association of Research Libraries in September 1983. Ninety, or 97 percent, responded. The Hewitt and Shipman survey provides a broad base of information about cooperative collection development activities in the larger academic libraries of the United States: Two-thirds were at that time involved in such programs, with very little special funding to support them; an additional nearly 50 percent were engaged in planning cooperative programs; both the largest and the smallest libraries in the group were more involved than the medium-sized libraries; the most common programs were the sharing of information on expensive items, serials selection, and joint acquisitions; the greatest difficulties encountered were administrative, rather than attitudinal. Hewitt and Shipman believe that in spite of the impressive number of cooperative collection development activities among these libraries, the operational programs are still "poorly delineated or even embryonic," reflecting their interpretation that the interest and activity revealed by the survey is directed more at the establishment of relationships rather than specific, active programs.[95]

With its focus entirely on the largest academic libraries, this survey does not provide a complete picture of academic library cooperative collection development, nor does it gather the information necessary to understand why the medium-sized ARL libraries are less likely to be involved in cooperative ventures than other libraries, as is revealed by the survey. Is this purely coincidental or is there something about the institutional psychology that would shed further light on decision making related to cooperation? In any case, this survey is an important contribution toward building a context in which specific experiments and research can be evaluated. The survey should be repeated.

Among the requirements, both evident and subtle, for successful cooperative collection development programs is the means or mechanism by which fundamental information about collections, and the plans and decisions surrounding their management, can be exchanged. The development of such a mechanism is bound to involve a good deal of research and experimentation in order to arrive at a medium that can convey the various kinds of information needed and do so reliably. In view of the pressure that has been mounting in the 1980s to establish cooperative collection development programs, the identification of an appropriate medium for these purposes has become a major issue. Two such research tools have presented themselves—the shelflist measurement and the conspectus—and they have undergone considerable experimentation.

Developed initially and in stages at Northwestern University, the University of Wisconsin, and the University of California at Berkeley, the procedure for monitoring and comparing size and growth of parts of a collection among libraries was brought to test phase in seventeen of the larger academic libraries in the United States in 1973. In the course of the ensuing dozen years, many more libraries joined the project.[96] The shelflist count is a fairly reliable instrument, whose final tallies are extrapolated from actual sample counts in about 500 classifications of the Library of Congress scheme. The procedure is time-consuming and cumbersome and applies only to cataloged materials, of course. Whether or not the subject breakdown is detailed enough is a matter of individual need. But the strength of this instrument often is seen to reside in its potential for comparability on the basis of data rather than on the basis of impression, and its focus is on what has occurred in the development of collections rather than on what has been or is intended to occur. As a mechanism by which to identify relative strengths and weaknesses among collections at the national level, the shelflist measurement project is no more and perhaps no less than its name indicates.

The conspectus offers a different and complementary approach. Developed in 1980 by the Research Libraries Group (RLG), conspectus is defined as a "breakdown of subject fields in such a way as to allow distributed collection responsibilities for as many fields as possible."[97] It is a very sophisticated planning and communications tool, for it records existing collections' strengths and intended collection development activity, both analyzed on the basis of a variety of considerations, such as language and country of origin, and spread across as many as 5,000 segments of the collection in as many libraries as are selected for participation. It is maintained online and incorporates information about local decisions on preservation. The RLG conspectus has been the nucleus of the North American Collections Inventory Project since 1983, having been pilot tested along the way to identify the many practical implications of adopting this management tool. Farrell describes such a test involving Indiana University, Purdue University, and the University of Notre Dame in which the chief positive result seems to be that the internal and external communications that are enhanced by the processes demanded in employing the conspectus help establish an environment that is conducive to the coordination of collection management among libraries.[98]

The sophistication and potential of the conspectus tool are offset to some degree by its reliance on professional judgment and impression, rather than on data, and by the subjective influences on the interpretation of varying levels of strength within and among libraries. Henige provides a thoughtful critique of this research tool, which was in wide use at the close of the 1980s.[99]

It is clear that a management tool intended to serve as the basis for coordinated collection management among a large number of libraries throughout North America—and beyond—will need to possess the positive characteristics of both the shelflist count and the RLG conspectus. If that is so, it would be desirable to direct research at a practical means of merging these two methods such that their complementarity could be mutually reinforcing. The result would be the development of a much-needed tool for the effective management of coordinated collection development. And, owing to the nature of the processes that then would be demanded by the adoption of such a powerful and reliable tool, that new instrument would also serve as a tool for research in a great many aspects of collection management.

Retrospect and Prospect

The observation was made at the beginning of this chapter that the literature surrounding selection, collection development, and collection management has expanded surprisingly in a relatively short time. Establishment of a body of research within that literature got off to a slower start, however, perhaps because the questions to be addressed had first to be identified. In fact, the field had to be defined. The accumulation of a great mixture of seemingly unrelated essays and reports became the context for research in collection management, and what was an amorphous assemblage of goals, strategies, problems, and viewpoints only a dozen years ago is beginning to be given order, a coherent significance.

Now we are at the point of crossing the threshold to a new era in research and thought devoted to collection management. We will need to determine the appropriateness of existing research and theory to an evolving kind of collection management wherein the fundamental considerations are global accessibility, rather than local ownership, and the generic book, rather than the paper codex; wherein scholarly communication, rather than librarianship, is our business, and distinctions between information and knowledge have a new importance. We will need to test old models, measures, and principles at a fortunate time when it seems likely that information systems made possible by technology will be of much greater value to collection management than they have been heretofore. Surely that technology lends itself more to research in collection management as a system than have other approaches in the past; and the system's perspective on collection management will be even more critical than ever before.

As we move in these directions, it is evident that research in collection management will need to be informed by theory and research in many other disciplines, largely because of the rapidly increasing interdependence of its relationship with a changing environment. Of the many weaknesses that can be ascribed to collection management research of the past, one of the most significant has been the failure to identify success in other than the most simplistic—and perhaps meaningless—terms. That failure cannot be repeated in an era in which collection management will necessarily be so tightly integrated into its environment. Consequently, it is likely in this new era that research will begin to both reflect and guide the proper blending of science and art that inherently is collection management.

Notes

1. *Guide for Writing a Bibliographer's Manual*, ed. Carolyn Bucknall et al. (Chicago: American Library Assn., 1987), v.

2. *Collection Development in Libraries: A Treatise*, ed. Robert D. Stueart and George B. Miller, Jr., 2 vols. (Greenwich, Conn.: JAI Pr., 1980). A completely revised edition of this collection of essays is to be published in 1990 as *Collection Management in Libraries: A Treatise*, ed. Charles B. Osburn and Ross W. Atkinson, 2 vols. (Greenwich, Conn.: JAI Pr., in preparation).

3. Rose Mary Magrill, "Collection Development in Large University Libraries," *Advances in Librarianship* 8 (1978): 1–54.

4. Alfred C. Potter, "Selection of Books for College Libraries," *Library Journal* 22 (October 1897): 39–44.

5. Douglas Waples and Harold D. Lasswell, *National Libraries and Foreign Scholarship* (Chicago: Univ. of Chicago Pr., 1936), especially pp. 74–75.

6. Gayle Edward Evans, "The Influence of Book Selection Agents upon Book Collection Usage in Academic Libraries" (Ph.D. diss., University of Illinois, 1969). This research was replicated and expanded a decade later, showing faculty to have greater success than the combination of librarians and faculty, but only in the areas of science and social science, not in the humanities. See Robbie Barnes Bingham, "Collection Development in University Libraries: An Investigation of the Relationship between Categories of Selectors and Usage of Selected Items" (Ph.D. diss., Rutgers University, 1979).

7. J. Periam Danton, *Book Selection and Collections: A Comparison of German and American University Libraries* (New York: Columbia Univ. Pr., 1963), pp. 37, 74.

8. Cecil K. Byrd, "Subject Specialists in a University Library," *College & Research Libraries* 27 (May 1966): 191–193.

9. Robert P. Haro, "The Bibliographer in the Academic Library," *Library Resources and Technical Services* 13 (Spring 1969): 163–169.

10. Helen Welch Tuttle, "An Acquisitionist Looks at Mr. Haro's Bibliographer," *Library Resources and Technical Services* 13 (Spring 1969): 170–174.

11. Eldred R. Smith, "The Impact of the Subject Specialist Librarian on the Organization and Structure of the Academic Research Library," in *The Academic Library: Essays in Honor of Guy R. Lyle*, ed. Evan Ira Farber and Ruth Walling (Metuchen, N.J.: Scarecrow, 1974), pp. 71–81.

12. Wilmer H. Baatz, "Collection Development in Nineteen Libraries of the

Association of Research Libraries," *Library Acquisitions: Practice and Theory* 2 (1978): 85–121.

13. Norman H. Dudley, "Organizational Models for Collection Development," in *Collection Development in Libraries: A Treatise*, ed. Robert D. Stueart and George B. Miller, Jr. (Greenwich, Conn.: JAI Pr., 1980), pt. A, pp. 19–33.

14. Dennis W. Dickenson, "A Rationalist's Critique of Book Selection for Academic Libraries," *Journal of Academic Librarianship* 7 (July 1981): 138–143; and "Six Responses to 'A Rationalist's Critique . . . ,'" *Journal of Academic Librarianship* 7 (July 1981): 144–151. Dickenson advanced many of his views in "Subject Specialists in Academic Libraries: The Once and Future Dinosaurs," in *New Horizons for Academic Libraries*, ed. Robert D. Stueart and Richard D. Johnson (New York: Saur, 1979), pp. 438–444.

15. Elaine F. Sloan, "The Organization of Collection Development in Large University Research Libraries" (Ph.D. diss., University of Maryland, 1973). An excellent and more recent summary of the literature, thinking, and research on the subject is provided by Bonita Bryant, "The Organizational Structure of Collection Development," *Library Resources and Technical Services* 31 (April-June 1987): 111–122.

16. Jeanne Sohn, "Collection Development: Organizational Patterns in ARL Libraries," *Library Resources and Technical Services* 31 (April-June 1987): 123–134. However, James A. Cogswell surveyed twenty ARL libraries at about the same time and was able to infer six models. His analysis is very useful because he discusses the advantages and disadvantages of each in "The Organization of Collection Management Functions in Academic Research Libraries," *Journal of Academic Librarianship* 13 (Nov. 1987): 268–276.

17. Manuel D. Lopez, "A Guide for Beginning Bibliographers," *Library Resources and Technical Services* 13 (Fall 1969): 462–470.

18. Anthony W. Ferguson, "University Library Collection Development and Management Using a Structural-Functional Systems Model," *Collection Management* 8 (Spring 1986): 13.

19. Dan C. Hazen, "Modeling Collection Development Behavior: A Preliminary Statement," *Collection Management* 4 (Spring-Summer 1982): 13.

20. Bonita Bryant, "Allocation of Human Resources for Collection Development," *Library Resources and Technical Services* 30 (April-June 1986): 149–162.

21. Charles B. Osburn, "Education for Collection Development," in *Collection Development in Libraries: A Treatise*, ed. Robert D. Stueart and George B. Miller (Greenwich, Conn.: JAI Pr., 1980), pt. B, p. 565.

22. In Russell Fischer, "Managing Research Libraries: An Interview with David Weber," *Wilson Library Bulletin* 59 (January 1985): 321.

23. Patricia Battin, "Developing University and Research Library Professionals," *American Libraries* 14 (January 1983): 22–25; and Edward G. Holley, "Defining the Academic Librarian," *College and Research Libraries* 46 (Nov. 1985): 462–468.

24. Fremont Rider, *The Scholar and the Research Library* (New York: Hadham Press, 1944), pp. 3–19. See especially the chapter titled "The Growth of American Research Libraries."

25. In a later, but much less known study, Rider discovered a decline in growth rate during the period from 1938 to 1947, "Recent Statistics of College Library Growth," *About Books at the Olin Library* 17 (1947): 1–6.

26. *The Past and Likely Future of Fifty-Eight Research Libraries, 1951–1980: A Statistical Study of Growth and Change* (West Lafayette, Ind.: University Libraries and Audio Visual Center, Purdue University, 1965–1973). 9 editions.

27. A member of the team, Miriam Drake, published subsequent studies that reinforce the findings of this study. Miriam A. Drake, *Academic Research Libraries: A Study of Growth* (West Lafayette, Ind.: University Libraries and Audio Visual Center, Purdue University, 1977).

28. Robert E. Molyneux, "Patterns, Process of Growth, and the Projection of Library Size: A Critical Review of the Literature on Academic Library Growth," *Library and Information Science Research* 8 (January-March 1986): 5–28, and "Growth of ARL Libraries, 1962/63–1983/84," *Journal of Academic Librarianship* 12 (Sept. 1986): 211–216.

29. Robert B. Downs, *Development of Research Collections in University Libraries*, University of Tennessee Library Lectures, no. 4 (Knoxville: University of Tennessee, 1954).

30. Verner W. Clapp and Robert T. Jordan, "Quantitative Criteria for Adequacy of Academic Library Collections," *College & Research Libraries* 26 (Sept. 1965): 371–380.

31. Melvin J. Voigt, "Acquisition Rates in University Libraries," *College & Research Libraries* 36 (July 1975): 263–271.

32. "Standards for College Libraries 1986," *College & Research Libraries News* 47 (March 1986): 189–200; "Standards for University Libraries," *College & Research Libraries News* 40 (April 1979): 101–110.

33. Rider, *The Scholar and the Research Library*, p. 8.

34. Clapp and Jordan, "Quantitative Criteria for Adequacy of Academic Library Collections," p. 373. In an earlier study of 119 privately supported four-year colleges, Jordan found correlations among volumes in the library, volumes per student, and library salaries per student. His criteria for quality were drawn from a mixture of his own criteria and published rankings. See Robert T. Jordan, "Library Characteristics of Colleges Ranking High in Academic Excellence," *College & Research Libraries* 24 (Sept. 1963): 369–376.

35. H. William Axford, "Rider Revisited," *College & Research Libraries* 23 (July 1962): 347.

36. George Piternick, "Library Growth and Academic Quality," *College & Research Libraries* 24 (May 1963): 229.

37. For example, see George Piternick, "ARL Statistics—Handle with Care," *College & Research Libraries* 38 (Sept. 1977): 419–423.

38. Robert E. Molyneux, "Patterns, Process of Growth, and the Projection of Library Size: A Critical Review of the Literature on Academic Library Growth," *Library and Information Science Research* 8 (January-March 1986): 5–28.

39. Allan M. Cartter, *An Assessment of Quality in Graduate Education: A*

Comparative Study of Graduate Departments in 29 Academic Disciplines (Washington, D.C.: American Council on Education, 1966), p. 114.

40. The proceedings are published as *Farewell to Alexandria: Solutions to Space, Growth, and Performance Problems of Libraries*, ed. Daniel Gore (Westport, Conn.: Greenwood Pr., 1976).

41. Michael K. Buckland, "An Operations Research Study of a Variable Loan and Duplication Policy at the University of Lancaster," *Operations Research*, ed. Don R. Swanson and Abraham Bookstein (Chicago: Univ. of Chicago Pr., 1972), pp. 97–106.

42. Gore, *Farewell to Alexandria*, p. 174. Published originally in his article "Zero Growth for the College Library," *College Management* 9 (August-September 1974): 12–14.

43. Robert N. Broadus, "Use Studies of Library Collections," *Library Resources and Technical Services* 24 (Fall 1980): 317–324.

44. For example, Line and Sandison conclude after a detailed study of the obsolescence factor, "It appears then that 'obsolescence' is not a concept of which librarians can make much practical use." Maurice B. Line and Alexander Sandison, "'Obsolescence' and Changes in Use of Literature with Time," *Journal of Documentation* 30 (Sept. 1974): 319.

45. Herman H. Fussler and Julian L. Simon, *Patterns in the Use of Books in Large Research Libraries* (Chicago: Univ. of Chicago Pr., 1961).

46. Allen Kent et al., *Use of Library Materials: The University of Pittsburgh Study* (New York: Marcel Dekker, 1979), especially p. vii and chapter II, "Circulation and In-House Use of Books," pp. 9–55.

47. Paul Metz, *The Landscape of Literature: Use of Subject Collections in a University Library* (Chicago: American Library Assn., 1983), pp. 56–57.

48. Richard William Trueswell, "User Behavioral Patterns and Requirements and Their Effect on the Possible Application of Data Processing Computer Techniques in a University Library" (Ph.D. diss., Northwestern University, 1964).

49. Richard W. Trueswell, "Determining the Optimal Number of Volumes for a Library's Core Collection," *Libri* 16 (1966): 58, 59.

50. S. C. Bradford, "Sources of Information on Specific Subjects," *Engineering* (January 26, 1934): 85–86.

51. Gertrude House Lamb, "The Coincidence of Quality and Quantity in the Literature of Mathematics" (Ph.D. diss., Case Western Reserve University, 1971). The correlation is challenged by Bert R. Boyce and Janet Sue Pollens, "Citation-Based Impact Measures and the Bradfordian Selection Criteria," *Collection Management* 4 (Fall 1982): 29–36.

52. William Goffman and Thomas G. Morris, "Bradford's Law and Library Acquisitions," *Nature* (June 6, 1970): 922–923.

53. James C. Baughman, "Toward a Structural Approach to Collection Development," *College & Research Libraries* 38 (May 1977): 241–248.

54. Francis K. W. Drury, *Book Selection* (Chicago: American Library Assn., 1930), p. 1.

55. Margit Kraft, "An Argument for Selectivity in the Acquisition of Materials for Research Libraries," *Library Quarterly* 37 (July 1967): 284–295.

56. Patricia A. McClung et. al., *Selection of Library Materials in the Humanities, Social Sciences, and Sciences* (Chicago: American Library Assn., 1985); Beth J. Shapiro, John Whaley, et. al., *Selection of Library Materials in Applied and Interdisciplinary Fields* (Chicago: American Library Assn., 1987).

57. Ross W. Atkinson, "The Citation as Intertext: Toward a Theory of the Selection Process," *Library Resources and Technical Services* 28 (April-June 1984): 109–119.

58. John Rutledge and Luke Swindler, "The Selection Decision: Defining Criteria and Establishing Priorities," *College & Research Libraries* 48 (March 1987): 123–131.

59. Hendrik Edelman, "Selection Methodology in Academic Libraries," *Library Resources and Technical Services* 23 (Winter 1979): 37.

60. Leon Raney, "An Investigation into the Adaptability of a Domestic Approval Plan to the Existing Pattern of Book Selection in a Medium-Size Academic Library" (Ph.D. diss., Indiana University, 1972).

61. Thomas W. Leonhardt, *Approval Plans in ARL Libraries. SPEC Kit #83* (Washington, D.C.: Association of Research Libraries, 1982).

62. Clinton Howard, *Approval Plans. Spec Kit #141* (Washington, D.C.: Association of Research Libraries, 1988).

63. Charles B. Osburn, "Planning for a University Library Policy on Collection Development," *International Library Review* 9 (April 1977): 209–224.

64. Elizabeth Futas, *Library Acquisition Policies and Procedures*, 2nd ed. (Phoenix: Oryx Pr., 1984).

65. Dorothy A. Koenig, "Rushmore at Berkeley: The Dynamics of Developing a Written Collection Development Policy Statement," *Journal of Academic Librarianship* (Jan. 1982): 344–350.

66. Ross W. Atkinson, "The Language of the Levels: Reflections on the Communication of Collection Development Policy," *College & Research Libraries* 47 (March 1986): 140–149.

67. Paul H. Mosher, "Quality and Library Collections: New Directions in Research and Practice in Collection Evaluation," *Advances in Librarianship* 13 (1984): 211–238; Eugene Wiemers, Jr., et. al., "Collection Evaluation: A Practical Guide to the Literature," *Library Acquisitions: Practice and Theory* 8 (1984): 65–76; Dorothy E. Christiansen, C. Roger Davis, and Jutta Reed-Scott, "Guide to Collection Evaluation through Use and User Studies," *Library Resources and Technical Services* 27 (Oct.-Dec. 1983): 432–440; Thomas E. Nisonger, "An Annotated Bibliography of Items Relating to Collection Evaluation in Academic Libraries, 1969–1981," *College & Research Libraries* 43 (July 1982): 300–311.

68. Mosher, "Quality and Library Collections," 233.

69. Elizabeth Futas and David L. Vidor, "What Constitutes a 'Good' Collection?" *Library Journal* 112 (April 15, 1987): 45–78.

70. M. Llewellan Raney, *The University Libraries* (Chicago: Univ. of Chicago Pr., 1933).

71. William Webb, "Project CoED: A University Library Collection Evaluation and Development Program," *Library Resources and Technical Services* 13 (Fall 1969): 457–462.

72. William J. Barrow, *Deterioration of Book Stock. Causes and Remedies*, ed.

Randolph W. Church (Richmond: State Library of Virginia, 1959), p. 16.

73. The report is reprinted in an edited but unabridged version by its original author, Gordon R. Williams, "The Preservation of Deteriorating Books," *Library Journal* 91 (January 1, 1966): 51–56; (January 15, 1966): 189–194.

74. Pamela W. Darling and Sherelyn Ogden, "From Problems Perceived to Programs in Practice: The Preservation of Library Resources in the U.S.A., 1956–1980," *Library Resources and Technical Services* 25 (January-March 1981): 9–29.

75. Christinger Tomer, "Identification, Evaluation, and Selection of Books for Preservation," *Collection Management* 3 (Spring 1979): 34–54.

76. Dan C. Hazen, "Collection Development, Collection Management, and Preservation," *Library Resources and Technical Services* 26 (January-March 1982): 6–10.

77. Ross W. Atkinson, "Selection for Preservation: A Materialistic Approach," *Library Resources and Technical Services* 30 (Oct.-Dec. 1986): 341–353.

78. Roger S. Bagnoll and Carolyn L. Harris, "Involving Scholars in Preservation Decisions: The Case of the Classicists," *Journal of Academic Librarianship* 13 (July 1987): 140–146.

79. Jasper G. Schad, "Allocating Materials Budgets in Institutions of Higher Education," *Journal of Academic Librarianship* 3 (January 1978): 328–332.

80. Gary M. Shirk, "Allocation Formulas for Budgeting Library Materials: Science or Procedure?" *Collection Management* 6 (Fall-Winter 1984): 37–47.

81. William E. McGrath, "A Pragmatic Book Allocation Formula for Academic and Public Libraries with a Test for Its Effectiveness," *Library Resources and Technical Services* 19 (Fall 1975): 356–368.

82. John Thomas Pierce, "The Economics of Library Acquisitions: A Book Budget Allocation Model for University Libraries" (Ph.D. diss., University of Notre Dame, 1976).

83. George V. Hodowanec, "Literature Obsolescence, Dispersion, and Collection Development," *College & Research Libraries* 44 (Nov. 1983): 421–443.

84. William McPheron et al., "Quantifying the Allocation of Monograph Funds: An Instance of Practice," *College & Research Libraries* 44 (March 1983):116–127.

85. Jasper G. Schad, "Fairness in Book Fund Allocation," *College & Research Libraries* 48 (Nov. 1987): 479–486. The importance of environmental considerations to the practitioner is made evident also by the research of Neuman, who studied the extent to which management information systems influence strategic planning in sixty-seven ARL libraries. She found that such systems have little influence, while environmental factors are considerably influential. See Susan Goldstein Neuman, "The Influence of Management Information Systems in Strategic Planning for Collection Development in Academic Libraries" (Ph.D. diss., University of Pittsburgh, 1986).

86. Voigt, "Acquisition Rates in University Libraries."

87. Fritz Machlup, *The Production and Distribution of Knowledge in the United States* (Princeton, N.J.: Princeton Univ. Pr., 1962). In collaboration with Kenneth Leeson, Machlup also attempted a much more comprehensive examination of the flow of information in the scholarly communication system, but it is disappointing in its unevenness and in the incomparability of its data. See Machlup and Leeson, *Information*

through the Printed Word: The Dissemination of Scholarly, Scientific, and Intellectual Knowledge, 4 vols. (New York: Praeger, 1978–80).

88. Bernard M. Fry and Herbert S. White, *Publishers and Libraries: A Study of Scholarly Research Journals* (Lexington, Mass: Lexington Books, 1976).

89. American Council of Learned Societies, *Scholarly Communication: The Report of the National Enquiry* (Baltimore: Johns Hopkins Univ. Pr., 1979).

90. Charles B. Osburn, *Academic Research and Library Resources: Changing Patterns in America* (Westport, Conn.: Greenwood, 1979).

91. *The Changing System of Scholarly Communication* (Washington, D.C.: Association of Research Libraries, 1986).

92. Herbert C. Morton et. al., *Writings on Scholarly Communication: An Annotated Bibliography of Books and Articles on Publishing, Libraries, Scholarly Research, and Related Issues* (Lanham, Md.: Univ. Pr. of America, 1988).

93. Under the auspices of ACLS, Morton and Anne Jamieson Price have also conducted a comprehensive survey of humanists and social scientists that addresses their concerns about a broad range of elements in the scholarly communication system. See their summary, "The ACLS Survey of Scholars: Views on Publications, Computers, Libraries," *Scholarly Communication* (Summer 1986): 1–16.

94. Among the reviews are Jeanne Sohn, "Cooperative Collection Development: A Brief Overview," *Collection Management* 8 (Summer 1986): 1–9; and David C. Weber, "A Century of Cooperative Programs among Academic Libraries," *College & Research Libraries* 37 (May 1976): 205–221.

95. Joe A. Hewitt and John S. Shipman, "Cooperative Collection Development among Research Libraries in the Age of Networking: Report of a Survey of ARL Libraries," *Advances in Library Automation and Networking* 1 (1987): 189–232.

96. Joseph J. Branin, David Farrell, and Mariann Triblin, "The National Shelflist Count Project: Its History, Limitations, and Usefulness," *Library Resources and Technical Services* 29 (Oct.-Dec. 1985): 333–342.

97. Nancy E. Gwinn and Paul H. Mosher, "Coordinating Collection Development: The RLG Conspectus," *College & Research Libraries* 44 (March 1983): 131.

98. David Farrell, "The NCIP Option for Coordinated Collection Development," *Library Resources and Technical Services* 30 (Jan.-March 1986): 47–56.

99. David Henige, "Epistemological Dead End and Ergonomic Disaster? The North American Collections Inventory Project," *Journal of Academic Librarianship* 13 (Sept. 1987): 209–213.

Elaine Svenonius

Bibliographical Control

The essential functions of any library, whether school, public, special, or academic, are to acquire, organize, and assist in the retrieval of bibliographic materials. The second of these functions, the topic of this chapter, is critical to the first and third. Effectiveness in the acquisition and retrieval of materials depends directly on the system of bibliographical control used to organize them.[1] While different systems of control are appropriate to different types of libraries, the economies of cooperation have led to the fairly widespread, albeit grudging, acceptance of the bibliographical control systems used in academic and research libraries as de facto standards. As most of the research on bibliographical control deals with such systems, this chapter focuses on academic libraries although it rarely mentions them specifically.

Bibliographical control will be used in this chapter conventionally to include descriptive cataloging, subject cataloging, and classification. The conventional categorization, while chosen here for simplicity, reflects two realities of the library world: the functional organization in technical service departments and the course organization of curricula in library schools. It might be argued that such a categorization is inadequate because the categories are neither exclusive or exhaustive, nor are they well-defined or conceptualized at a level of generality appropriate for serious research. The shifting boundaries of bibliographical control itself constitute an area of research.

Descriptive Cataloging

At the beginning of the 1980s, when the second edition of the *Anglo-American Cataloguing Rules* (AACR2) was about to be implemented, many librarians were alarmed, fearing that perhaps as many as 49 percent of the headings in library catalogs would need alteration.[2] The outcry was loud: Such a cost was not be be tolerated! Some of the more expensive rules had to be rescinded! Hereafter, every rule change had to be accompanied by an impact statement! The fact that there was such consternation is telling for several reasons. First, it demonstrates quite clearly that cataloging practice is driven by cost considerations. Change is inevitable if there is to be progress; it is also inevitably expensive. Thus, practicing librarians tend to be opposed to change. Does it follow as well that they are opposed to research that might instigate change? A little research on the impact of AACR2 actually had a calming effect. Arlene Taylor demonstrated that the initial fears attending implementation of AACR2 were much exaggerated.[3]

A second reason why the outcry over AACR2 is telling is that it raises the question on what basis are changes made to the catalog code? Why, for instance was the rule for main entry under editor dropped? Akos Domanovsky argued that no prevailing user expectations existed regarding editor entry; but was there empirical evidence for this?[4] Why were corporate bodies dropped as authors? Presumably curtailing entry under corporate bodies would have the effect of entering most serials under title (a good thing?); but what alternative means to the same end were considered and what research was undertaken to see how access generally would be affected by the change? (This change, implemented in 1981, has recently been studied by Dorothy McGarry and Martha Yee.[5]) Without the interest and support of administrators or code designers, it is not surprising that there is a paucity of empirical research on the evaluation of catalog code design.

Data Elements

One aspect of code design that has been investigated, perhaps because it seems not overly difficult, concerns the data elements to be included in a bibliographic record. Research in this area began in 1958 with the American Library Association's *Catalog Use Study*, which found that for the most part library patrons make use of only a handful of data elements, usually author, title, publisher, and place of publication.[6]

Multiple replication of this research has produced essentially the same results.[7] The most recent and possibly most sensational example was performed at Bath by Alan Seal.[8] He used a methodology that involved monitoring parallel catalogs, a normal one and an experimental one, in a polytechnic library consisting of 320,000 books and 160,000 nonbook materials. The normal catalog consisted of full bibliographic records, while the experimental catalog, which was in COM form, contained only brief records. Excluded from these brief records were statements of responsibility, edition author statements, notes, ISBNs, places of publication, publisher, and series statements. Cross-references were also eliminated, and personal name headings were reduced to initials plus surnames. For a one-month period users of the library were requested to use the experimental catalog; only if their needs were not met in the experimental catalog should they consult the normal catalog. Surprisingly, the failure rate in use of the experimental catalog was calculated at 8 percent, where failure was defined as (1) inability to locate an item that could be located in the normal catalog; (2) inability to distinguish between similar bibliographic records; or (3) inability to retrieve specific details about a given item. Failure in any of these three respects was perceived as failure in meeting catalog objectives.

Seal's study lacked external validity. Generalizing about the data elements to be included in bibliographic records from the behavior of a sample of university students ignores the fact that the catalog must be designed for the most exacting user demands. Such demands are more likely to come from reference and acquisition librarians and from serious scholars than from casual users of the catalog. Further, generalizing from a small collection where confusion among the various editions of a work may not often occur is questionable. The need for a "full and accurate" catalog was argued eloquently by Panizzi more than a century ago.[9] His arguments, based on reason and an understanding of both users and the items populating the bibliographic universe, remain the most cogent rebuttal to the recent claims emanating from Bath.

That empirical research relating to the data elements to be included in a bibliographic record is flawed does not, however, mean that such research should be eschewed. Full-level cataloging, particularly as rendered in the MARC bibliographic formats, is probably wasteful and excessive; it is certainly redundant. The present demand is for simpler and cheaper cataloging. The demand has been steadily gathering force and was recently articulated at the 1989 IFLA Cataloging Section meeting in the form of a request that a minimal level ISBD be developed.[10] The demand is reasonable; the danger is that the development of such an ISBD might either ignore empirical research or be based on flawed research. The data elements to be included in a bibliographic record must be necessary and sufficient to meet the needs of all users of the catalog. No comprehensive study has directly addressed the question of bibliographic information needed by acquisition and reference librarians, although studies relating to the problem of duplicates impinge on it.

Duplicates, Versions, and Editions

A key objective in descriptive cataloging is to create bibliographic records of sufficient fullness to distinguish disparate items in a collection. Exactly what constitutes sufficient fullness is at the heart of the problem of duplicates. The problem occurs when a database contains two or more bibliographic records that represent items that are copies of each other—two items stand in the copy relationship if they share key attributes. Not surprisingly, the concept of copy is viewpoint-dependent. What a bibliographer would view as a copy differs from the view of a naive user, a reference librarian, or a scholar. These perceptions, in turn, differ from what the input standards of various bibliographic utilities, which do not agree among themselves, regard as copies. The ambiguity is not of academic interest alone. If indeed there is no agreement on what constitutes the copy relationship, then there is consensus neither on what constitutes a unique bibliographic item nor on when to enter a new record in a database.

Early work on the problem of duplicates was carried out at the Library of Congress and reported in Appendix D of the Library of Congress's *Studies in Descriptive Cataloging.*[11] It was undertaken to refute the assertion that full title-page transcription was necessary to guard against the confusions of different editions of a work. Examination of 2,504 bibliographic records representing 198 works showed that the simplified cataloging proposed by Lubetzky could sufficiently distinguish editions and issues of a work. Further, it was shown that number of pages was a good predictor of edition variation within a given work.

With the advent of global catalogs that merge the holdings of many libraries, the problem of duplicates has become exacerbated. Global catalogs not only contain a great many records for the same work, significantly more than would be encountered in the largest of research libraries, but they also contain records created by different cataloging conventions. To the confusion of editions of a work is added the confusion of different methods of bibliographic description. Most studies addressing the problem of duplication in large databases define the goal of duplicate detection as the reduction in the amount of human intervention needed to expunge duplicate records. They define duplicate records as those that match partially or exactly a defined set of data elements, for instance, title, date of publication, and number of pages.

Duplicate detection algorithms have been evaluated in terms of either their ability to discriminate perfectly each individual record in the database or their ability to emulate duplicate detection performed by humans comparing bibliographic records.[12] Both approaches are open to criticism. The first algorithm assumes, falsely, that items in the database are unique. (Indeed, one measure of a good duplicate algorithm is that it succeeds in conflating like items.) The second algorithm assumes, falsely, that bibliographic records correctly reflect actual item differences as perceived by users of the items. To incorporate a user's perspective, research would have to look at the actual items referenced by the records and ask if the actual texts referenced by the so-designated duplicate records were substitutable for the purposes to be served. This approach, in turn, requires an independent conceptual definition of item equivalence, or rather several such definitions, allowing for different user views.

Related to the duplicate problem are the problems of multiple versions and multiple editions. While these problems have always existed, the emergence of global catalogs has made them obtrusive.The problem of multiple versions is how to represent in bibliographic records items that have the same content but appear in different physical formats. [13] The problem of multiple editions is how to display, in a form palatable to the user, a large number of records representing variant editions of one work, e.g., the more than 100 records in the OCLC database for *Humphry Clinker*.[14]

Code Design in a Machine Environment

It hardly seems possible that less than a decade ago technology-driven research in the area of bibliographical control was looking at such issues as (1) the optimal kind of catalog (COM, online or book); (2) the cost-effectiveness of an online catalog; (3) the bibliographic utility that offered the best service; and (4) the costs of cataloging with copy. Research questions relating to administrative concerns triggered by the implementation of online catalogs are necessarily of more temporal duration than those relating to fundamental issues of system design. Foremost among the latter is how to design a cataloging code that truly exploits computer capabilities. The relevance of AACR2 in a computer environment has been challenged; for instance, it is believed by some that the concept of main entry is no longer necessary.[15] Even the framers of AACR2 are apologetic on this point, noting that while they considered designing a main entry–free code, there was not sufficient time to research the considerable implications of such a move.[16]

Some research relating to the question of a main entry–free code was undertaken by Betty Baughman and Elaine Svenonius. Following the code's suggestion that Chapter 21 be used by those preferring alternative entry cataloging, the authors looked at the consequences of systematically substituting "access point" for every occurrence in the code of the words "main entry" or "added entry."[17] They concluded that while main entry construed as "focal access point" is probably no longer needed in retrieval in an online environment, it (or something like it) is still needed for the citing function of the catalog and also for the display function. Part of the difficulty in understanding the considerable implications of abandoning the main entry is that the concept is ambiguous. An attempt to unravel the various meanings of "main entry" has recently been made by Michael Carpenter.[18]

A recently published volume, *The Conceptual Foundations of Descriptive Cataloging*, addresses the main entry question as well as other issues relating to code design in an automated environment.[19] Contributors speculate about the objectives of the catalog; the nature of bibliographic structures; the concepts of authorship, main entry, standards, and integration; and the effect of technology on code design. The volume embodies research of a conceptual nature, that is, research characterized by asking questions, defining terms, imagining possibilities, and analyzing concepts. Activities such as these are sometimes passed over by researchers in their eagerness to gather empirical data. However, the data gathered in empirical research are only as good as the constructs used to interpret them. Conceptual research is needed, particularly to address comprehensive questions such as the design of an optimal set of rules for organizing information in the online environment.

Bibliographic and Authority Relationships

Daniel Bell observed that the information age is characterized by the pre-eminence of theoretical knowledge.[20] Evidence of this trend in bibliographical control research is the appearance of formalistic approaches to deal with the structural aspects of the catalog. By these are meant the relationships exhibited in a catalog, e.g., relationships among items (bibliographic relationships) and relationships among names (authority relationships).

Authority relationships have been the target of recent research that questions the relevance in the computer environment of present practices for *see* and *see also* relationships.[21] The idea behind this research is that where computers can automatically make such linkages, for instance between syntactic variants, there is no need to expend intellectual effort on the task. Further research is needed on automatic ways to achieve authority control, not only for names of persons but also for titles of works and series. Many bibliographic databases incorporate merged files and are threatened with a loss of integrity due to the presence of records reflecting variant authority practices. The post-hoc collocation of like titles and names is a necessary first step in quality control. The concern is that if it cannot be done automatically it will not be done at all.

Other questions relating to authority control have not been researched and need to be. One is simply how much of it to do. The "other side" of cataloging, and the most expensive, is authority control and is worth examining for possible cost savings.[22] Also worth exploring is the issue of providing access to names that are in part controlled and in part uncontrolled. John Duke has looked at this issue and suggested a means of providing enhanced access without incurring additional authority work.[23] Conceptual research is also needed in the area of authority control. Barbara Tillett has observed that the rationale of when to collocate using added entries and when to employ references is shaky at best, and confuses the function and thereby the definition of bibliographic and authority records.[24]

Until recently the literature dealing with bibliographic relationships was largely limited to discussions of the single most important of these relationships, the relationship between manifestations of a given work. This topic has not diminished in importance; indeed it would appear that it is becoming even more debatable as the advent of online catalogs forces a reassessment of the functions of the catalog.[25] Other bibliographic relationships are assuming more importance than they have had previously partly because the bibliographic universe is perceived as becoming increasingly complex and partly because the problem of representing bibliographic data in machine-readable form is becoming focal. Barbara Tillett elaborated a taxonomy of bibliographic relationships and surveyed their frequency of occurrence in the LCMARC database.[26] Melissa Bernhardt developed a methodology for retrieving, formatting, and displaying serial records that graphically show relationships among them.[27] Significantly, Bernhardt's methodology does not rely on a passive use of bibliographic records but upon a manipulation of these records that creatively exploits the sophisticated retrieval and display capabilities of the computer.

Another topic in relationship research, one addressed by John Attig, is how to communicate bibliographic records.[28] Since the MARC format was designed for communicating data elements, it is not adequate to communicate bibliographic relationships. In his assessment of this limitation Attig considers such fundamental matters as the objects that qualify for bibliographic description and the difference between holding records and bibliographic records.

Automatic and Expert Systems

Another instance of technology driving bibliographical control is the recent interest in developing automatic and expert systems to perform catalog construction and maintenance functions. Strictly defined, there is a difference between automating the algorithmic components of a function, e.g. automatic cataloging, and developing a computer consultant to supply expert information to assist in carrying out a function. While the term "expert system" applies only to the latter and assumes the existence of a knowledge base, it tends to be used somewhat indiscriminately to cover automated systems generally.

Mention has already been made of computer techniques for assisting in certain areas of cataloging, such as detecting duplicates, linking syntactic variants of names, and displaying related serial titles. The idea of automating cataloging as a whole was probably first advanced by Martha Sandberg Fox in her doctoral dissertation in 1972.[29] Fox compared the AACR1 and ALA cataloging rules from the perspective of which set of rules was most amenable for automation.

During the 1980s, interest in automatic cataloging revived, with projects initiated at OCLC, the University of Texas, and UCLA, and in England and Sweden. While related, these projects have had various aims: (1) to automatically derive name access points from machine-readable title pages of English language monographs; (2) to construct automatic procedures to produce a first-level bibliographic description consistent with the rules for AACR2; (3) to develop automatic procedures for identifying titles proper based on title page data; (4) to automatically derive access points from machine-readable bibliographic descriptions; and (5) to represent *if-then* algorithms for choice of access points as a series of menus.[30]

Recently, the Library of Congress has been exploring the potential of applying expert systems to assist in performing functions carried out in its Processing Department.[31] The function singled out for development is one of the most complex and problem riddled—series authority work. While no attempt was made to describe in detail how an automated series consultant might work, enough was imagined to conclude that it would be able to perform the kinds of activities normally found in successful expert systems: design, diagnosis, debugging, repair, and instruction. Interestingly, the delivery of descriptive cataloging information is not singled out for expert-system development because this function consists of a large number of finite steps, each of which can be accomplished quickly by an experienced cataloger. The next decade will undoubtedly reveal the appropriateness of expert systems to various bibliographic domains, especially with respect to the dimensions of costs and effectiveness.

Classification

The focus of most recent work in classification has been on automation: developmental work in automating the Dewey Decimal (DDC) and the Library of Congress (LCC) classifications; experimentation with classification in online information retrieval; and speculation and analysis relating to the possible uses of online classifications. There has been some work, but relatively little, in other areas, such as evaluation of classifications, experimentation to understand how humans classify, and the development of methods for automatic and machine-aided classification.

Developmental Work

The actual automating of DDC and LCC has been driven primarily by the economic advantages of updating and publishing the schedules. The nineteenth edition of DDC was published in machine-readable form in 1979. In 1984, development began on a support system for the DDC editorial office at LC. The system included development of a database of records as well as appropriate software for accessing and editing the database. John Finni and Peter Paulson examined the possibility of using the DDC editorial system as part of an integrated cataloger's work station.[32] To realize this possibility, however, requires research into the ways catalogers and classifiers jointly use the various tools that would be included in a cataloger's work station, e.g. the different authority files, sets of rules, and databases.

Despite the enormity of the undertaking, exploratory work began in 1988 to study the feasibility of "automating" LCC. The first step in such a study was to develop a standard generalized format for the communication of classification data. Anticipated in 1985 by Pauline Cochrane and Karen Markey, the USMARC format for authority data for classification schedule data was completed in 1988 and is currently going through a review process. The design of the format was predicated on the objectives of distributing LCC data in machine-readable form (as well as printed), using these data in online information retrieval, and developing an LCC editorial support system. In the course of the development of the format, Nancy Williamson conducted a detailed analysis of the LCC schedules in order to determine characteristics affecting the format design.[33] Insofar as this work is revelatory of inconsistencies in the LCC hierarchies, irregularities in instructions, and anomalies in vocabulary that need resolution before automation can begin, it contributes to the improvement of LCC and to our general understanding of classification systems.

Classification in Online Information Retrieval

The earliest experimental study of the use of traditional classifications online retrieval was the UDC project conducted by Freeman and Atherton in the middle sixties.[34] The goal of this project was to determine whether the Universal Decimal Classification (UDC) could be used in a mechanized retrieval system. One phase of the project consisted of programming various strategies for accessing either the UDC schedules or, through them, a bibliographic database of 2,330 items on nuclear science. Another phase of the Freeman and Atherton project focused on the UDC notation, with a view to exploiting it in a batch retrieval system. In this system, queries were expressed in Boolean combinations of facets of a UDC number; retrieved were documents in the database classified with numbers containing those facets. Problems with the UDC notation (e.g., the ambiguity of certain facet indicators) and with the UDC syntax rules (e.g., their lack of specificity and the fact that they could lead to synonymous constructions) led the researchers to conclude that while UDC can be used as an indexing language in a mechanized system, it cannot function efficiently in such a system.

The Freeman and Atherton work was seminal in its definition of search strategies utilizing UDC numbers and its demonstration of the programming involved therein. The project gave direction to future research in the mechanization of UDC, suggesting that it include (1) experimentation with the use of UDC in conjunction with a detailed thesaurus, using the former to narrow a file and the latter to perform precision searches; (2) evaluation of the UDC as a switching language; and (3) revision of the UDC to emend its structural faults. These suggestions were acted upon within five or six years following the Freeman and Atherton work.[35]

The most recent experimental study examining the use of traditional classifications online is the Dewey Decimal Classification project conducted by Karen Markey and her associates at OCLC.[36] This study took the form of comparing two online catalogs, a subject online catalog (SOC) and a Dewey online catalog (DOC). The latter differed from the former by containing bibliographic records enhanced by verbal matter from the Dewey schedules. Both catalogs permitted call number searching (with subsequent schedule browsing) and keyword searching of the subject-rich fields in bibliographic records. The SOC catalog permitted alphabetic scanning of the Library of Congress Subject Headings (LCSH) with left-most matching, and the DOC catalog permitted scanning of the Dewey Relative Index. Where the DOC catalog differed most from the SOC catalog was in provision of a search strategy called a subject outline search. This search strategy, based on correlations between class numbers and keywords, is similar to the one used in the Freeman and Atherton study. Basically, it "automates" a traditional manual search procedure wherein a user searches the card catalog under subject, writes down the class numbers associated with the subject, and then goes to the shelves to browse. The difference here is that the browsing is done online and the culling of related class numbers is done automatically.

Interpreting the results of the Markey study poses problems because three of the evaluation measures used—precision, recall, and "led directly to relevant items"— were defined with respect to items displayed rather than items retrieved. With this caveat, the major results were the following: (1) Alphabetical searching, requiring exact matching, of either LCSH or the Dewey relative index is virtually useless. In SOC this strategy led to relevant items 5 percent of the time; in DOC, 0 percent of the time. Such a result is hardly surprising; exact matching is a stringent retrieval condition. Refiguring retrieval based on "close matching" gave somewhat better results. (2) Keyword searching of the subject-rich portions of bibliographic records was the search option most frequently used. Not unexpectedly, it produced better precision and poorer recall in SOC than in DOC, whose vocabulary was enhanced by the addition of verbal matter from the DDC schedules. (3) Call number searching, which assumes the user has identified a number of interest, seemed to give better results in SOC than in DOC: 18 percent of patrons' call number searches led to relevant items in SOC; in DOC the number was 7 percent. After being directed to a call number search, few users opted to browse the schedules generically or specifically. (4) The percentage of subject outline searches that led to relevant items directly or in combination with other strategies was 29 percent, a disappointingly low figure, especially since this search strategy makes the most characteristic use of the classification. The problem, however, may lie not so much in the idea of such a strategy, but in its application. For instance, one difficulty with these searches was that users were directed to class numbers that were often too broad; e.g., a user interested in karate was directed to the general number for jujitsus (yawara), which contained items on karate along with 100 others. Another difficulty was that users seemed not know how to choose among the different class numbers correlated with their search terms.

Online experiments with traditional classifications have defined certain options. Schedules can be searched by call number or keyword. Searches can be performed using Boolean combinations of the components or facets of classification numbers. Bibliographic records can be enhanced by verbal text from classification schedules to improve keyword retrieval. Classification indexes can be browsed. Users' search terms can be correlated with classification numbers, by way of schedule captions, notes, index entries, or vocabulary in the subject-rich portions of bibliographic records. The experiments, however, do not tell us conclusively whether pursuing these options would be worthwhile. Access to a relative index using an exact match condition may be ineffective, but keyword access might work. A subject outline search as defined in the Markey study may be ineffective, but this does not preclude the workability of another method of correlating verbal and class headings. Users may seldom choose search strategies exploiting classificatory information, but this does not mean such strategies are not useful; it could mean only that users fail to understand the power of these strategies. Interfaces might be designed whereby such strategies could be exploited to help the user without explicit user awareness. More importantly, such experiments do not tell us what other search strategies might be designed. Search strategies exploiting the aspects of classifications that uniquely distinguish them from systems based on verbal headings alone, e.g., notation and structural properties, need to be developed. Prerequisite to this development is basic research into the nature of classification, as called for by Ranganathan in the 1960s.[37]

Analytic and Speculative Studies Relating to Automation

Conceptualization of the problems to be expected and the potentialities that might be achieved in automating classification can be found not only in the reports of implementation and experimentation, but also in writing of an analytic or speculative nature. Following Douglas Waples, such writing might be characterized as the "look before the leap," in that it provides visions, warnings and frameworks for research.[38]

Phillip Immroth's examination of the indexing of the LCC is an old but still relevant example of an analytical-conceptual study.[39] Immroth demonstrated that the Library of Congress subject headings provide a very inadequate index to the LCC. Such a finding is useful as it bears on present efforts to develop online search strategies that correlate subject headings and class numbers. The implication is not that such efforts should be abandoned but that more sophisticated correlation methods should be explored. For example, probabilistic methods and strategies that seek to predict class numbers using combined information from a variety of sources (not subject headings alone) deserve exploration. Immroth's study is valuable as well for its vision, particularly the suggestion of a chain index for the LCC. An argument can be made that the effective use of classification in online retrieval will ultimately depend upon the existence of adequate indexes to the classification. The feasibility of chain indexing needs reexamination, since it has the potential for improving both precision and recall.[40]

In several papers Lois Chan examined the possibility of using LCC as an online retrieval tool. She looked at both possibilities and limitations within the context of the broad question: what features of classification systems affect their usefulness in online subject retrieval? Identified features include the structure of a classification (largely enumerative vs. largely synthetic), the tables, notation, vocabulary and indexes of a classification, and the degree of call number integrity in a classification over time and across libraries. Chan raised questions for further research: Does the LCC favor precision over recall and DDC recall over precision? What is the impact on retrieval of a largely enumerative scheme?[41]

Arnold Wajenberg considered how structural information encoded in Dewey numbers could be used in online retrieval.[42] Structural information may be divided into two categories: hierarchical and synthetic. Unfortunately, the DDC class numbers do not always express hierarchy (e.g., the DDC class number for chain hoists is the same length as that for hoisting equipment); nor, lacking a consistent method of facet indication, do they reflect synthetic structure. Wajenberg proposes a method whereby these lapses in DDC notation could be remedied by encoding in the 082 field information about broader terms and about the number-building process that results in a given class number. While some question remains about the proper locus of structural information—in the 082 field of a particular bibliographic record, in an authority record for a class number or elsewhere—Wajenberg's work is a tour de force, demonstrating what must be done to exploit classificatory structure in online information retrieval.

Janet Swan Hill wrote a cautionary paper in which she pointed out obstacles to the use of traditional classification in an online environment and argued that automating traditional classifications should not be a high priority in classification research.[43] Four of these obstacles are: (1) users do not understand classification numbers; (2) traditional classifications are illogical; (3) a shelf-ordering classification does not work for information retrieval; and (4) classification numbers change.

How formidable these obstacles are is open to question and research. Probably the most serious is that classification numbers change. Macrochanges affecting classification numbers, such as the development of a phoenix schedule, perhaps can be dealt with by creating automatic mapping procedures that utilize clues on bibliographic records, e.g., subject headings, title words, and possibly keywords from tables of contents and indexes. More insidious and difficult to handle are microchanges, the minor changes in shelf-listing procedures that often result from copy-cataloging decisions to accept "as-is" class numbers. Although the economics of shared cataloging make standardization desirable, acceptance of copy cataloging without reclassification when helpful order is eroded is a threat to shelf-list integrity and to the potential use of classification online. A study of the degree, kind, and cost of quality control needed to prevent DDC and LCC from degenerating into mark and park systems, probably more than any other kind of research, would furnish evidence on the viability of these systems for online browsing.

It is probably possible to develop for online use classifications more appropriate than DDC or LCC, which were designed primarily for shelf arrangement. With a view to providing a direction for future research and development as well as a measure by which to assess the online potentialities of present schemes, Svenonius speculated upon what an ideal general classification might look like, one that was designed expressly for a full-featured online catalog.[44] Svenonius raises questions that need research: (1) how to strike a balance between synthesis and enumeration; (2) how to make different classifications compatible; and (3) how to create an ideal notation that in addition to meeting the criteria of expressivity, hospitality, and brevity can also be generated automatically.

Comparative and Evaluative Research

Perhaps because libraries in this country are locked into a particular classification, DDC or LCC, there is is little motivation for research that examines the comparative effectiveness of different classifications. A notable exception to this generalization is the work of Edward O'Neill, Martin Dillon, and Diane Vizine Goetz, in which the collocatability, or rather its reverse, class dispersion, is compared in LCC and DDC.[45] The question these authors asked was "Are there patron needs, queries or retrieval situations that would be better served by one classification rather than another?" This work is significant in the area of evaluation; it has implications for LCC and DDC convertibility; it is, moreover, an example of the abstract study of classification called for by Ranganathan. Further progress in this area of research will depend upon development of an articulate language of description, comparison, and evaluation, a kind of metalanguage, as it were, that has classificatory and indexing languages as its objects.

Research in User Behavior

Another subject of classification research probes the user's mind to ascertain processes and sequences that may be relevant to the construction of classification schemes. It is not unusual for reference to the imagined mind of the user to be invoked in the justification of design decisions in the realm of bibliographical control. One of the arguments in favor of a classified catalog over an alphabetic subject one is that the order in which it presents ideas in some way reflects the logic of the user's mind. In the design of faceted schemes, the problem of citation order often is rationalized on the basis of some theory of how users think, e.g., engineers are interested more in processes than in things or objects.

To be taken seriously, views about the classificatory behavior of users must have empirical warrant. Such warrant can be found in the fields of individual and developmental psychology. Suzanne Najarian looked at the evidence in these fields which supports the hypothesis that human memory makes use of hierarchical structuring.[46] She recommended systems that adopt hierarchical organizations familiar to users, that permit search strategies similar to those facilitating retrieval from memory, and that take into consideration the amount of information a person can attend to at one time. Before these recommendations can be put into effect, more research using specific methodologies designed to study the nature of human categorizing and remembering is needed.

Eleanor Rosch, in an attempt to understand the nature of human categorization, speculated about the specificity level at which people articulate concepts.[47] She hypothesized that there is a certain specificity or abstraction level at which most people operate. To test this hypothesis she asked subjects to list attributes for objects at each of three levels in nine different taxonomies. An example of a taxonomy is: furniture: chair: kitchen chair. The object in each chain that was assigned the most attributes in common was the middle level; the middle level was, therefore, deemed the basic level of abstraction. Problems with this experiment encompass the operational definition of basic level (the logic of classification presumes a subordinate class has more attributes than the class including it) and lack of control of variables that could affect a person's verbal behavior, variables such as culture, intelligence, experience, knowledge, and imagination. Further, it is dangerous to generalize from behavior vis-a-vis nine three-member (incommensurable) taxonomies in an artificial environment to real world behavior, particularly to information-seeking behavior.

Studies in the field of library and information science have indicated great variability in the specificity of user's search language.[48] Indeed, this is a raison d'etre for a classified approach to subject retrieval, an approach that, moving up and down hierarchies, can gear a user's vocabulary to that of the system. Nevertheless, Rosch's research is an example of the type of investigation that is needed. Other inventive methodologies, perhaps linguistically and psychologically based, are needed to study human categorizing and retrieval processes. An example of a linguistic approach to the study of human categorization is the work of Clare Beghtol.[49] Interested in linguistic constructions of "aboutness," she proposed the interesting hypothesis that a classifier's perception of what an article is about is a function of the classification systems used.

Methods for Automatic and Semiautomatic Classification

Space constraints preclude a comprehensive review of the vast literature relating to automatic classifications. (For an excellent overview of recent work in this area, see Peter Willett.[50]) However, research on automatically classifying documents into existing classifications will be considered briefly. A variety of interesting systems for automatically classifying documents has been implemented with nontraditional classifications. These systems include the BIOSIS system constructed by Vleduts Stokolov, the chemical abstracts system devised by K. A. Hamill and A. Zamora, and the energy database system designed by Claudio Todeschini and Michael Farrell.[51] Irene Travis recently reviewed examples and discussed the potentiality of different knowledge-base systems in classification.[52]

In the area of classification, the LC report on expert systems mentioned above singled out shelf-listing for expert system development.[53] Envisioned is an automatic shelf-listing assistant which would supply cuttering data once class numbers have been completed. For the most part, cuttering would be done completely automatically; but where anomalies existed in shelf-listing patterns, these would be brought to the attention of the cataloger. The report also specified an expert system to aid in actual assigning of class numbers to documents. Once a subject heading had been assigned to a document, the system would perform a thesaurus-assisted search of the classification schedules to determine its appropriate class number.

An expert system for classifying books using DDC was described by Charles Jewitt in an article entitled "Subject Indexing Engine."[54] Jewitt envisioned a subject indexing engine as a component of a cataloger's workstation receiving as input a cataloger's verbal description of a topic, theoretically in any language, and producing as output a DDC number. Jewitt's examples of mappings from verbal descriptions to class numbers clearly illustrate the complexity of the DDC number-building rules. The attempt to develop such an indexing engine reveals directions for future DDC revision and clarifies some of the problems involved in using the DDC as a switching language.

Kathleen Garland considered the possibility of automatically classifying documents into LCC classes.[55] Using keywords from subject headings and titles, she experimented with automatically clustering 416 monographs that had already been assigned to the class Q (Science) by LC catalogers. Clusters obtained using different criteria for threshold similarity were compared with existing LC classes. At high thresholds, an automatically generated cluster was likely to fall neatly within a single LC class; however, many documents in a given LC class were not among those automatically clustered there. Garland called for further study with automatic classification, using as clustering points data elements other than keywords in titles and subject headings. She also called for exploration of the differences between manual and automatic classification methods.

Subject-Heading Assignment

The 1980s have been a period of unprecedented interest and activity in the area of subject access. Marking the beginning of this period was a meeting held in Dublin, Ohio, in June 1982.[56] Sponsored by the Council on Library Resources (CLR), it brought together twenty-three persons representing bibliographic utilities, research libraries, library schools, and indexing and abstracting agencies for the purpose of discussing critical problems in subject access to bibliographic records and arriving at strategies for resolution. The meeting produced a number of recommendations, short-term and long-term, for improving subject access.

The lead recommendation called upon CLR to assume a leadership role in the improvement of subject access, and indeed it has in the areas of research funding and sponsorship of research forums.

Another recommendation specified that the Library of Congress Subject Headings should be made available in machine-readable form with current and regular updates. This recommendation, implemented in 1987, spawned a number of new research problems, the most obvious being how to incorporate the machine-readable LCSH into online catalogs in an effective manner. Locally, this problem is being addressed by systems designers at individual institutions, and a number of different solutions will likely be formulated. Generally, it is being addressed in a CLR research project directed by Karen Markey and Diane Vizine-Goetz.[57] Markey and Vizine-Goetz have already completed the first phase of this project, a study of the characteristics of LCSH authority records for topical and geographic headings. In subsequent phases of the project they will evaluate automated techniques to link the natural language terms entered by online catalog users with the LCSH.

One particularly knotty problem attending the use of LCSH online, the display of assigned subject headings, deserves special mention. The sheer number of subject headings that begin with the same word (e.g., in the ORION database, 584 headings begin with "Aeronautics") combined with the confusing ordering of headings produced by machine-filing rules result in displays that would frustrate even the most sophisticated catalog users. An ALA subcommittee is analyzing problems resulting from machine-filing rules, particularly cases where subdivisions of headings are interrupted by phrase headings, inversions, or parenthetical qualifiers.[58] The problem of redundancy in headings has been addressed at OCLC by Edward O'Neill and quite recently by Mia Massicotte, who proposed a method of compressing subject heading displays.[59] Further work is needed in creating helpful orderings of subject headings.

Still another CLR recommendation addressed creation of a mechanism for libraries to contribute new subject headings and see references to LC for inclusion in LCSH. In 1982, under the rubric Entry Vocabulary Project, a cooperative subject authorities program was implemented, with catalogers at the University of California at Berkeley, Duke, Harvard, and the National Library of Canada sending suggestions to the Subject Catalog Division of the LC.[60] As was the case with the distribution of LCSH in machine-readable form, the implementation of cooperative subject authority work created new areas for research and problem solving. Development of protocols for making cooperative projects cost effective is urgently needed. It seems clear that the distributed creation of subject headings cannot succeed unless there is a manual of rules and guidelines to insure a uniform practice. Nudged by the CLR, LC has produced such a manual, but it is still only partially complete.[61] Much work remains to rationalize the creation and assignment of LCSHs and to transform LCSH from being a precedence-based index language into a rule-based language. Ideally, the development of any particular index language, like LCSH, should be informed by the results of basic conceptual research into index language design. Recently, development of a subject heading manual that is independent of any specific index language has received some attention.[62]

Quality control is another area for research generated by the prospect of cooperative subject heading creation and assignment. Particularly needed are measures for improving the consistency of assigned subject headings. Inconsistency is of two kinds: (1) the same subject heading, because of spelling errors, omissions, additions, or inversions, is represented in a database in different forms, and (2) books on the same subject are assigned different subject headings by different catalogers. The extent of the first type of inconsistency is astonishing; the single subheading "Addresses, Essays and Lectures" (no longer used) appears in the OCLC database under 100 different guises.[63] Obviously, the effect of such inconsistencies on ordered displays is disastrous. The degree to which automatic procedures can be developed to correct these inconsistencies is being pursued by O'Neill and others at OCLC.[64]

The second type of inconsistency, intercataloger inconsistency, has recently been studied by Lois Chan, who compared subject headings on 100 MARC records assigned by non-LC libraries and LC respectively.[65] Only fifteen pairs represented perfect matches; eighty pairs had at least one matching heading, and five had no matches at all. The obvious message here is that perfect matches in LCSH heading assignment by different catalogers are hard to achieve. Constance McCarthy has characterized the obstacles that prevent materials on the same subject being located under the same heading and suggested such possible solutions as providing more subject headings per record, improving the LCSH cross-reference structure, enlarging the LCSH entry vocabulary, and when assigning a given subject heading, routinely checking its suitability by reviewing its past use.[66] Research is needed to test the viability of these approaches to improved consistency and, thereby, improved collocatability.

One of the recommendations emanating from the CLR Dublin meeting endorsed development of a strategy for integrating LCSH with other thesauri and with classification schedules to make combined use of these bibliographical tools possible in online searching. As the first step to impose a more thesaural structure on LCSH, a program was written that would automatically analyze the LCSH see-also references in order to isolate the BT-NT relationships from the RT ones. Unfortunately, the theoretical principle underlying the computer program (a two-way see-also indicates a related term and a one-way see-also indicates a hierarchical relationship) did not work well in practice. A considerable amount of human drudge work now needs to be done to introduce consistency and predictability into the LCSH syndetic structure. Distributing this work outside of LC is a possibility, but to realize it, protocols would have to be developed, and, prior to that, index language design rationalized.

To explore in a general way the compatibility of LCSH with other indexing vocabularies, LC commissioned a study to review how multiple thesauri are accommodated in seven large online catalogs.[67] The integration of indexing vocabularies, the compatibility of indexing languages, or the use of multiple thesauri, whatever the research area is called, constitutes one of the more theoretically challenging areas in index language research.

Another of the CLR recommendations asked that funding agencies support research into how people adapted to online catalogs. It was stressed that results of this research should be actionable, that is capable of being used by those designing systems. A number of studies of online catalogs have been conducted recently, the most notable being one funded by CLR itself.[68] In this study 8,094 online catalog users and 3,981 nonusers in 29 libraries, a quarter of them public libraries and a half large research libraries, were asked about their use of and attitudes toward online catalogs. Various research methodologies were employed in this study, including questionnaire surveys, focus group interviews, and transaction log analyses. The most cited finding to emerge from the study was the great number of subject searches conducted. In those online catalogs that provided subject searches, 59 percent of users searched for subject information; presumably, a significantly larger number than performed subject searches in card catalogs. Reaction to this finding was, on the one hand, doubtful (might the results be biased by the great number of undergraduate students who responded?) and, on the other, jubilant (there has been a paradigm shift in catalog searching).[69]

Some research carried out since the CLR study has confirmed the replicability of this finding. Carolyn Frost looked at subject searching of 196 faculty members at an academic research library.[70] Contrary to expectation, 90 percent conducted subject searches to some extent in the online or card catalog. Though statistical tests were not performed, the amount of subject searching in the two catalogs did not appear to differ significantly. The belief that subject searching is more prevalent in online catalogs and the conjecture raised by some that "the performance of known-item searches in the card catalog was a user adaptation to the difficulty of doing effective subject searching with this tool" needs further corroboration.[71]

Much of the reporting on the results of the CLR study centered on problems that users experienced with online catalogs. Users have difficulty in (1) finding correct subject terms; (2) increasing a search when too little is retrieved; and (3) limiting a search when too much is retrieved. The actionable results of the study were, therefore, that subject access should be both enriched and simplified. The CLR study results were mostly descriptive. Matthews and Lawrence, however, attempted some relationship research when they looked at independent variables that might be linked with the dependent variables success and user satisfaction in searching online catalogs.[72] Among the types of independent variables they examined were (1) characteristics of users; (2) the task; (3) the interface;and (4) the library setting. More research is needed that goes beyond mere description to the level of explanation. Progress in any field depends on identifying significant variables, operationally defining them (in a creative way) and specifying how they are related. Additional variables that might affect user performance in online systems have been suggested by Charles Meadows: experience, skill and language complexity; Raya Fidel has suggested type of request.[73]

As noted previously, the CLR study recommended that subject access be enriched and simplified. Suggestions for bibliographic record enhancement have centered on two approaches: either adding more controlled vocabulary (e.g., more LCSH headings) or making available more subject-rich fields for free-text searching (e.g., table of contents data or publisher's abstracts could be added to records).[74] In 1983, Mandel counseled that the various alternatives for subject enhancement be tested with respect to their effectiveness and costs.[75] In 1988 the first experimental data relating to this issue appeared. The Australian Defense Force Academy tested the retrieval effectiveness of adding an average of 21 multiword terms from the table of contents or index to the 653 field of the MARC record for each of 6,000 books.[76] The results were noteworthy: the cost of adding the new terms, at a rate of 1,000 per month, was the salary of one paraprofessional; retrieval increased 300 percent; and of the 318 documents retrieved by matching on only the added terms (i.e., neither title terms or words in LCSHs), 69 percent were relevant. This last finding is in accord with other studies carried out on the abstracting and indexing databases, showing that free-text searching retrieves relevant material not retrieved using controlled vocabularies, and vice versa.[77] Given that expert opinion favors a combination of controlled vocabulary and free-text searching and that free-text searching can be made cost-effective for large files, the question that needs to be addressed now is how much and what kind of free text to add to bibliographic records. Adding too much of it (the contents pages of a book?) or adding poor quality text (publisher's blurbs?) could deteriorate search performance, especially precision.

As to simplifying subject access, the provision of keyword searching is probably the preferred choice. Another method offering promise is to assist users with query formulation. In a recent paper, Lois Chan introduced the term "synonym operator."[78] Employing a synonym operator, a user looking for aeroplanes is automatically shown items indexed with airplanes. Several writers have speculated on the advantages of using a transparent or interactive online thesauri in the search process.[79] The design of such thesauri poses a challenge; it seems likely that a more imaginative structure than is attained by following conventional thesaurus guidelines is needed.[80]

The integration of such thesauri into the search process is a challenging area of research. A factor that presently inhibits the use of thesauri in information retrieval is that they are usually index-language specific and in order to search a number of databases simultaneously, searchers are forced to use free-text or natural language rather than controlled vocabulary terms.[81] A notable exception is the BRS/TERM thesaurus, which merges the controlled vocabularies of several index languages by forming concept clusters of terms that are loosely related. The BRS/TERM approach is one solution to the multiple thesauri problem. Another approach is the construction of a "universal thesaurus."[82]

A third approach to simplifying subject access is to provide a structure that can help a user navigate through query and command formulations in an online catalog. Just as a classification structure, like the DDC, can guide a user's shelf browsing without his or her ever knowing the meaning of class numbers or the principles on which the classificatory structure is based, other types of interactive and transparent bibliographic structures can be devised to guide online browsing. The OKAPI online system is an example of a system that is beginning to experiment with simple navigational techniques.[83] For example, if a query input by the user fails in one type of match, the system follows a decision tree and automatically executes another type of match. The execution of decision trees, like the transparent switching of user vocabulary to controlled vocabulary, holds both the promise of simplifying and the danger of misconstruing a user's search.

In the interest of simplifying subject access, experimentation is needed with different search and display strategies. Obstacles to such experimentation are the present limitations of many online catalogs and the lack of funding to develop new capabilities, especially experimental ones. There are, however, some innovative model catalogs that can serve as prototypes for research and development. The CITE system at the National Library of Medicine, which features probabilistic and associative retrieval, ranked display output, and relevance feedback, is one such system.[84] It would seem that there is a danger of overcomplication when options are added to a system to make it more pliable and powerful. The results of one study show users prefer larger databases to more sophisticated ones.[85] Surely the implication is not that sophisticated interfaces should not be developed, but rather that different interfaces should be developed for novices and experts.

Since the time of Cutter, sensitivity to the user has guided the design of bibliographical tools. Some recent studies of users' searching behavior have been reviewed by Karen Markey.[86] A prominent class of such studies is matching studies, in which users' query formulations are analyzed from the point of view of how well they match terms in the LCSH vocabulary. In a recent study of this sort, Allyson Carlyle examined user expressions on transaction logs from ORION, UCLA's online information system.[87] She found significantly higher match rates than have been found in previous studies.

It would appear that much depends on how matches are defined. The match categories used in Carlyle's study were more refined than those previously used; even so, she advises that they could be expanded still further. She also recommends a deeper level of analysis of users' queries, an analysis at a semantic level in order to understand the connection between what users say and what they mean. Transaction-log studies provide a good source of data about users' searching behavior. Such studies are limited, however, insofar as most transaction logs do not show clearly when a given search begins and ends. The cooperation of systems personnel in developing logs better suited for analysis, and even interactive questionnaires, would be very helpful to researchers studying users' query language.

A different type of user study, self-styled a "holistic" approach to understanding user behavior, is represented by the work of Micheline Hancock.[88] Using a methodology that combined user questionnaires as well as participant observation, she studied users' subject searching strategies at the catalog and at the shelves. She speculates that subject searching in libraries may have been underestimated since, in her data, one in three searches initiated as a specific item search was in fact a subject search.

It is useful to explore a variety of research methodologies—analytical, observational, survey and experimental—to study users' searching behavior in that different methodologies are appropriate to different research questions and productive of different findings. It seems worth mentioning again, however, that more attention needs to be paid to developing methodologies that explore not just how users behave but why they behave the way they do. It will be an indication that the field of bibliographical control is becoming more scientifically based when its research becomes less descriptive and more explanatory.

Finally, as with cataloging and classification, there is in the subject heading area an interest in expert systems. An early example is Field's experimentation with the automatic generation of subject headings.[89] The LC report on expert systems calls for a subject heading consultant that would replace all of the present documentation issued by LC to support the subject cataloging function: the bibliographic, name, subject, and classification authority files, as well as databases for the LCSH subdivisions.[90] Given any subject term as input, the system would then suggest appropriate subject headings to the cataloger. Again, how exactly such a consultant would work is left to future research. Some related research currently underway is being done by Gary Strawn, who is testing the possibility of automatically verifying LCSH.[91]

An example of a semideveloped expert system was described by Susanne Humphrey and Nancy Miller.[92] The system is a prototype interactive knowledge based system for computer-assisted assignment of MeSH headings. Its knowledge base consists of the MeSH headings supplemented by additional semantic relationships and a set of procedural rules encoded in a data structure called frames. Procedural rules specify actions to be taken once certain conditions are met, e.g., "if the purpose of the procedure is diagnosis and the age of the patient is fetus, then add the heading Prenatal diagnosis." The development of expert systems, such as that of Humphrey and Miller, forces an analysis of existing practice and, in so doing, leads to a better understanding of exactly what is involved in the provision of a given form of bibliographical control. In other words, expert systems have a theoretical function to play in research as tools of analysis in addition to their practical function of lightening work burdens.

Conclusion

Throughout this chapter, research lacunae have been identified. Needed in the area of cataloging is empirical research on code design, including studies of the impact of changes in the code in terms of both effectiveness and cost. An example of a research question in this area is, which elements should be included in a bibliographic record? The computer has brought to cataloging potentialities and difficulties, both occasioning the need for research. An example of the latter is the problem of duplicates attending the emergence of global catalogs and retrospective conversion projects. As to the former, the question of central interest is how to design a code that effectively exploits machine capabilities. Related to this is the question of how to develop expert systems to assist in the process of descriptive cataloging.

In the area of classification as well, the research agenda has been largely dictated by the potential of the computer to provide better or cheaper means to achieve bibliographical control. The rendering into machine-readable form of the DDC and eventually the LCC has raised the need for a conceptual reevaluation of classificatory principles and practice. It has generated research into how traditional bibliothecal classifications might be implemented in online information retrieval and in cataloger's workstations. Work done so far in this area has opened a Pandora's box of research issues, making the study of online classifications one of the most fruitful areas of current bibliographical control research. Other promising areas for classification research include (1) experimentation with methods for automatic and machine-aided classification, and (2) psychological and linguistic explorations into the human classificatory process.

Directions for improving access to library materials through subject headings were formulated in a CLR– sponsored meeting in Dublin, Ohio, in 1982. Chief among them was the directive to make LCSH available in machine-readable form, giving rise to questions about how to incorporate LCSH into online catalogs effectively. Among these are the following: (1) how to display subject headings; (2) how to link users' queries, expressed in natural language with the language of LCSH; (3) how to enhance the LCSH vocabulary; (4) how to formalize subject heading assignment, in the form of protocols, for the sharing of subject-authority work; (5) how to improve consistency in subject heading assignment; and (6) how to integrate LCSH with other thesauri. Research addressing how people adapt to online catalogs has shown that subject access needs to be enriched and that it needs to be simplified. Opportunities for developmental research in these areas abound. In following them, it is necessary to heed research findings that exist and to base system development upon studies of user behavior that go beyond mere description to seek explanations. Finally, in the area of subject headings access, a promising avenue of research is the designing of expert and automatic systems to aid in the process of providing subject access. The development of expert systems in all areas of bibliographical control is clearly emblematic of a trend. It is a trend that promises not only to ease the economic burden of bibliographical control, but also to rationalize its conceptual foundations and improve its effectiveness.

Notes

1. Seymour Lubetzky, *Principles of Cataloging, Final Report: Phase I: Descriptive Cataloging* (Los Angeles: University of California Institute of Library Research, 1969), pp. 1–4.

2. *Library of Congress Information Bulletin* 37 (March 3, 1978): 153.

3. Arlene G. Taylor, *AACR2 Headings: A Five-Year Projection of Their Impact on Catalogs* (Littleton, Colo.: Libraries Unlimited, 1982).

4. Akos Domanovsky, "Editor Entries and the Principles of Cataloguing," in *Foundations of Cataloging: A Sourcebook,* ed. Michael Carpenter and Elaine Svenonius (Littleton, Colo.: Libraries Unlimited, 1985), pp. 192–207.

5. Dorothy McGarry and Martha Yee, "Conference Proceedings with a Generic Term

for Meeting and the Name of a Corporate Body: A Survey and Comments," to be published in *Libraries Resources and Technical Services.*

6. *Catalog Use Study,* ed. Vaclav Mostecky (Chicago: American Library Assn., 1958).

7. James Krikelas, "Catalog Use Studies and Their Implication," *Advances in Librarianship,* vol. 3, ed. Mel Voigt (New York: Seminar Pr., 1972), pp. 195–220.

8. Alan Seal, "Experiments with Full and Short Entry Catalogues: A Study of Library Needs," *Library Resources and Technical Services* 27 (April/June 1983): 144–155.

9. Anthony Panizzi, "Mr. Panizzi to the Right Hon. the Earl of Ellesmere, Jan. 29, 1848," *Foundations of Cataloging: A Sourcebook,* ed. Michael Carpenter and Elaine Svenonius (Littleton, Colo.: Libraries Unlimited, 1985), pp. 15–47.

10. International Federation of Library Associations and Institutions, "Minutes of the Meetings: Monday, 29 August 1988 and Saturday, 3 September 1988," 54th General Conference, Sydney, August 29–September 3, 1988, p. 3.

11. Elizabeth G. Pierce, "Appendix D: Testing the Value of Full Title-Page Transcription in Cataloging," *Descriptive Cataloging: A Report to the Librarian of Congress by the Director of the Processing Department* (Washington, D.C.: Government Printing Office, 1946), pp. 36–39.

12. Pankaj Goyal, "Duplicate Record Identification in Bibliographic Databases," *Information Systems* 12: 239-242 (1987); Thomas B. Hickey, "Automatic Detection of Duplicate Monographic Records," *Journal of Library Automation* 12 (June 1979): 125–142.

13. Library of Congress, *Discussion Paper No. 21: Communication of Records for Multiple Versions,* typescript.

14. Elaine Svenonius, "Clustering Equivalent Bibliographic Records," *Annual Review of OCLC Research, July 1987–June 1988* (Dublin, Ohio: OCLC Online Computer Library Center, 1988), pp. 6–8.

15. Michael Gorman, "AACR 2: Main Themes," paper read at the International Conference on AACR2, Florida State University, 1979, in *The Making of a Code: The Issues Underlying AACR2,* ed. Doris H. Clack (Chicago: American Library Assn., 1980), p. 46.

16. Michael Gorman and Paul Winkler, eds., *Anglo-American Cataloguing Rules,* 2nd ed. (Chicago: American Library Assn., 1978).

17. Elizabeth Baughman and Elaine Svenonius, "AACR2: Main Entry Free?" *Cataloging and Classification Quarterly* 5 (Fall 1984): 1–15.

18. Michael Carpenter, "Main Entry," in *The Conceptual Foundations of Descriptive Cataloging,* ed. Elaine Svenonius (San Diego: Academic Pr., 1989), pp. 73–95.

19. Elaine Svenonius, ed., *The Conceptual Foundations of Descriptive Cataloging* (San Diego: Academic Pr., 1989).

20. Daniel Bell, *The Coming of the Post-Industrial Society: A Venture in Social Forecasting* (New York: Basic, 1976).

21. Arlene Taylor, "Authority Files in Online Catalogs: An Investigation of Their Value," *Cataloging and Classification Quarterly* 4 (Spring 1984): 1–17; Catherine M. Thomas, "Authority Control in Manual vs. Online Catalogs: An Examination of 'See' References," *Information Technology and Libraries* 3 (December 1984): 393–398.

22. Frances Ohmes and J. F. Jones, "The Other Half of Cataloging," *Library Resources and Technical Services* 17 (Summer 1973): 320–329.

23. John Duke, "Access and Automation," in *The Conceptual Foundations of Descriptive Cataloging*, ed. Elaine Svenonius (San Diego: Academic Pr., 1989), pp. 117–128.

24. Barbara Tillett, "Bibliographic Structures: The Evolution of Catalog Entries, References and Tracings," in *The Conceptual Foundations of Descriptive Cataloging*, ed. Elaine Svenonius (San Diego: Academic Pr., 1989), pp. 149–165.

25. Patrick Wilson, "The Second Objective"; Edward T. O'Neill and Diane Vizine-Goetz, "Bibliographic Relationships: Implications for the Function of the Catalog"; and Sara Shatford Layne, "Integration and the Objectives of the Catalog," all in *The Conceptual Foundations of Descriptive Cataloging*, ed. Elaine Svenonius (San Diego: Academic Pr., 1989).

26. Barbara Tillett, "Bibliographic Relationships: Toward a Conceptual Structure of Bibliographic Information Used in Cataloging" (Ph.D. diss., University of California, Los Angeles, 1987).

27. Melissa M. Bernhardt, "Dealing with Serial Title Changes: Some Theoretical and Practical Considerations," *Cataloging and Classification Quarterly* 9 (Winter 1988): 25–39.

28. John Attig "Descriptive Cataloging Rules and Machine-Readable Record Structures: Some Directions for Parallel Development," in *The Conceptual Foundations of Descriptive Cataloging*, ed. Elaine Svenonius (San Diego: Academic Pr., 1989), pp. 135–148.

29. Martha Sandberg Fox, "The Amenability of a Cataloging Process to Simulation by Automatic Techniques" (Ph.D. diss., University of Illinois, 1972).

30. Elaine Svenonius and Mavis Molto, "Studies in Automatic Cataloging," to be published in *Journal of the American Society for Information Science*; *Annual Review of OCLC Research: July 1985–June 1986* (Dublin, Ohio: OCLC Online Computer Library Center Inc., 1986), p. 9; Ling Hwey Jeng "An Expert System for Determining Title Proper in Descriptive Cataloging: A Conceptual Model," *Cataloging and Classification Quarterly* 7 (Winter 1986): 55–70; Roy Davies, "Outlines of the Emerging Paradigm in Cataloguing," *Information Processing and Management* 23 (1987): 1–10; Roland Hjerppe and B. Olander, *Artificial Intelligence and Cataloging* (Linkoping, Sweden: Linkoping University, 1985).

31. Charles Fenly and Howard Harris, *Expert Systems: Concepts and Applications* (Washington, D.C.: Library of Congress, Cataloging Distribution Service, 1988).

32. John J. Finni and Peter J. Paulson, "The Dewey Decimal Classification Enters the Computer Age: Developing the DDC Database (TM) and Editorial Support System," *International Cataloguing* 16 (October/December 1987): 46–48.

33. Pauline A. Cochrane and Karen Markey, "Preparing for the Use of Classification in Online Cataloging Systems and in Online Catalogs," *Information Technology and Libraries* 4 (June 1985): 91–109; Library of Congress, *Classification Data* (Washington, D.C.: Library of Congress, 1988), typescript; Nancy Williamson, "The Library of Congress Classification: Problems and Prospects in Online Retrieval, "*International Cataloguing* 15 (October/December 1986): 45–48; Nancy Williamson, "The Library of

Congress Classification in the Computer Age," *Proceedings of the Conference on Classification Theory in the Computer Age,* Albany, November 1988 (Albany: State University of New York, 1989).

34. Robert R. Freeman and Pauline Atherton, "File Organization and Search Strategy Using the Universal Decimal Classification in Mechanized Reference Retrieval Systems," in *Mechanized Information Storage, Retrieval, and Dissemination: Proceedings of the FID/IFIP Joint Conference,* ed. Kjell Samuelson (Amsterdam: North-Holland Publishing Co., 1986), pp. 122–152; Robert R. Freeman and Pauline Atherton, "AUDACIOUS—an Experiment with an On-line, Interactive Reference Retrieval System Using the Universal Decimal Classification as the Index Language in the Field of Nuclear Science," in *Information Transfer: Proceedings of the 31st ASIS Annual Meeting* (New York: Greenwood, 1968), pp. 193–199.

35. Anthony C. Foskett, *The Universal Decimal Classification: The History, Present Status and Future Prospects of a Large General Classification Scheme* (London: Bingley, 1973); Hans Wellisch, "UDC: Present and Potential," *Drexel Library Quarterly* 10 (October 1974): 75–89.

36. Karen Markey, and Anh Demeyer, *Dewey Decimal Classification Online Project: Evaluation of a Library Schedule and Index Integrated into the Subject Searching Capabilities of an Online Catalog: Final Report to the Council on Library Resources* (Dublin, Ohio: OCLC Online Computer Library Center Inc., 1986) OCLC Report No. OCLC/OPR/RR-86/1.

37. S. R. Ranganathan, "Library Classification," in *Classification Research: Proceedings of the Second International Study Conference on Classification Research,* ed. Pauline Atherton (Copenhagen: Munksgaard, 1965), p. 33.

38. Douglas Waples, "The Graduate Library School at Chicago," *Library Quarterly* 1 (January 1931): 26–36.

39. John Phillip Immroth, *Analysis of Vocabulary Control in Library of Congress Classification and Subject Headings* (Littleton, Colo.: Libraries Unlimited), 1971.

40. Elaine Svenonius, "Bibliothecal Classifications," *Proceedings of the International Conference on Library Classification Function,* University of Alberta, Edmonton, June 20 and 21, 1989, ed. Andre Nitecki and Tony Fell (Edmonton: Faculty of Extension, University of Alberta, 1990), pp. 22–53.

41. Lois Chan, "Library of Congress Classification as an Online Retrieval Tool: Potentials and Limitations," *Information Technology and Libraries* 5 (September 1986): 181–192, paper read at the Conference on Classification as Subject Enhancement in Online Catalogs, sponsored by OCLC and the Council on Library Resources, Dublin, Ohio, January 1986; Lois Chan, "Library of Congress Class Numbers in Online Catalog Searching," *RQ* 28 (Summer 1989): 530–536.

42. Arnold Wajenberg, "MARC Coding of DDC for Subject Retrieval" *Information Technology and Libraries* 2 (September 1983): 246–251.

43. Janet Swan Hill, "Online Classification Number Access: Some Practical Considerations," *Journal of Academic Librarianship* 10 (March 1984): 17–22.

44. Elaine Svenonius, "An Ideal Classification for an Online Catalog,"*Proceedings of the Conference on Classification Theory in the Computer Age,* Albany, November 1988 (Albany: State University of New York, 1989), pp. 35–43.

45. Edward T. O'Neill, Martin Dillon, and Diane Vizine-Goetz, "Class Dispersion between the Library of Congress Classification and the Dewey Decimal Classification," *Journal of the American Society for Information Science* 38 (May 1987): 197–205.

46. Suzanne E. Najarian, "Organizational Factors in Human Memory: Implications for Library Organization and Access Systems," *Library Quarterly* 51 (July 1981): 269–291.

47. Eleanor Rosch, "Human Categorization," in *Studies in Cross-Cultural Psychology*, vol. 1, ed. N. Warren. (London: Academic Pr., 1977), pp. 1–67.

48. Marcia J. Bates, "Factors Affecting Subject Catalog Search Success" *Journal of the American Society for Information Science* 28 (May 1977): 161–169.

49. Clare Beghtol, "Bibliographic Classification Theory and Text Linguistics: Aboutness Analysis, Intertextuality and the Cognitive Act of Classifying Documents," *Journal of Documentation* 42 (June 1986): 84–113.

50. Peter Willett, "Recent Trends in Hierarchic Document Clustering: A Critical Review," *Information Processing and Management* 24 (1988): 577–597.

51. Natasha Vleduts-Stokolov, "Concept Recognition in an Automatic Text-Processing System for the Life Sciences," *Journal of the American Society for Information Science* 38 (July 1987): 269–287; Karen A. Hamill and Antonia Zamora, "The Use of Titles for Automatic Document Classification," *Journal of the American Society for Information Science* 31 (November 1980): 396–402; Claudio Todeschini and Michael P. Farrell, "An Expert System for Quality Control in Bibliographic Databases," *Journal of the American Society for Information Science* 40 (January 1989): 1–11.

52. Irene Travis, "Applications of Artificial Intelligence to Bibliographic Classification," *Proceedings of the Conference on Classification Theory in the Computer Age*, Albany, November 1988 (Albany: State University of New York, 1989).

53. Fenly and Harris, *Expert Systems.*

54. Charles Jewitt, "A Subject Indexing Engine," in *Proceedings of 8th International Online Information Meeting, London, 4–6 December, 1984* (Oxford: Learned Information (Europe), 1984), pp. 151–160.

55. Kathleen Garland, "An Experiment in Automatic Hierarchical Document Classification," *Information Processing and Management* 19 (1983): 113–120.

56. Keith W. Russell, ed., *Subject Access*. Report of a meeting sponsored by the Council on Library Resources, Dublin, Ohio, June 7–9, 1982 (Washington, D.C.: Council on Library Resources, 1982).

57. Karen Markey and Diane Vizine-Goetz, *Characteristics of Subject Authority Records in the Machine-Readable Library of Congress Subject Headings* (Dublin, Ohio: OCLC Online Computer Library Center, 1988), OCLC Research Report No. OCLC/OR/RR-88/2.

58. SAC Subcommittee on the Display of Subject Headings, "Report of the Meeting of the SAC Subcommittee on the Display of Subject Headings in Subject Indexes in Online Public Access Catalogs," July 8, 1988. Typescript.

59. Mia Massicotte, "Improved Browsable Displays for Online Subject Access," *Information Technology and Libraries* 7 (December 1988): 373–380.

60. Pauline A. Cochrane, *LCSH Entry Vocabulary Project: Final Report to the*

Council on Library Resources and to the Library of Congress (ERIC ED 233746).

61. Library of Congress, Subject Cataloging Division, Processing Services, *Subject Cataloging Manual: Subject Headings,* rev. ed. (Washington, D.C.: Library of Congress, 1985).

62. William E. Studewell and Paule Rolland Thomas, "The Form and Structure of a Subject Heading Code," *Library Resources and Technical Services* 32 (April 1988): 167–169.

63. Anna Lantz, Edward T. O'Neill, and Diane Vizine-Goetz. " 'Addddrdsses, Elctures, Esssays' and Other Variant Subject Headings," in *Academic Libraries: Myths and Realities: Proceedings of the Third National Conference of ACRL* (Chicago: ACRL, 1984), pp. 183–186.

64. Ed O'Neill and Rao Aluri, *A Method for Correcting Typographical Errors in Subject Headings in OCLC Records* (Dublin, Ohio: OCLC Online Computer System, 1980), OCLC Report No. OCLC/OPR/R-80/3; ERIC ED 215680.

65. Lois Chan, *Variations in Subject Cataloging in Non-LC Cataloging Records in the OCLC Database* (Dublin, Ohio: OCLC Online Computer Library Center, Inc., 1989) OCLC/OR/RR-89/1.

66. Constance McCarthy, "The Reliability Factor in Subject Access," *College & Research Libraries* 47 (January 1986): 48–56.

67. Carol A. Mandel, *Multiple Thesauri in Online Library Bibliographic Systems: A Report Prepared for Library of Congress Processing Services* (Washington, D.C.: Library of Congress, 1987).

68. Joseph Matthews, Gary Lawrence, and Douglas Ferguson, ed., *Using Online Catalogs: A Nationwide Survey* (New York: Neal Schuman, 1983); Neal K. Kaske, et al., *A Comprehensive Study of Online Public Access Catalogs: An Overview and Application of Findings* (Dublin, Ohio: OCLC Online Computer Library Center, Inc., 1983), OCLC Report No. OCLC/OPR/RR-83/4; ERIC ED 231404. Vol. 3, *Final Report to the Council on Library Resources.*

69. Robert N. Broadus, "Online Catalogs and Their Users," *College & Research Libraries* 44 (November 1983): 458–467; Pauline A. Cochrane, "A Paradigm Shift in Library Science," *Information Technology and Libraries* 2 (March 1983): 3–4.

70. Carolyn O. Frost, "Faculty Use of Subject Searching in Card and Online Catalogs," *Journal of Academic Librarianship* 13 (May 1987): 86–92.

71. Ray Larson, "The Decline of Subject Searching: Long-Term Trends and Patterns of Index Use in an Outline Catalog," to be published.

72. Joseph R. Matthews and Gary S. Lawrence, "Further Analysis of the CLR Online Catalog Project," *Information Technology and Libraries* 3 (December 1984): 354–376.

73. Charles T. Meadow, *A Survey of User Adaptation to an Interactive Information Retrieval System* (Dublin, Ohio: OCLC Online Computer Library Center, Inc., 1983), OCLC Report No. OCLC OPR RR-83/6; Raya Fidel, "What Is Missing in Research about Online Searching Behavior?" *Canadian Journal of Information Science* 12 (1987): 54–61.

74. Pauline Atherton, *Books Are for Use: Final Report of the Subject Access Project to the Council of Library Resources* (Syracuse, N.Y.: Syracuse University, 1978), ERIC ED 156131; Barbara Settel, ed., *Subject Description of Books: A Manual of Procedures*

for Augmenting Subject Descriptions in Library Catalogs (Syracuse, N.Y.: Syracuse University, 1977).

75. Carol A. Mandel and Judith Herschman, "Online Subject Access—Enhancing the Library Catalog," *Journal of Academic Librarianship* 9 (July 1983): 148–155.

76. Alex Byrne, and Mary Micco, "Improving OPAC Subject Access: The ADFA Experiment," *College & Research Libraries* 49 (September 1988): 432–441.

77. Elaine Svenonius, "Unanswered Questions in the Design of Controlled Vocabularies," *Journal of the American Society for Information Science* 37 (September 1986): 331–340.

78. Lois Chan, "Library of Congress Subject Headings as an Online Retrieval Tool: Structural Considerations," in *Improving LCSH 20for Use in Online Catalogs* (Littleton, Colo.: Libraries Unlimited, 1986), pp. 123–133.

79. Anne B. Piternick, "Searching Vocabularies: A Developing Category of Online Search Tools," *Online Review* 8 (October 1984): 441–449 ; Marcia Bates, "Subject Access in Online Catalogs: A Design Model," *Journal of the American Society for Information Science* 37 (November 1986): 357–376.

80. Elaine Svenonius, "Design of Controlled Vocabularies," *Encyclopedia of Library and Information Science,* vol. 45, ed. by Allen Kent, Harold Lancour, and Jay E. Daily (New York: Marcel Dekker, 1990), pp. 82–109.

81. Raya Fidel, Private communication reporting work in progress.

82. Dagobert Soergel, *Indexing Languages and Thesauri: Construction and Maintenance* (Los Angeles: Melville, 1974).

83. Nathalie Nadia Mitev et al., *Designing an Online Public Access Catalogue: OKAPI, a Catalogue on a Local Area Network* (London: British Library, 1985), Library and Information Science Report No. 39.

84. Tamas E. Doszkocs, "CITE NLM: Natural Language Searching in an Online Catalog," *Information Technology and Libraries* 2 (December 1983): 364–380.

85. David W. Lewis, "Research on the Use of Online Catalogs and Its Implications for Library Practice," *Journal of Academic Librarianship* 13 (July 1987): 152–157.

86. Karen Markey, *Analytical Review of Catalog Use Studies* (Dublin, Ohio: OCLC Online Computer Library Center, 1980) OCLC Research Report No. OCLC/OPR/RR-80/2.

87. Allyson Carlyle, "Matching LCSH and User Vocabulary in the Library Catalog," *Cataloging and Classification Quarterly* 10 (1989): 37–63.

88. Micheline Hancock, "Subject Searching Behaviour at the Library Catalogue and at the Shelves: Implications for Online Interactive Catalogues," *Journal of Documentation* 43 (December 1987): 303–321.

89. B. J. Field, "Towards Automatic Indexing: Automatic Assignment of Controlled-Language Indexing and Classification from Free Indexing" *Journal of Documentation* 31 (December 1975): 246–265.

90. Gary L. Strawn, Letter to Dee Michel, 2 November 1987.

91. Fenly and Harris, *Expert Systems.*

92. Susanne M. Humphrey and Nancy E. Miller, "Knowledge-Based Indexing of the Medical Literature: The Indexing Aid Project," *Journal of the American Society for Information Science* 38 (May 1987): 184–196.

Jo Bell Whitlatch

Access Services

Professional concerns of academic librarians are shifting from collection building to providing access to information for users. Stayner notes that the change in emphasis from ownership to access can be attributed to at least two factors: the decline in funds available to purchase materials and the effects of technological changes, which have expanded accessibility to users without requiring ownership by the user's primary library.[1] This chapter describes the various dimensions of access and reviews research findings related to accessibility and use of information sources, user interface with library staff and bibliographic systems, physical access to libraries, and physical retrieval of material from libraries.

Research conducted primarily in the United States during the past twenty years is emphasized here. Studies that address explanation and prediction, thereby enhancing our understanding of the role of academic libraries in society, are highlighted. Although descriptive surveys of professional practices in academic libraries are interesting for comparative purposes, they have limited explanatory power and are not examined here. Priority is given to studies based on several libraries, with more limited coverage of important studies conducted in a single institution. Studies conducted in one institution are included when the results would have implications for professional practice if the studies were successfully replicated in other academic libraries.

Dimensions of Access

Blair distinguishes physical access from logical access.[2] Logical access is concerned with how to find the address of the desired information—the discovery of which information source contains the desired information and, if the library is selected, which book in the library will be likely to satisfy a particular information need. Physical access concerns how desired information is retrieved and represented physically to the inquirer once the address of the information is known. In the library, physical access involves discovering the location of a book with a particular call number and locating the material on the shelf. Blair notes that problems of logical access must be addressed first because one must know what kind of information answers a particular question.

Buckland identifies four types of accessibility relating to retrieval and the state of becoming informed by documents: (1) indicative access, or the problem of defining documents containing the information; (2) physical access; (3) linguistic access; and (4) conceptual access or the ability to comprehend the text.[3] He observes that libraries tend to focus on indicative and physical access and therefore are primarily concerned with information retrieval rather than with communication generally. Culnan suggests that the concept of accessibility provides a unifying theme for designing information services and for gathering feedback from users for evaluation and improvements in the service.[4] Her research provides support for accessibility as a multidimensional concept, which includes: (1) physical access to the information system; (2) interface or bibliographic access to the source; and (3) the ability to physically retrieve potentially relevant information.

This essay first discusses research related to accessibility and information source use in order to explore the role accessibility plays in determining information source use. Then, two dimensions of accessibility are discussed as they apply to libraries. The first dimension, logical or indicative access, focuses on analysis of research on user interaction with library staff and library bibliographic systems. The second dimension, physical access to information, focuses on analyzing research on physical access to library buildings by users and research related to users obtaining documents, both within libraries and from remote locations.

Accessibility and Information Source Use

Research in organizational behavior suggests that although both quality and accessibility influence use of information sources, accessibility rather than quality consistently determines information usage. O'Reilly found that accessibility predicted frequency of information source use independent of other variables, such as uncertainty in the task, education, and tenure on the job.[5] In the last two decades, a number of studies which focus on use of information sources also confirm the importance of accessibility in determining information source selection. These studies are summarized in Table 1 and furnish convincing evidence that personal collections of scholars are the primary source used in conducting research.

Lack of time and the volume of literature were cited by many respondents as important information difficulties.[6] Time appears to be the major factor in the nonuse of the library by academic physicists and chemists. Distance was also a factor indicated by some.[7] Special information problems reported by historians were lack of time and money for research, distance from a good research library, lack of knowledge of a language, lack of knowledge of existence of material, restrictions on physical access such as failure to declassify documents, lack of specialized guides, and interlibrary loan restrictions.[8]

Scholars interviewed by Soper cited convenience as the reason for putting effort and money into personal collections.[9] Personal collections were easier to use, flexible, and responsive to individual research interests because they have been developed and arranged to meet those interests. They were also housed in preferred working environments. Personal collections accounted for the largest percentage of the works cited in scholarly articles. The only locations important as sources of cited works were personal collections (59 percent), the main institutional library (23.1 percent), and libraries in other cities or counties (9.5 percent).

Respondents in the humanities answered significantly differently from respondents in other disciplines. They reported citing as many works in libraries as in their personal collections, and a substantial proportion of works cited were located in libraries far from their home institutions. Soper concluded that the establishment and maintenance of personal collections appeared to be more closely related to convenience than to inadequacy of institutional collections. Personal collections were found to contain materials very similar to library collections.

These case studies and surveys of how practitioners and scholars use information demonstrate that understanding and evaluating accessibility are essential to designing information services, including such academic library services as reference, circulation, reserves, and interlibrary loan. Comprehending access services requires a holistic view of the information user. This perspective shifts the focus from an examination of information sources and systems to an investigation of the role of information in users' everyday lives, work, or social settings.[10] Dervin's view of information as that which informs is also essential. It is the individual who makes sense of the information, constructs reality, and decides the utility of the information in a given situation.[11]

Progress in effective design of access services, therefore, requires looking at the library as a system functioning in an environment. In this environment, users select the library to meet certain types of demands. Buckland notes that studies of the dynamics and sensitivity of demand have been seriously neglected.[12] Buckland suggests that individuals have desires that, in their own perceptions, could probably be satisfied by using the library. Individuals weigh

TABLE 1
ACCESSIBILITY AND INFORMATION SOURCE USE

Study	*Sample*	*Method*	*Main Results*
Bowden & Bowden (1971)	400 randomly selected members of the American Psychiatric Association	Survey	Materials for work-related projects primarily obtained by purchase (67%); minority from libraries (28%)
Chen (1974)	500 academic physicists and chemists in greater Boston area	Survey	Time major factor in nonuse of the library
Soper (1976)	300 authors of scholarly journals of general scope from sciences, social sciences and humanities	Interview	Convenience primary reason for money and effort invested in developing personal collections
Scholarly Comm. (1979)	Sample of scholars representing 7 disciplines in humanities and social sciences	Survey	Majority (74%) of references cited came from personal collections; use library as a supplement for costly, specialized and less frequently used materials
Stieg (1981)	767 historians listed in *Directory of American Scholars*	Survey	Preference for highly evaluative sources for discovering information: references in books/journals, book reviews, and specialized bibliographies

Bowden, Charles L. and Virginia M. Bowden. "A Survey of Information Sources Used by Psychiatrists." *Bulletin of the Medical Library Association* 59 (October 1971): 603–608.

Chen, Ching-chih. "How Do Scientists Meet Their Information Needs?" *Special Libraries* 65 (July 1974): 272–280.

Soper, Mary Ellen. "Characteristics and Use of Personal Collections." *Library Quarterly* 46 (October 1976): 397–415.

Scholarly Communication: The Report of the National Enquiry. Baltimore: Johns Hopkins, 1979.

Stieg, Margaret F. "The Information Needs of Historians." *College & Research Libraries* 42 (November 1981): 549–560.

the perceived price of using the library against the perceived probable benefit of doing so. Buckland identifies many aspects of price that must be considered to understand demand. These aspects include reliability or consistency of service, delay, environmental noise, distractions, other physical annoyances, monetary cost, travel time, cultural and educational barriers, hours of service, library arrangement of services, and service policies and procedures.

TABLE 1—*Continued*

Study	*Sample*	*Method*	*Main Results*
O'Reilly (1982)	163 employees in 4 branch locations of a county welfare agency	Survey	Accessibility predicted information source use
Baughman (1983)	258 social science researchers in 5 greater Boston-area universities	Survey	Personal collections most important place to obtain information for contract research; library is second place and most needed for investigating new areas
Price (1987)	3,835 scholars	Survey	Personal library collection and materials purchased in past year ranked by majority (76% & 62%) as of great importance for teaching and research. Slightly less than half ranked library of great importance

O'Reilly, Charles A. "Variations in Decision Makers' Use of Information Sources: Impact of Quality and Accessibility of Information." *Academy of Management Journal* 25 (December 1982): 756–771.

Baughman, Susan. "Social Science Sponsored Researchers: Their Use of Academic Libraries." *Collection Management* 5 (Fall/Winter 1983): 53–68.

Price, Anne J. "Librarians and Scholars: The Need for Channels of Communication," in *SPEC Kit on Library-Scholar Communication.* Washington, D.C.: Association of Research Libraries, 1987.

The Logical Dimension of Access

The logical or indicative dimension of accessibility involves users forming queries in the language of the library retrieval system. This dimension encompasses both library staff assistance and direct user interface with retrieval systems. It includes staff training and user ability to use catalogs and printed indexes. This section first reviews studies related to user interface with library staff and then reviews research related to direct user-library retrieval system interface.

User Interface with Library Staff

The research related to library staff assistance to users and the influence of such assistance upon effectiveness of library access services can be discussed under six headings: models of the reference process, reference effectiveness, interpersonal communication issues, service desk staffing, referral services, and librarians as intermediaries to bibliographic systems. For purposes of this chapter, reference service is defined as the personal assistance given by library staff to users.

Models of the Reference Process

Jahoda tested a six-step model of the search strategy process.[13] After testing, the model was revised to include the following steps: (1) message selection; (2) selection of types of answer-providing tools; (3) selection of specific answer-providing tools; (4) selection of search headings; (5) answer selection; and (6) negotiation and renegotiation. Jahoda then tested an instructional module for each step. The answer selection test concerned two types of problems: numbers and complete bibliographic citations selected as answers. Test results suggested that students have difficulties in selecting answers from tables, charts, and graphs.

Wilkinson and Miller analyzed reference service in terms of the number of steps necessary to provide information. A step is regarded as a distinct judgment leading to a decision, action, or recommendation. At a technical library, questions with three or more steps constituted less than one-quarter of the sample. The two-step question was the modal question for all user status groups. In a follow-up study on questions at a liberal arts college, the one-step question accounted for 60 percent of all questions asked.[14]

Reference Effectiveness

Effectiveness may be defined as how well an organization is doing relative to some set of standards.[15] Because organizational effectiveness is inherently subjective and based upon the personal values and preferences of individuals, understanding organizational effectiveness requires understanding multiple models of organizational effectiveness.[16] This view is essential to the study of reference effectiveness because each of the different constituencies of a library will use different standards in the evaluative process. The difficulty of developing accurate and reliable measures of accomplishments of multiple sets of objectives has often led to the use of substitutes, such as measuring actual system use and user satisfaction with service, as a way of evaluating reference assistance.

In recent years, research in this area has moved beyond counting types of questions or simple global measures of user satisfaction and begun to employ a number of interesting and useful alternative measures of reference effectiveness. Three particularly important measures are: accuracy of answers, librarian judgments, and joint user and librarian judgments. Major studies using these measures are summarized in Tables 2 and 3.

Accuracy of Answers

Perhaps the greatest single advance has been the development of the method of unobtrusive observation as a means of assessing the outcome of the reference transaction.[17] In unobtrusive observation, proxies present factual test questions

TABLE 2
REFERENCE EFFECTIVENESS — ACCURACY MEASURES

Study	*Sample*	*Method*	*Main Results*
Myers (1983)	14 fact-type inquiries tested in 40 Southeastern United States academic libraries	Unobtrusive	50.4% of all test questions answered correctly
Jirjees in Myers & Jirjees (1983)	Five 4-yr. state colleges with graduate programs in Northeast United States	Unobtrusive testing by telephone; case studies	56.6% of all test questions answered correctly
Hernon & McClure (1986)	15 factual and bibliographic inquiries tested in 13 academic and 13 public libraries	Unobtrusive testing in person	61.8% of all test questions answered correctly; no significant differences between type of library
McClure, Hernon & Purcell (1986)	12 academic and public libraries	Unobtrusive testing in person, interviews, surveys, daily logs of questions	53% of all test questions answered correctly in academic libraries; 30% in public libraries
Benham (1987)	12 factual questions administered to 244 reference librarians with MLS earned between 1-1-75 and 5-30-79 and working in public or academic library with 100,000 volumes or more	Obtrusive testing	52.7% of all test questions answered correctly; low response rate (25%) may have inflated results
Hernon and McClure (1987)	63 questions administered in one library	Unobtrusive testing in person, an experimental design to test effect of 2 learning interventions	63.5% of all pretest questions answered correctly; 52.4% of all posttest questions answered correctly

Myers, Marcia J. and Jassim M. Jirjees. *The Accuracy of Telephone Reference/Information Services in Academic Libraries.* Metuchen, N.J.: Scarecrow, 1983.

Hernon, Peter and Charles R. McClure. "Unobtrusive Reference Testing: The 55 Percent Rule." *Library Journal* 111 (April 15, 1986): 37–41.

McClure, Charles R., Peter Hernon, and Gary R. Purcell. *Linking the U.S. National Technical Information Service with Academic and Public Libraries.* Norwood, N.J.: Ablex, 1986.

Benham, Frances. "A Prediction Study of Reference Accuracy among Recently Graduated Working Reference Librarians (1975–1979)," in *Success in Answering Reference Questions.* Metuchen, N.J.: Scarecrow, 1987.

Hernon, Peter and Charles R. McClure. *Unobtrusive Testing and Library Reference Services.* Norwood, N.J.: Ablex, 1987.

TABLE 3
REFERENCE EFFECTIVENESS — LIBRARIAN AND USER JUDGMENTS

Study	*Sample*	*Method*	*Main Results*
Kantor (1980)	2,000 reference queries collected from 16 self-selected libraries	Analysis of conditions based on librarian judgments	Conditions causing most failures were collection and source failures
Bunge (1985)	50 questions each at 18 academic libraries	Librarian and user surveys	55% of users reported finding just what they wanted and being satisfied
Murfin and Gugelchuk (1987)	50 questions each at 15 academic libraries (excludes medical and undergraduate)	Librarian and user surveys	55.8% of users reported finding just what they wanted and being satisfied for all types of questions; 46.7%, for facts and statistics types of questions
Whitlatch (1987)	257 reference queries received in 5 academic libraries in Northern California	Librarian and user surveys	66% of users reported success in locating material needed; 57% of users reported locating material and being highly satisfied

Kantor, Paul B. "Analyzing the Availability of Reference Services," *Library Effectiveness: A State of the Art.* pp. 131–149. Chicago: American Library Association, 1980.
Bunge, Charles A. "Factors Related to Reference Question Answering Success: The Development of a Data-Gathering Form." *RQ* 24 (Summer 1985): 482–486.
Murfin, Marjorie E. and Gary M. Gugelchuk. "Development and Testing of a Reference Transaction Assessment Instrument." *College & Research Libraries* 48 (July 1987): 314–338.
Whitlatch, Jo Bell. *The Role of the Academic Reference Librarian.* New York: Greenwood, 1990.

at the reference desk by phone or in person. Unobtrusive studies have focused on one aspect of evaluating reference service—the accuracy of responses that staff give to questions administered to them.

The unobtrusive methodology was first applied by Crowley and Childers in a public library setting. This methodology was then applied to academic libraries by Myers and Jirjees.[18] Myers found that a higher level of acceptable answers was positively associated with number of volumes in the reference collection and number of hours of service. University libraries also had the best performance score as opposed to community college or college libraries.

In more recent unobtrusive study, Hernon and McClure ascertained that the most frequent reasons for incorrect answers were: (1) the library gave the wrong data (64 percent of cases); (2) the staff indicated they didn't know and did not suggest any referral (20.1 percent); and (3) staff claimed the library did not own a source that would answer the question, although in fact, the library owned the source (15.4 percent). Hernon and McClure have determined that additional training furnished through learning interventions failed to improve accuracy of answers to test reference questions.[19] The two intervention strategies used between the pretest and posttest were a four-hour workshop that provided an overview of basic United States statistical sources and a slide presentation that reviewed basic United States statistical sources.

In a study exploring the use of National Technical Information Services (NTIS) publications by academic and public library staff and users, McClure, Hernon, and Purcell contributed valuable insights to the study of reference accuracy.[20] Combining additional data collection techniques with unobtrusive testing, they were able to study reasons for inaccurate answers in more depth than is possible with unobtrusive testing alone. Proxies had a considerably higher probability of obtaining a correct answer from a government documents department than the main reference desk. However, they found that reference staff generally lacked awareness and in-depth knowledge of NTIS services, lacked immediate physical access to publications, and perceived the price structure as excessive. Also contributing to failures was the isolation of NTIS publications from the mainstream of bibliographic control techniques.

Benham employed factual test questions but used an obtrusive methodology.[21] Benham notes that the average accuracy level would have been 7.48 percent higher had respondents obtained a correct answer each time they named a correct source. Benham's best combination of independent variables was able to explain 53 percent of the variation in reference accuracy. These seven variables were correct sources named, correct sources available, graduate record examination quantitative score, degree to which reference and bibliography courses were interesting, hours on the reference desk per week, number of years in reference work since earning the master's in library science, and the degree to which reference work is satisfying.

Because Benham's results are in the same range as studies using the unobtrusive methodology, the results suggest that there may be no need for additional research to establish this low performance rate as typical of public and academic libraries on factual questions. Findings by Hernon and McClure and Benham strongly support each other in suggesting that many of the failures to provide correct answers are related to the librarian's lack of knowledge of appropriate sources and the librarian's inability to deal carefully with quantitative or other types of specific factual data. These conclusions are also supported by Jahoda's findings concerning the difficulty library students have selecting answers from statistical material.[22]

Librarian Judgments

Another recent model of evaluation employs the judgment of the librarian to determine reference effectiveness. Kantor argues, based on other research, that about 75 percent of the time users are at least as satisfied as librarians think they are. Recent research by Whitlatch substantiates these earlier studies.[23] Whitlatch concluded that for approximately 83 percent of the reference transactions, librarian judgments of success are an adequate substitute for user judgments because librarian ratings on all aspects of service were identical to or lower than those of users. In the majority of cases, then, expert librarian judgment can serve as a substitute for surveying users.

Kantor analyzed the reference process and identified a chain of essentially independent conditions that must be met in order for users to obtain the information they seek.[24] The five conditions used in the analysis were communication (question not understood), knowledge (cannot think of a source), collection (do not have the source), source (source does not have the information), and patron (information located but patron not satisfied). Results indicated that for sixteen self-selected libraries, the two conditions causing the most failures were not having the source and locating a source that did not have the information.

Joint User and Librarian Judgments

Murfin and Bunge developed and field tested a form that gathers data from both reference librarians and library users on success in answering reference questions. The criterion for complete success is rigorous in that users must mark that they found just what was wanted, they must indicate satisfaction, and they must not check any of the reasons for dissatisfaction.[25] Success rates are comparable to accuracy rates obtained by testing reference librarians with preselected factual questions. When a semifinal version was tested, 55 percent of users reported finding just what they wanted and being satisfied; however, user reports of finding exactly what they wanted rose to 65.13 percent when librarians did not report being busy and reported searching with the user for answers.[26] Exploratory cluster analysis provided evidence that users appear to distinguish between their satisfaction with the service provided and satisfaction with the information they obtained. Only 16 percent of the variance in service satisfaction could be explained by users' evaluation of the quality of information received.[27]

Whitlatch tested a model of variables influencing academic library reference service effectiveness by using three separate measures of effectiveness: (1) librarian judgments of the value of service; (2) user judgments of the value of service; and (3) user success in finding needed information.[28] Correlations between user value of service and user success were moderate, whereas correlations between librarian value and the two other measures, user value and user success, were weak. These relationships and statistical tests indicating that the three measures were not redundant strongly support the importance of developing multiple measures of reference effectiveness. Further, classes of variables related to feedback, service orientation, time constraints, and task uncertainty had the most significant effects on reference service success.

Contrary to results by Murfin and Bunge, the degree to which the librarian was busy or the type of assistance (personal versus referral) did not significantly explain variations in any of the user or librarian measures of reference effectiveness. Users expected to be provided with quick, concise information at the reference desk. Study results also suggested reasons for the relatively low accuracy rates found in unobtrusive studies: librarians answered a relatively small proportion (11.3 percent) of factual questions and viewed the task of answering factual queries as somewhat less routine than answering subject or instructional questions, because factual questions involved the use of less frequently used sources, were less similar to other types of questions, and involved less subject familiarity.[29]

Interpersonal Communication

Communication and its relationship to reference effectiveness have been subjects of continual interest throughout the last decade. However, given the frequency with which communication issues have been discussed in the literature, surprisingly little empirical work has been conducted, as shown in Table 4. One of the earliest explorations of the issue is work by Swope and Katzer testing reasons for library users' reluctance to ask questions of library staff.[30] Major reasons given for not asking a librarian questions were that users had been dissatisfied with the past service of the librarian, the question was thought to be too simple, or the question was too much of a bother for the librarian.

In other early exploratory work, Nelson tested faculty awareness of thirteen different reference services and found that faculty from the humanities and education had a statistically significant higher level of average awareness than faculty from science.[31] Nelson also found that faculty from one of the six colleges tested had an average level of awareness that was substantially higher than faculty from any of the other colleges. Follow-up interviews indicated that librarians from this college were the most active in book selection and collection development and seemed to display a higher degree of personal initiative in establishing and maintaining contact with faculty members.

Kazlauskas classified common nonverbal behaviors as positive or negative.[32] Positive staff behaviors included immediate eye contact, nodding, and slight smiling. Negative staff behaviors included lack of the staff's immediate nonverbal acknowledgment of a user waiting, staff engrossed in reading, filing, tapping fingers, or pacing. Kazlauskas found that when a user had a choice of staff to approach, the user always approached the staff member demonstrating receptivity. Users also tended to approach staff who were standing rather than

TABLE 4
INTERPERSONAL COMMUNICATION

Study	*Sample*	*Method*	*Main Results*
Swope & Katzer (1972)	119 users at Syracuse University's Carnegie Library	Interview, survey	Of 41% of users with questions, only 35% would ask a librarian
Nelson (1973)	694 faculty in 6 California State Colleges	Interview, survey	Higher level of awareness reference service in one college
Howell, Reeves & Van Willigen (1976)	97 reference encounters at one institution	Observation, survey	One-third of encounters involved question negotiation; instruction may contribute to user satisfaction
Kazlauskas (1976)	148 service transactions at 4 institutions in Southern California	Observation at reference and circulation points	Users approached staff who demonstrated receptivity and were standing
Hernon & Pastine (1977)	362 students at the University of Nebraska, Omaha	Survey	Students generally preferred to locate materials without librarian assistance
Halperin & Strazdon (1980)	100 Drexel University students	Conjoint analysis and survey	Completeness of answer most significant factor in student rankings of reference service; factors related to speed of service ranked last
Collins (1985)	43 reference supervisors from 19 academic libraries in the greater Boston area	Interview, critical incident analysis	Social skills occur with greater frequency in general than in specialized academic reference settings

Swope, Mary Jane and Jeffrey Katzer. "Why Don't They Ask Questions?" *RQ* 12 (Winter 1972): 161–166.

Nelson, Jerold. "Faculty Awareness and Attitudes Toward Academic Library Reference Services: A Measure of Communication." *College & Research Libraries* 34 (September 1973): 268–275.

Howell, Benita J., Edward B. Reeves, and John Van Willigen. "Fleeting Encounters—A Role Analysis of Reference Librarian-Patron Interaction." *RQ* 16 (Winter 1976): 124–129.

Kazlauskas, Edward. "An Exploratory Study: A Kinesic Analysis of Academic Library Service Points." *Journal of Academic Librarianship* 2 (July 1976): 130–134.

Hernon, Peter and Maureen Pastine. "Student Perceptions of Academic Librarians." *College & Research Libraries* 38 (March 1977): 129–139.

Halperin, Michael and Maureen Strazdon. "Measuring Students' Preferences for Reference Service: A Conjoint Analysis." *Library Quarterly* 50 (April 1980): 208–224.

Collins, John William III. "A Critical Incident Analysis of the Behavior of Academic Reference Librarians: Implications for Inservice Training." Ed.D. diss., Boston University, 1985.

sitting. He also found that reference personnel tended to exhibit positive behaviors a higher percentage of the time than circulation personnel.

Collins analyzed behavior of librarians related to effective and ineffective reference services by interviewing reference supervisors.[33] Behavioral categories were grouped into four general categories of behavior: organizational knowledge, technical skills, personal qualities, and social skills. His exploratory work found that critical incidents involving social skills occur with greater frequency in general academic and research libraries than they do in science or law libraries.

Service Desk Staffing

Reference staffing has been the topic of considerable research. Areas tested by research can be classified into two groups: type of staff and quantity of staff.

Type of Staffing

Twenty years ago, Lawson found that less than 40 percent of reference staff time was spent performing professional activities, whereas over 60 percent of reference staff were professional librarians. In case studies of four college libraries, Mech found that the libraries studied, for the most part, failed to examine their priorities, programs, and the effectiveness of their use of professional and support staffs.[34] Although Lawson's classification of some activities as subprofessional might invoke much controversy in the field today, studies at individual libraries have tended to support Lawson's conclusions about the mix of questions at reference desks. Heinlen and St. Clair and Aluri reported case studies that utilized nonprofessional library employees extensively in answering reference questions.[35]

Other studies, however, have found that library support staff do not provide the same quality of answers as librarians. Halldorsson and Murfin found that professionals were clearly superior to nonprofessionals in achieving successful solutions to faulty information questions.[36] They found that nonprofessionals referred or consulted with further sources for only 28 percent of questions they were initially unable to answer. The lower performance of nonprofessionals appeared to be due primarily to lesser personal knowledge of the subject matter of questions and of reference materials. Professional failures appeared to be related to a reluctance to respond to questions that depended primarily on difficult interviews for solutions and to a lack of time to conduct proper interviews and examine reference sources.

In twenty academic libraries, the average success score for paraprofessional staff members was 50.5 percent, and for professionals, 60.4 percent.[37] Users reported needing more in-depth information or wanting a different viewpoint significantly more often when they were assisted by paraprofessionals. Paraprofessionals experienced more communication difficulties and performed more poorly on complex questions than professionals. Murfin and Bunge found that only four of the twenty libraries used paraprofessional staff members with considerable effectiveness. In these four libraries, paraprofessionals directed users less often, searched with their users more often, handled questions of less complexity, and consulted other staff members more frequently.

Demand for Reference Services

Regazzi and Hersberger tested four models in order to develop alternative staffing patterns that might increase the effectiveness of service.[38] The formula used in the cost analysis assumed that it was as important not to have users waiting as it was not to have staff idle. A two-stage model, with the nonprofessional making the first contact with the user and the necessary referrals to the librarian, provided the highest cost effectiveness rating.

Murfin found the most important factor explaining the variation in number of reference transactions was turnstile count, and that the number of transactions was highly dependent on the number of reference staff hours provided.[39] Therefore, reference transaction totals represent only demand demonstrated and met with present staffing limitations. Brooks found that reference-type statistics related strongly to other reference-type statistics, and not at all to circulation and in-library use counts, which correlated with each other.[40] He suggested that reference counts were reflecting a library use phenomenon that differed from the phenomenon being measured by circulation and in-library use.

Referral Services

Referral between information services must be studied as a two-way process. Staff referring users must be able to identify sources with the required information and the staff receiving referrals must make information and appropriate assistance available to users. Referral services have received surprisingly little attention.[41] This may be because relatively little referral takes place as part of academic library reference services.

In five academic libraries studied by Whitlatch, assistance to users seldom involved consultation with other librarians (7 percent of all questions). [42] In those reference encounters where users reported not being able to locate needed materials, librarians reported consulting only 17.6 percent of the time. Hernon and McClure found that approximately 9 percent of all questions involved referral to library staff within the library or other depository libraries.[43] Only 37 percent of the 340 test questions were correctly answered. Further, only 27.6 percent of documents personnel who failed to find acceptable answers made referrals. In 24 percent of cases where documents personnel responded that they did not know the answer, they also made no referral suggestions. Of the 127 correctly answered questions, only three involved referrals.

Henderson found that fewer presidents, academic deans, and librarians were interested in offering community telephone reference service than were library directors.[44] Referral services in this and other settings may be limited by lack of top administrative support for making the community college library more accessible to the larger community.

Hawley's exploratory study of referrals found that the central need was for the librarian to know of outside resources that could offer assistance.[45] Primary concerns of librarians in making referrals were efficiency and equity, that what people receive should be proportional to what they contribute. His findings suggested that librarians tended to limit referral to other libraries because of the expectation that the library being asked for assistance should receive reimbursement from the requesting library. Relationships with users, however, unlike those with other libraries, appeared to be influenced by the contributions of the user, the interest and respect granted the librarian, and idealism and empathy. Results from Henderson and Hawley both strongly suggest that formal reciprocal arrangements for referral are necessary for referral to be used as a regular part of reference service.

Librarians as Intermediaries to Bibliographic Systems

Packer and Soergel tested current awareness methods and concluded that selective dissemination of information (SDI) services should concentrate efforts on serving scientists in specialties with high scatter of information. Librarian intermediaries would be most valuable in these areas because of the difficulties involved in designing profiles to search across conventional disciplines and specialties.[46] However, their results also indicated that scientists were unlikely to subscribe to SDI services because they were doubtful about the possibility of designing a profile that would identify relevant material and suppress irrelevant material.

Morris, Holtum and Curry found that users clearly preferred to be present during the search and that the number of relevant citations and user satisfaction were significantly higher with the user present.[47] Their work also indicated that the value of the user's presence was due to the user's opportunity to refine the search while it was being processed. Results from the Council on Library Resources online project also indicate that users who received at least some initial training and assistance were more satisfied and successful than those who did not; the best sources appeared to be library staff, friends, or other nearby users of the catalog and online assistance. Users who neither sought nor received assistance were less likely to report satisfaction or success. The most effective forms of assistance appeared to be printed or online sources. Obtaining aid from library staff was not always regarded as helpful.[48]

Librarian service orientation and effective bibliographic access may be linked. Williams found an interesting positive relationship between the service orientation of government documents librarians and bibliographic access via commercialized systems, public catalogs and commercially produced indexes.[49] The greater the bibliographic control over government documents collections, the higher the score on positive attitudes toward working with people.

Nielsen's results indicated that users paying fees received more responsive service from librarians than users who received free service.[50] Librarians who charged a fee tended to spend more time with a library user than librarians who performed free searches, and librarians who charged a fee also participated more in continuing education.

One of the primary ways in which librarians assist users in locating information is through the use of books located in the reference collection. Bates collected data on file structures of books in an academic library, a public library, and a special library to verify a descriptive definition of reference books that distinguished them from stack books.[51] She proposed that if the function of reference books was their use for referral purposes, then reference books ought to overwhelmingly contain a characteristic file structure that was not the same as books designed for reading through. Through systematic sampling she examined 343 books and measured the percentage of book length in pages devoted to files and lists. Reference books were operationally defined as books that contained 60 percent of their length in files or lists. Of all works housed in the reference collection, 85.9 percent met her operational definition, whereas 93.6 percent of stack books did not. Exceptions in the reference collection tended to be canonical texts or highly demanded stack items stored in reference for protection. Further study of file structures of manual and automated reference sources should be valuable in clarifying the role reference file structures play in human search strategies.

Direct User Interface with Library Systems

This section briefly summarizes the most important research related to direct user access to library bibliographic systems. Studies that evaluate individual catalog systems or CD-ROM systems are not included.

Document Availability

Document availability studies conducted in many individual academic libraries have provided a composite picture of user success and failure in locating books known to be held by the library. These studies have most commonly studied user searches for known items in open stack libraries.

The past two decades have seen the development by Saracevic, Shaw and Kantor, of a widely accepted methodology which is based on earlier research conducted by Morse and Buckland.[52] Saracevic, Shaw, and Kantor's method measures the performance of users and libraries separately but provides an overall measure of total success. Categories are arranged in the sequence in which users searching for materials would usually encounter the following barriers to access: (1) item not acquired by library; (2) user catalog error; (3)

in circulation; (4) library maintenance error (e.g., missing, misshelved); and (5) user bookstack error. Two other categories have sometimes been included in availability studies: bibliographic citation errors, and errors in the library catalog. However, these two types of errors tend to be relatively rare and, if included, are often grouped with another category such as user catalog error. This technique is extremely useful for comparing performance of one library with other libraries, determining reasons for nonavailability of books within an individual library, and comparing performance for the same library over time. Mansbridge compared availability rates for seventeen document availability studies.[53] Availability levels for ownership of library materials ranged from a low of 74 percent to a high of 98.1 percent, with an average of 90.6 percent. Availability levels related to user catalog skills ranged from a low of 88 percent to a high of 97.9 percent, with an average of 93.6 percent. In a series of book availability studies, Shaw provided an excellent analysis of decreases in acquisitions performance and relationships to declining book funds.[54]

Serials have been less commonly studied. Two studies conducted at single institutions by Golden, Golden, and Lenzini and Adalian, Rockman, and Rodie have found success rates for collection ownership and user catalog skills comparable to those in book availability studies.[55]

Subject Access

Before the introduction of online catalogs, research studies of card catalog use found that people were searching catalogs primarily by author or title. Document availability studies tended to confirm high success rates for author-title searches. Early studies of online catalogs, however, provided consistent evidence that the majority of searches were by subject. The new capabilities of the online catalog appear to have increased demand for subject searching. This change in function of the catalog has resulted in significant, much needed research on subject access to bibliographic systems.

Results of the Council on Library Resources online catalog project study of academic and public libraries with subject searching capability in their online catalogs suggested that topic searching was more prevalent among those who were less experienced with the library and its catalogs.[56] The results also indicated that topical searching was linked with lower levels of perceived search success and satisfaction, and that systems displaying subject headings were particularly effective in improving user satisfaction with subject searching features and in reducing user impatience with the system. Also, systems with keyword searching received more subject searching than those not offering keyword searching.

Analysis of online transaction logs has also provided very valuable information regarding problems with bibliographic access. Low output from online catalog searches has been a widespread and prevalent problem. Results from studies of online catalogs at University of Washington, Syracuse

University, Northwestern University, and University of California provided zero postings for 35 to 57.5 percent of all subject searches: On the other hand, high search output has also been a problem, with from 8 to 14 percent of all searches resulting in over 100 retrievals.[57]

Sullivan and Seiden employed verbal protocols to study how new users behaved when they used the catalog.[58] Verbal protocols are spoken records of people talking aloud as they work and are a very promising methodology for exploring user behavior with online systems. Each subject was asked five questions related to locating material in the catalog. Success for subject-related questions was 69.2 percent. Strategic errors occurred at all stages of the search process, including problem formulation, design, and implementation of the search. Strategic errors were difficult to overcome because they involved lack of library knowledge, lack of system knowledge, or lack of subject knowledge. The authors noted that users were extremely persistent and creative in trying to recover from errors, perhaps because the users were under observation and the online catalog was still an attractive novelty to many users.

Bates found a low match between terms students selected for subject searching and library subject headings. She indicated that her results were supported by findings of numerous other researchers which indicated low interindexer consistency and high variability in patterns of association in the human mind.[59] Carlyle observed that exact matches with subject headings ranged from 25 to 57 percent; Lester studied sample transaction logs and found that users' terms matched Library of Congress subject headings 40.1 percent of the time.[60] By applying three search match processes—right truncation, adjacent string searching, and keyword and Boolean searching—she was able to increase the total match success to 78 percent. Adding subject authority, the capability of searching anywhere in the full MARC record and spelling correction further increased the match success to 92.7 percent.

A serious limitation of transaction log studies is that results tell only whether users found something that matched the terms they entered and not whether they found catalog information satisfying their true requests. Results of matching studies also cannot be compared across studies because of great differences in study methodologies and environments.

Rao and Knutson found no significant correlation between subject access points and recorded use.[61] In retrospect these results should not be surprising. Many variables may be more influential than number of catalog access points in determining use. The number of subject access points are extremely restricted and probably quite inadequate for almost all titles. Further inquiries along these lines do not appear likely to add much to our understanding.

User Fees for Direct Bibliographic Access

Introduction of new online services without additional public funding has resulted in many libraries charging some direct monetary costs to the services' users. Little research exists regarding how these fees influence access and satisfaction with service.

The University of Delaware Library conducted a survey of library-subsidized online searches and found that there was no relationship between monetary cost to the student and satisfaction with the search.[62] Instead, the two factors significantly related to student satisfaction were retrieval of at least forty relevant citations and student estimate of time saved. Students in this study reported saving more than 1,000 hours of search time.

The Logical Dimension—Future Research

Substantial progress in the last two decades has been made in research on reference effectiveness. Researchers have designed studies that employ measures in addition to user satisfaction and have often studied more than one library, as shown in Tables 2 and 3. The most frequent measurement of reference effectiveness has been accuracy of answers, with the academic library reference staff providing correct and complete answers to factual and bibliographic questions only 50 to 60 percent of the time. Through use of multiple measures, it has been determined that for all types of reference questions users may agree that they find just what they wanted and are fully satisfied only 55 percent of the time. Although it is less certain how to improve reference effectiveness, studies indicate that in some situations, effective reference service is positively related to larger institutions, institutions granting higher degrees, librarian service orientation, interpersonal communication skills, instruction, staff training and education. Relationships between effective reference service and levels of demand, lack of personal assistance and referrals appear to be complex and deserving of further study.

Future research should be carefully tied to work that has already been done. Existing measures should be replicated and further developed rather than totally new measures being developed to study old concepts. Promising areas for future research include: (1) small scale studies to identify appropriate and effective measures of service orientation of library staff and to evaluate training methods for interpretation of statistical and factual material and for communication skills; (2) more tightly structured studies of referral that build upon the findings of the exploratory studies and determine how the institutional, social, and technical abilities of staff affect the quality of referral services; (3) more explicity relating studies of monetary costs, user time, user effort of use, and the tradeoffs among these different areas to the study of personal assistance; and (4) improving information access by designing studies that compare the cost effectiveness of different methods of user assistance, such as staff instruction of catalog users and interface design for direct use of catalogs.

User searches of catalogs for known items are quite successful. However, recent research indicates that subject searches constitute the majority of searches, and these tend to be much less successful. The degree of match between user subject requests and assigned subject headings is relatively low, with many subject requests producing no results and some producing too many items. Keyword indexing in combination with subject authority in online catalogs provides exciting new capabilities. Most online bibliographic databases have used keyword indexing extensively, but these systems are not designed for nor used extensively by infrequent and often novice users. The combination of keyword indexing and subject headings under authority control provides an excellent opportunity to improve the understanding of system designs, which will enhance effectiveness of subject access for users.

Promising avenues for research appear to be designing a dense semantic network as a front-end user thesaurus, designing systems that use a searching hierarchy of assigned subject headings and then keyword searching, and designing systems which enter summaries of book contents, or tables of contents or book indexes.[63] Controlled experiments should be made to test the effectiveness of these different system designs in improving subject access for users.

Finally, improving bibliographic access to materials in the book collection has the potential for improving reference effectiveness. Enhanced semantic networks, book contents, and indexes should be useful not only for improving direct access by users to subjects but also for improving performance levels for reference service. Lack of librarian knowledge of sources is known to be related to lower reference success levels. Improved bibliographic access has the potential for enabling librarians to identify more effectively appropriate sources containing answers to all types of queries. Consequently, catalog system designs should be tested using success levels in reference assistance as measures of catalog effectiveness. In comparison to user searching in online catalogs, much less is known about the effectiveness of subject searching in online literature retrieval systems, particularly CD-ROM. A study similar to that designed by the Council on Library Resources should be conducted across many CD-ROM systems and several libraries.

The Physical Dimension of Access

The second dimension of accessibility concerns physically obtaining a book, periodical, or other material from the library collection. This section describes research related to effectiveness of branch libraries, library circulation programs, library stack maintenance programs, user skills, and interlibrary loan.

Branch Libraries

In academic settings, the study of physical access to libraries has focused primarily on branch libraries. Seal summarized the literature related to academic branch libraries and noted that most of the statements regarding branch libraries were based upon extensive experience and observation with relatively few systematic research studies.[64] Research studies that have been conducted, however, tend to form a consistent and coherent pattern of the costs and benefits of branch libraries. The most important research related to access to library buildings is summarized in Table 5.

Raffel and Shishko used location theory to study comparative costs of centralized and decentralized libraries.[65] They concluded that a decentralized system was more costly to the library, but centralized systems often involved hidden costs in user time, energy, and decreased use. Waldhart and Zweifel observed that location theory provided limited insight because the concept of accessibility, not distance, was central to most arguments for decentralization of libraries.[66] They suggested three dimensions of accessibility that should be studied—distance, time, and familiarity. Accessibility was viewed as a perceptual problem influenced by such factors as ease of use, experience with an information source, and climatic conditions. For faculty altering their patterns of library use due to a document delivery service, explanations were related to savings in time, easier access which increased use, and greater convenience.[67]

Dougherty and Blomquist provided what is still the major study addressing the dilemma of increased library costs involved in maintaining many decentralized libraries and increased user costs related to centralized library systems. The use of a variety of data collection methods greatly strengthened their findings by providing a multifaceted view of an individual's library use and attitudes toward the library system and its services.

The major conclusion of their studies at Syracuse University and Ohio State University was that many Syracuse University researchers placed greater importance upon ease of use and convenience of access to the library collection than upon the depth and range of holdings. The library use pattern of faculty did not appear to be influenced by the percentage of potentially relevant documents housed in any specific location. Interviews suggested that significant variables important to users' satisfaction were parking facilities, geographical layout of the campus, number of branches and their location, service orientation of library staff, and attractiveness and comfort of the library.

The Dougherty and Blomquist study also found that library materials at Syracuse University were dispersed through several locations in campus libraries. On the average, researchers frequented two libraries, far below the mean of seven libraries housing potentially relevant materials. Faculty who used branch libraries in the same building exhibited a much higher expectation of obtaining documents (73.9 percent) than faculty who used the central library (48.8 percent).

The study concluded that greater perceived effectiveness of branches must be derived from factors other than concentration of holdings. Data from faculty

TABLE 5
PHYSICAL ACCESS TO LIBRARIES

Study	*Sample*	*Method*	*Main Results*
Dougherty (1973)	208 faculty users of document delivery service of University of Colorado	Survey	Majority (54%) of users altered patterns of library use. One-day delivery service achieved for 69% of requests in first year of service
Dougherty & Blomquist (1974)	Syracuse & Ohio State Universities	Personal interviews, subject interest profiling shelf location counts, distance measurements, surveys	Researchers placed greater importance upon ease of use and convenience of access than depth and range of holdings
Greene (1975)	Faculty at Georgia Institute of Technology	Circulation stats, faculty surveys and interviews	Remote physical access increased faculty use of the collection
Genaway & Stanford (1977)	University of Minnesota academic dept. heads	Survey	Most frequent cited advantages of "unofficial" dept. reading rooms were convenience of location and unique materials (25% +)
Manikas (1981)	Dept. shop collections in public 2 yr.-colleges in 6 Southern states	Survey	Twice as many faculty as librarians agreed that there would be greater use of some library materials if housed in classroom or shop collections

Dougherty, Richard M. "The Evaluation of Campus Library Document Delivery Service." *College & Research Libraries* 34 (January 1973): 29–39.

Dougherty, Richard M. and Laura L. Blomquist. *Improving Access to Library Resources.* Metuchen, N.J.: Scarecrow, 1974.

Greene, Robert J. "LENDS: An Approach to the Centralization/Decentralization Dilemma." *College & Research Libraries* 36 (May 1975): 201–207.

Genaway, David C. and Edward B. Stanford. "Quasidepartmental Libraries." *College & Research Libraries* 38 (May 1977): 187–194.

Manikas, Jennifer Karen. "The Shop Collection in Vocational Technical Programs: A Perceptual Study of Two-Year Faculty and Librarians." Ph.D. diss., Florida State University, 1981.

TABLE 5—*Continued*

Study	*Sample*	*Method*	*Main Results*
Shoham (1982)	40 users of University of California library school	Survey	Preferred accessibility of decentralized library system despite disadvantages of limited hours and collections
Metz (1983)	Virginia Polytechnic Institute and State University and University of Nebraska library system	Analysis of circulation data	Faculty at institution with decentralized libraries relied primarily on one library and much more on subject literature in primary research field
D'Elia & Hutkins (1986)	582 faculty at all University of Minnesota campuses served by document delivery services	Survey	Reasons for use related to convenience and thoroughness of service; nonuse related to need to browse, ease of self-service, immediacy of need — not to cost
Jackson (1982)	173 4-year college and university libraries with major construction 1974–1980	Existing printed sources	Size of parent institution was principal variable contributing to library accessibility for disabled persons

Shoham, Snunith. "A Cost-Preference Study of the Decentralization of Academic Library Services." *Library Research* 4 (Summer 1982): 175–194.
Metz, Paul. *The Landscape of Literatures.* Chicago: American Library Association, 1983.
D'Elia, George and Charla Hutkins. "Faculty Use of Document Delivery Services: The Results of a Survey." *Journal of Academic Librarianship* 12 (May 1986): 69–74.
Jackson, Katherine Morgan. "A Study of the Accessibility of College and University Libraries to Handicapped Students since the Passage of the Rehabilitation Act of 1973." Ph.D. diss., Texas A & M University, 1982.

interviews indicated that convenience of location, accessible and service-oriented branch librarians, and the ease of becoming familiar with smaller branch libraries were influential factors. Because study findings related to document delivery at Ohio State were based on a nonrandom sample of users, study results may not have been representative of faculty as a whole. However, for faculty interviewed, library document delivery services available at Ohio State University had improved the perceived accessibility of materials and increased faculty use of library resources.[68]

Greene also studied the trade-off between library costs in supporting decentralized systems and users' costs involving centralized systems.[69] A remote physical access delivery system provided by a centralized library appeared to moderate some of the disadvantages of centralized collections, such as lower use. Greene found that remote bibliographic and physical access increased faculty use of the collection. Distance also proved to be a significant use factor as the study results indicated that faculty located farthest from the library were more likely to be users of the remote physical access system.

Metz conducted a comparative study between Virginia Polytechnic Institute and State University and the University of Nebraska library systems.[70] The data collection method was a snapshot of circulation data at a given time. He found that at the University of Nebraska, an institution with a large number of branch libraries, the faculty borrowed primarily from one library and relied much more heavily upon the subject literature in their primary research field than faculty at Virginia Polytechnic, an institution with only two branch libraries. Metz concluded that branch libraries may inevitably interfere with cross disciplinary reading. He also found important differences between disciplines. The literatures of the life and physical sciences were reasonably independent of other disciplines, but because of the high incidence of cross disciplinary use, it would be difficult to identify discrete literature groups in the social sciences that could be physically grouped together.

Seal noted that for large institutions, total centralization of library facilities was not desirable.[71] The current recommended solution was planned decentralization, in which large multidisciplinary collections were created. Research studies support this conclusion and also suggest that remote bibliographic and delivery services within the campus can greatly increase faculty utilization of collections.

Book Circulation

Mansbridge summarized the results from seventeen document availability studies and concluded that overall availability rates ranged from 47.7 percent to 72.7 percent, with an average of 59.4 percent. In the typical academic library, the average user successfully retrieves 60 percent of books originally desired. As noted previously, the three categories identified as barriers to physical retrieval of material after users identified items owned by the library are: in circulation, library stack maintenance errors, and user bookstack errors. Mansbridge reported circulation performance levels ranging from a low of 77 percent to a high of 95 percent, with an average of 86.6 percent.[72] Therefore, the average probability of items being available for circulation rather than charged to another borrower was 86.6 percent. In his longitudinal studies at Case Western, Shaw has identified increases in circulation performance which were related to revisions in loan policies.[73]

Buckland conducted the most important work on loan and duplication policies and the effect of these library policies on book availability. As a result of an operations research study conducted at the University of Lancaster, Buckland simulated the availability level of books based on various combinations of different lengths of loan, degree of duplication, and levels of popularity. For loan and duplication policies in effect in 1967 and 1968, he estimated availability or success levels to be 60 percent. Buckland calculated that adoption of a variable loan policy, with 10 percent of books most in demand assigned a one-week loan period and the rest having four return dates a year would raise the availability level to 86 percent. Implementation of a variable loan policy at Lancaster was followed by a dramatic increase in use. Borrowing from the open shelves increased by 200 percent over two years, although the user population increased by only 40 percent.[74] Availability levels also increased in the short term. By 1970 success level was at 80 percent; however, by 1972 the success level was down to 60 percent.[75]

These results suggest strongly that user demand for books is sensitive to the availability level. The level of demand may depend on the chance of success (i.e., availability level) experienced by the user. Buckland's results were supported by findings from a study in the Physics Library at Ohio State University.[76] Data collected in Buckland's study clearly indicated that there was a marked tendency for borrowed books to be returned when they were due, regardless of the length of the loan period.[77] Goehlert and Baaske, Tolliver and Westerberg also published findings from single institutions that suggested that enforcing the loan period was important in maintaining book availability.[78]

Document availability studies focus on immediate availability. The extent and effect of delays upon book availability have been less frequently studied than immediate availability. Goehlert used data collected through a book delivery service for faculty to study both immediate book availability and delays.[79] He found that only 41 percent of books requested were immediately available. Books circulating to other users accounted for 55 percent of the cases of unavailability, and the number of books published within the last five years not immediately available was significantly greater than books over five years old. The main cause of immediate nonavailability was waiting for recalled books to be returned. A semester-long study showed that students returned recalled books roughly six days after the notice was sent, and faculty returned them seventeen days later. Eventual availability rate was 93.1 percent.

Another access issue of great concern to users is remote storage of library collections. Stayner developed a model which illustrated the relationship between storage and retrieval costs.[80] The model identified two components for determining the cost of access for a particular item: (1) a fixed storage cost per period; and (2) a retrieval cost that varied directly with the number of times the item was retrieved from storage. As Stayner noted, the model should be expanded to include costs borne by the system's users, which will be difficult to estimate, especially costs including delay and loss of browsing capability.

Book availability must also include the study of browsing and in-house use. Buckland noted that the variable loan period reduced collection bias for the browser because there was less systematic bias toward least frequently used materials when browsing at the shelf. Greene found that references in publications were responsible for almost as much borrowing as browsing, but that books borrowed because of references in publications were much more likely to be rated as essential than books discovered through browsing. Shill's results suggested that an important change in user search behavior occurred once stacks have been opened.[81] By browsing more books at the shelf users were able to be more selective about books they checked out.

The effectiveness of reserve systems for improving access to materials in libraries has been questioned. In studies at single institutions, Carmack and Loeber and Marshall found that higher circulation was linked to instructor use of shorter reserve lists.[82]

Automation of systems may have a positive effect on staff attitudes toward users. Getz analyzed the effect of automating circulation on demand and time savings for users. After automation of the Colorado State University Library circulation system, Mosley found substantial savings in user time, and an initial decrease in circulation, followed by a subsequent increase.[83]

Library Maintenance of Book Stacks

Mansbridge reported library stack maintenance performance levels averaging 87 percent, with ranges from 75.7 percent to 95 percent.[84] Therefore, the average probability of finding the book on the shelf rather than lost or misshelved was 87 percent. In his longitudinal studies Shaw has identified changes in the library stack maintenance performance levels as related to collection security and replacement policies.[85] The range in library maintenance levels provided evidence that stack maintenance and related collection security issues were a serious problem in some libraries.

Shill reported a mild increase in book availability from 65.8 percent to 70.9 percent, indicating that close supervision of shelf readers and security desk checking were effective in minimizing adverse effects of direct shelf access. In studies at single institutions, Michalko and Heidtmann, Kaske, and Beach and Gapen found significant reductions in loss of books after installation of electronic theft detection systems. Greenwood and McKean found that library exit modification, combined with more rigorous checking and an effective book loss publicity program, significantly reduced book loss. Unfortunately, problems of data collection and electronic security system installation problems did not permit the authors to determine whether the electronic security system reduced book loss.[86]

Identifying missing materials needing replacement has been a serious problem, particularly in large libraries where regular inventories of the entire collection are extremely costly. Kohl found that the percentage of patron reports of missing materials and the percentage of circulation activity within Library of Congress classification subgroup were significantly positively correlated with the percentage of missing materials in a subgroup.[87] Results suggested that a profitable approach to inventorying large collections would be employing user reports of missing materials and circulation statistics to determine inventory needs of classification subgroups.

Studies conducted at single institutions concerning user behavior and book loss have provided little useful information related to improving the effectiveness of library maintenance programs. Zelkind and Sprug did find that installation of a self-service charge-out system reduced book loss. This finding could be valuable if true in other settings. We have also determined that libraries cannot expect much help from other users in reporting mutilation. Theft may be related to material deprivation, or academic achievement.[88]

User Skills in Bookstacks

Mansbridge reported user skill levels ranging from 79 percent to 98.3 percent, with an average of 90.3 percent. Shaw noted that user performance can have a significant effect upon book availability in libraries. Shaw found that over time, performance of users in one library was consistently higher than that of another library in the same university. He suggested that it may be the library's type of clientele which accounted for the consistently higher performance.[89]

Searching in libraries provides considerable opportunity for errors. When attempting to locate items in catalogs, users may fail because they have incorrect or incomplete bibliographic citations, and they may miss citations in the catalog through carelessness. Users fail to locate items in the bookstacks because they copy call numbers incorrectly, are not familiar with library classification systems, or misinterpret special location information, such as folio or oversize. When these user errors are compounded, even libraries with high levels of user skills in the various categories may find that user errors account for a significant proportion of total failures. For example, user errors at the University of California, Santa Cruz accounted for 18.5 percent of all failures because of incorrectly copied call numbers, items present but not located in the catalog, and items present but not located on the shelf.[90]

Rinkel and McCandless found that prior use of the library had a positive effect on the availability of materials to a user. Results by Whitlatch and Kieffer suggested that unsuccessful users were unlikely to ask for assistance.[91]

Serials

Studies conducted with serials have been less frequently reported in the literature. Studies conducted at single institutions have found that availability of periodicals was limited because of administrative and bindery reasons and user errors. Hanson and Serebnick found that users who posed precise questions in a knowledgeable fashion were more likely to obtain useful information. Higher class rank, more frequent use of libraries, and more intensive bibliographic instruction distinguished the successful from the less successful group of students. In one institution, the greatest cause of user error was related to the separation of microform and bound serials collection.[92]

Users may also be reluctant to use microforms. When asked if the availability of more government publications on microforms would increase or decrease their use, the consensus of faculty document users was that use would decrease.[93] A small minority (11.2 percent) thought that availability of more source material would increase use. Reasons related to decreased use were eyestrain and headaches from prolonged reading, lack of convenient access to viewing equipment, time-consuming and less convenient for browsing, and hard to read, scan, and transcribe.

Another major access barrier for users has been missing and mutilated periodical issues. Publicity concerning expense and difficulty of replacement may be useful. One study indicated that students who mutilated materials also believed that issues got replaced much faster and more cheaply than did students who did not mutilate issues. A careful repair and replacement program may also be worthwhile: Obviously mutilated periodical volumes were more likely to be further damaged. Effectiveness of theft detection systems has been little studied, and with conflicting findings. Electronic theft systems have been found to reduce periodical loss at one institution. At another institution, Sleep concluded that the security system neither eliminated nor greatly decreased problem periodical losses and vandalism actually increased.[94]

Interlibrary Loan

Several studies have reported on library size relationship to interlibrary loan patterns. Schmidt and Shaffer found that amount of use by different libraries of an interlibrary loan and reference service at Ohio State University was not related to size of the libraries' collections. Trudell and Wolper found that very large libraries were net lenders, but that for libraries below 300,000 volumes, borrowers and lenders were distributed randomly rather than being grouped by size.[95]

Materials published in the last three years made up 40 percent of all requests. Dougherty reported that sampling of interlibrary loan requests at both the University of Illinois, Urbana-Champaign and University of Michigan revealed that one half of the requests were for items owned but not available at the library.[96] These results strongly suggested that most interlibrary lending requests can be satisfied by local networks and that resources of large university libraries were required only for a minority of lending requests.

Paustian tested the influence of collection size on lending and borrowing activities by analyzing the statistics of members of the Association of Research Libraries (ARL).[97] He found a moderately strong correlation between library size and lending, that explained about 25 percent of the variation in lending volume. Library size explained only about 10 percent of the variation in amount of borrowing. He found that the largest private academic libraries did not lend proportionately as much as some of the largest public universities.

Waldhart also found that private ARL libraries lend substantially fewer items than would be expected based on their size alone.[98] He also found a drop in lending activities of ARL members corresponding with the introduction of OCLC's interlibrary loan module. This suggested that the OCLC system has allowed libraries to gain access to holdings of more libraries and reduced demand for materials from the large university libraries. Glasco in her survey of ARL members also reported that patterns of borrowing and lending have shifted the concentration away from a few large research libraries.[99]

Delivery time remains fairly slow. In two studies, median turnaround times for OCLC requests were found to be eleven days and thirteen days. The median turnaround time of five to six days for a state interlibrary loan network was much shorter. One study found that higher costs were not related to faster delivery. Fill rates may also be lower for academic libraries, compared to other types of libraries.[100]

Difficulties in increasing reliance on interlibrary loan for access to library materials are related to monetary costs to libraries and to costs to users in the form of delays. An Association of Research Libraries survey of members found that although 39 percent of libraries chose speed of delivery as the major factor influencing their choice of supplier, 37 percent preferred to base their decision on charges.[101] User dependence upon interlibrary loan can be increased and speed of delivery improved by providing direct and simple access to interlibrary loan systems for users. Introduction of a user friendly interface for interlibrary loan ordering in the Library Computer System network increased interlibrary loan borrowing at the University of Illinois, Urbana–Champaign, from 3 to 8 percent of the total circulation in two years.[102]

Serious study of the acceptability to faculty of remote access as a substitute for ownership has just begun. Warner reported some faculty support for relying on interlibrary loan in lieu of continuing subscriptions; 26.1 percent were willing to rely on interlibrary loan for titles judged to be of moderate value, and 77.2 percent for titles judged to be of marginal value.[103] Discipline appeared influential on faculty attitudes toward remote access versus ownership. Stansbery found that guaranteed online access to scholarly journal articles with full text printing capabilities was regarded as an acceptable substitute for ownership by the majority of faculty (77.9 percent); however full-time biology faculty members were significantly more favorable than full-time history members.[104]

The Physical Dimension—Future Research

Research studies concerning branch libraries clearly support the proposition that decentralized access to materials increases utilization of library materials by users. However, decentralization of materials also decreases users' exposure to the full range of potentially relevant materials. The next decade will bring increasingly diverse options for user access to library materials. Scholars' workstations operating from remote locations will be able to provide online full text access to journal articles and research reports. Designing innovative services to enhance accessibility should be based on the research of the past. The cost effectiveness of different modes of access for both libraries and users must be investigated. Among the key research questions that must be addressed are how to design systems to minimize access time and effort, how to obtain greatest benefit from library expenditures, and how to maximize potential exposure to systems containing relevant documents.

In another chapter in this volume, Paul Metz summarizes considerable research that indicates that most demand falls on a relatively small proportion of the entire collection. Book document availability studies show that competing demands from other users seriously lower availability rates. Research indicates that libraries can improve the availability of materials by assigning a short loan period to high demand materials. Buckland's findings also suggest that these remedies will create further demand and that this additional demand will cause availability levels to sink back to previous levels.

The role of open stack browsing in accessing materials has been largely ignored. More studies on browsing should be conducted across several institutions. These studies should attempt to identify variables linked to browsing as a substitute and a supplement to use of bibliographic access systems. There is a need to determine if browsing is so crucial for many users in the selection of materials that remote bibliographic access will be more limited in value than might be assumed. Studies should also explore how clues used in browsing the shelves might be incorporated into online catalogs.

Costs to users in terms of delays have been little studied and would be a valuable addition to document availability studies. In order to collect more in-depth information about tolerance for delays, interviews rather than questionnaires are preferred. Circulation performance levels are available from several institutions. The relationship of availability levels to institutional variables, such as library funds per student, number of items circulated per student and type of institution, in addition to loan and duplication policies, should be investigated.

In some situations electronic security systems improve book loss rates. However, there are no good studies that look at loss rates across many libraries and systematically identify variables influencing book loss rates. Variables that should be studied include door guards, measures of demand likely to be related to missing rates such as number of books circulated per student enrolled, electronic theft systems, other security devices such as video cameras, and publicity campaigns aimed at reducing book theft. Large studies of entire collections would be expensive to conduct, especially because sample inventories would be required to assess the level of book loss in each library. Studies limited to a few selected high-use areas, such as women's studies, Chicano studies, and computer programming, and conducted across institutions with similar curricula would control study costs and begin to improve the understanding of variables related to rate of book loss.

In the average library, lack of user skills tends to lower book availability rates somewhat less than circulation or library maintenance failures. Relationships between user performance levels and institutional variables, such as library physical organization of services, type of institution, arrangement of library stack assistance programs, and library sign programs, should be studied.

Overall availability levels for serials may average around 60 percent, which is comparable to books. Restricted lending reduces availability problems related to circulation, but library maintenance practices, such as binding, shelving in separate locations by format, and theft and mutilation, reduce serials availability levels. More libraries should conduct studies of journal availability. With a large investment in printed and microform periodical collections, libraries need to monitor availability levels.

Full-text retrieval for selected reference works and serials is already available in libraries. Facsimile transmission will undoubtedly impact serials first. The new technology provides an exciting opportunity to improve availability for journals and research reports in the short term and for books eventually. Online access to full texts of periodicals from remote sites is now a reality for several current journals. As access becomes easier and technology makes locally accessible, inexpensive databases available simultaneously to multiple end-users, libraries will have an outstanding opportunity to improve availability rates of journals by eliminating conditions of failure related to stack maintenance and circulation programs. As the new capabilities become more readily available, there is a need to continue surveying users, both on and off library sites, in order to monitor availability levels and conditions creating failures.

Large academic libraries appear to be valuable resources for esoteric material sometimes requested on interlibrary loan. On the other hand, recent studies have found that much of the material requested is current material often owned but not available at the home library. Studies indicate that local resource-sharing networks can provide effective access to much of this material.

Delivery times are consistently slow, with local networks able to achieve one week and national systems, two weeks. Improved facsimile technology and online full-text databases for serial literature appear likely to reduce significantly delivery times for certain types of materials. However, as with online searching, there may be additional costs related to these services that are passed on in part to users.

An understanding of how monetary charges influence access would be improved with studies concerning trade-offs to users between monetary costs and costs of delay. Identification of variables related to tolerance for delays, such as status of user, currency of material, and type of material, would be very useful. Will further research find that most frequently material owned but not available and material published within the last five years are the materials for which little delay can be tolerated by the average user?

Conclusion

Many previous studies have relied too heavily upon one source of data, often user questionnaires. The recent development of a variety of appropriate methodologies is very encouraging. Unobtrusive studies, joint user and librarian questionnaires with the query as the unit of analysis, statistical counts of reference volume, analysis of complexity of reference queries, and interviews are appropriate, particularly when used in conjunction with one another. Interviews, analysis of actual use of materials, transaction logs, diaries of information source use, and observation by third parties are also valuable methods when used in conjunction with one another. All methods possess differing strengths and weaknesses and at the present time such methodological weaknesses can best be countered by using other methodologies without the same weaknesses. Therefore, future studies should incorporate more than one research method, represent multiple viewpoints of users and libraries, and collect data from several libraries.

As society enters the electronic age, librarians must be prepared to respond actively to the swift and dynamic changes in information retrieval technologies. Libraries must also face the enormous fixed costs associated with the large valuable collections of printed materials that must be preserved. The profession confronts exciting but extremely difficult economic challenges in continuing to provide academic library users with adequate access to rapidly diversifying forms of information.

One cannot hope to predict exactly how these changes will impact access to library information. However, the profession can learn from past research. Considerable data have been gathered regarding user and library costs in fees, time, and effort that create serious barriers to information access. As technology makes innovations in information access possible, studies are needed to examine the impact of these innovations upon access to information. Innovations will change user expectations regarding access to information and will result in users questioning whether present levels of access to information are acceptable. Many innovations may create unexpected and surprising new economic and social barriers to information access. Identifying and minimizing the impact of new barriers upon access and using innovations to eliminate old barriers are essential and very challenging tasks for the profession.

Studies must examine interactions among the various access systems, including physical locations of on-site and remote terminals, the design of library bibliographic systems, and the structure of document retrieval systems. Studies also must consider the total effects of these interactions upon the level of access provided by libraries. For example, the impact of remote bibliographic access upon use and physical retrieval of documents is an important topic deserving serious study. Remote access capabilities will make the study of effectiveness of access services more difficult. At the present time, access to library systems is conveniently studied in the library and thus usually limited to studying current user demand. For reasons of convenience and economy, access studies have most often focused on use of bibliographic systems and materials within library buildings. In the 1990s, a significant number, perhaps even a majority of users, will gain bibliographic access to collections from terminals located outside the library and will use electronic document delivery services to obtain many documents. With increasing opportunities for remote access, more library access studies must center on the user. This development should facilitate more effective and generalizable studies to document the library's role in the life of the user.

Notes

1. Richard A. Stayner, "Economic Characteristics of the Library Storage Problem," *Library Quarterly* 53 (July 1983): 313–327.

2. David C. Blair, "The Management of Information: Basic Distinctions," *Sloan Management Review* 26 (Fall 1984): 13–23.

3. Michael K. Buckland, *Library Services in Theory and Context* (New York: Pergamon, 1988).

4. Mary Culnan, "The Dimensions of Perceived Accessibility to Information: Implications for the Delivery of Information Systems and Services," *Journal of the American Society for Information Science* 36 (September 1985): 302–308.

5. Charles A. O'Reilly, "Variations in Decision Makers' Use of Information Sources: Impact of Quality and Accessibility of Information," *Academy of Management Journal* 25 (December 1982): 756–771.

6. Charles L. Bowden and Virginia M. Bowden, "A Survey of Information Sources Used by Psychiatrists," *Bulletin of the Medical Library Association* 59 (October 1971): 603–608.

7. Ching-chih Chen, "How Do Scientists Meet Their Information Needs?" *Special Libraries* 65 (July 1974): 272–280.

8. Margaret F. Stieg, "The Information Needs of Historians," *College & Research Libraries* 42 (November 1981): 549–560.

9. Mary Ellen Soper, "Characteristics and Use of Personal Collections," *Library Quarterly* 46 (October 1976): 397–415.

10. T. D. Wilson, "On User Studies and Information Needs," *Journal of Documentation* 37 (1981): 3–15.

11. B. Dervin, "Communication Gaps and Inequities: Moving toward a Reconceptualization," in *Progress in Communication Sciences*, vol. 2., ed. B. Dervin and M. J. Voigt (Norwood, N.J.: Ablex, 1980), pp. 73–112.

12. Buckland, *Library Services.*

13. Gerald Jahoda, *The Process of Answering Reference Questions: A Test of a Descriptive Model* (Washington, D.C.: Educational Resources Information Center, 1977) ED 136 769.

14. John P. Wilkinson and William Miller, "The Step Approach to Reference Service," *RQ* 17 (Summer 1978): 293–300.

15. W. Richard Scott, *Organizations: Rational, Natural and Open Systems* (Englewood Cliffs, N.J.: Prentice-Hall, 1981).

16. K. S. Cameron and D. A. Whetten, *Organizational Effectiveness: A Comparison of Multiple Models* (New York: Academic Pr., 1983).

17. Marjorie E. Murfin and Gary M. Gugelchuk, "Development and Testing of a Reference Transaction Assessment Instrument," *College & Research Libraries* 48 (July 1987): 314–338.

18. Terence Crowley and Thomas Childers, *Information Service in Public Libraries: Two Studies* (Metuchen, N.J.: Scarecrow, 1971); Marcia J. Myers and Jassim M. Jirjees, *The Accuracy of Telephone Reference/Information Services in Academic Libraries* (Metuchen, N.J.: Scarecrow, 1983).

19. Peter Hernon and Charles R. McClure, "Unobtrusive Reference Testing: The 55 Percent Rule," *Library Journal* 111 (April 15, 1986): 37–41; Peter Hernon and Charles R. McClure, *Unobtrusive Testing and Library Reference Services* (Norwood, N.J.: Ablex, 1987).

20. Charles R. McClure, Peter Hernon, and Gary R. Purcell, *Linking the U.S. National Technical Information Service with Academic and Public Libraries* (Norwood, N.J.: Ablex, 1986).

21. Frances Benham, "A Prediction Study of Reference Accuracy among Recently Graduated Working Reference Librarians (1975–1979)," in *Success in Answering Reference Questions* (Metuchen, N.J.: Scarecrow, 1987).

22. Jahoda, *The Process of Answering.*

23. Paul B. Kantor, "Quantitative Evaluation of the Reference Process," *RQ* 21 (Fall 1981): 43–52; Jo Bell Whitlatch, *The Role of the Academic Reference Librarian* (New York: Greenwood, 1990), p. 86.

24. Paul B. Kantor, "Analyzing the Availability of Reference Services," in *Library Effectiveness: A State of the Art* (Chicago: American Library Assn., 1980), pp. 131–149.

25. Murfin and Gugelchuk, "Development and Testing."

26. Charles A. Bunge, "Factors Related to Reference Question Answering Success: The Development of a Data-Gathering Form," *RQ* 24 (Summer 1985): 482–486.

27. Murfin and Gugelchuk, "Development and Testing."

28. Whitlatch, *The role of the Academic Reference Librarian.*

29. Jo Bell Whitlatch, "Unobtrusive Studies and the Quality of Academic Library Reference Services," *College & Research Libraries* 50 (March 1989): 181–194.

30. Mary Jane Swope and Jeffrey Katzer, "Why Don't They Ask Questions?" *RQ* 12 (Winter 1972): 161–166.

31. Jerold Nelson, "Faculty Awareness and Attitudes toward Academic Library Reference Services: A Measure of Communication," *College & Research Libraries* 34 (September 1973): 268–275.

32. Edward Kazlauskas, "An Exploratory Study: A Kinesic Analysis of Academic Library Service Points," *Journal of Academic Librarianship* 2 (July 1976): 130–134.

33. John William Collins III, "A Critical Incident Analysis of the Behavior of Academic Reference Librarians: Implications for Inservice Training" (Ed. diss., Boston University, 1985).

34. Abram Venable Lawson, "Reference Service in University Libraries: Two Case Studies" (D.L.S. diss., Columbia University, 1971); Terrence Mech, "The Realities of College Reference Service: A Case Study in Personnel Utilization," *The Reference Librarian* 19 (1987): 285–308.

35. William F. Heinlen, "Using Student Assistants in Academic Reference," *RQ* 15 (Summer 1976): 323–325; Jeffrey W. St. Clair and Rao Aluri, "Staffing the Reference Desk: Professionals or Nonprofessionals?" *Journal of Academic Librarianship* 3 (July 1977): 149–153.

36. Egill A. Halldorsson and Marjorie E. Murfin, "The Performance of Professionals and Nonprofessionals in the Reference Interview," *College & Research Libraries* 38 (September 1977): 385–395.

37. Marjorie E. Murfin and Charles A. Bunge, "Paraprofessionals at the Reference Desk," *Journal of Academic Librarianship* 14 (March 1988): 10–14.

38. John J. Regazzi and Rodney M. Hersberger, "Queues and Reference Service: Some Implications for Staffing," *College & Research Libraries* 39 (July 1978): 293–298.

39. Marjorie E. Murfin, "National Reference Measurement: What Can It Tell Us about Staffing?" *College & Research Libraries* 44 (September 1983): 321–333.

40. Terrence A. Brooks, "The Systematic Nature of Library-Output Statistics," *Library Research* 4 (1982): 341–353.

41. Peter Hernon and Charles R. McClure, "Referral Services in U.S. Academic Depository Libraries: Findings, Implications and Research Needs," *RQ* 22 (Winter 1982): 152–163.

42. Whitlatch, *The Role of the Academic Reference Librarian*, p. 44.

43. Hernon and McClure, "Referral Services."

44. Mary Emma Henderson, "The Role of the Georgia Public Junior College Library in the Community" (Ph.D. diss., Florida State University, 1985).

45. George S. Hawley, *The Referral Process in Libraries: A Characterization and an Exploration of Related Factors* (Metuchen, N.J.: Scarecrow, 1987).

46. Katherine H. Packer and Dagobert Soergel, "The Importance of SDI for Current Awareness in Fields with Severe Scatter of Information," *Journal of the American Society for Information Science* 30 (May 1979): 125–135.

47. Ruth Traister Morris, Edwin A. Holtum, and David S. Curry, "Being There: The Effect of the User's Presence on MEDLINE Search Results," *Bulletin of the Medical Library Association* 70 (July 1982): 298–304.

48. Joseph R. Matthews and Gary S. Lawrence, "Further Analysis of the CRL Online Catalog Project," *Information Technology and Libraries* 3 (December 1984): 354–376.

49. Lauren S. Williams, "The Service Orientation of Government Documents Librarians in Academic Libraries of the Southeastern United States" (Ph.D. diss., Florida State University, 1984).

50. Thomas Brian Nielsen, "The Impact of a User Fee on Librarian Responsiveness: An Examination of Online Bibliographic Searching and Reference Practice" (Ph.D. diss., University of North Carolina, 1983).

51. Marcia J. Bates, "What Is a Reference Book? A Theoretical and Empirical Analysis," *RQ* 26 (Fall 1986): 37–57.

52. T. Saracevic, W. M. Shaw, Jr., and P. B. Kantor, "Causes and Dynamics of User Frustration in an Academic Library," *College & Research Libraries* 38 (January 1977): 7–18; P. M. Morse, *Library Effectiveness: A Systems Approach* (Cambridge, Mass.: MIT Pr., 1968); Michael K. Buckland, *Book Availability and the Library User* (New York: Pergamon, 1975).

53. John Mansbridge, "Availability Studies in Libraries," *Library and Information Science Research* 8 (1986): 299–314.

54. W. M. Shaw, Jr., "Longitudinal Studies of Book Availability," in *Library Effectiveness: A State of the Art* (New York: Library Administration and Management Assn., 1980).

55. Gary A. Golden, Susan U. Golden, and Rebecca T. Lenzini, "Patron Approaches to Serials: A User Study," *College & Research Libraries* 43 (January 1982): 22–30; Paul T. Adalian, Jr., Ilene F. Rockman, and Ernest Rodie, "Student Success in Using Microfiche to Find Periodicals," *College & Research Libraries* 46 (January 1985): 48–54.

56. Matthews and Lawrence, "Further Analysis."

57. Karen Markey, "Integrating the Machine-Readable LCSH into Online Catalogs," *Information Technology and Libraries* 7 (September 1988): 299–312.

58. Patricia Sullivan and Peggy Seiden, "Educating Online Catalog Users: The Protocol Assessment of Needs," *Library Hi Tech* 3 (1985): 11–19.

59. Marcia J. Bates, "Factors Affecting Subject Catalog Search Success," *Journal of the American Society for Information Science* 28 (1977): 161–169.

60. Allyson Carlyle, "Matching *LCSH* and User Vocabulary in the Library Catalog," *Cataloging & Classification Quarterly* 10 (1989): 37–63; Marilyn A. Lester, "Coincidence of User Vocabulary and Library of Congress Subject Headings: Experiments to Improve Subject Access in Academic Library Online Catalogs" (Ph.D. diss., University of Illinois, Urbana-Champaign, in progress), summarized in Roose, Tina, "Online Catalogs: Making Them Better Reference Tools," *Library Journal* 113 (December 1988): 76–77.

61. Pal V. Rao, "The Relationship between Card Catalog Access Points and the Recorded Use of Education Books in a University Library," *College & Research Libraries* 43 (July 1982): 341–345; Gunnar Knutson, "Does the Catalog Record Make a Difference? Access Points and Book Use," *College & Research Libraries* 47 (September 1986): 460–469.

62. Pamela Kobelski and Jean Trumbore, "Student Use of Online Bibliographic

Services," *Journal of Academic Librarianship* 4 (March 1978): 14–18.

63. Marcia J. Bates, "Subject Access in Online Catalogs: A Design Model," *Journal of the American Society for Information Science* 37 (1986): 357–376; Markey, "Integrating the Machine-Readable LCSH"; Alex Byrne and Mary Micco, "Improving OPAC Subject Access: The ADFA Experiment," *College & Research Libraries* 49 (September 1988): 432–441.

64. Robert A. Seal, "Academic Branch Libraries," in *Advances in Librarianship*, vol. 14, ed. Wesley Simonton (Orlando, Fla.: Academic Pr., 1986) pp. 175–209.

65. Jeffrey Raffel and Robert Shishko, "Centralization vs. Decentralization: A Locational Analysis Approach for Librarians," *Special Libraries* 63 (March 1972): 135–143.

66. Thomas J. Waldhart and Leroy G. Zweifel, "Organizational Patterns of Scientific and Technical Libraries: An Examination of Three Issues," *College & Research Libraries* 34 (November 1973): 426–435.

67. Richard M. Dougherty, "The Evaluation of Campus Library Document Delivery Service," *College & Research Libraries* 34 (January 1973): 29–39.

68. Richard M. Dougherty and Laura L. Blomquist, *Improving Access to Library Resources* (Metuchen, N.J.: Scarecrow, 1974).

69. Robert J. Greene, "LENDS: An Approach to the Centralization/Decentralization Dilemma," *College & Research Libraries* 36 (May 1975): 201–207.

70. Paul Metz, *The Landscape of Literatures* (Chicago: American Library Assn., 1983).

71. Seal, "Academic Branch Libraries."

72. Mansbridge, "Availability Studies."

73. Shaw, "Longitudinal Studies."

74. Michael K. Buckland, "An Operations Research Study of a Variable Loan and Duplication Policy at the University of Lancaster," *Library Quarterly* 42 (January 1972): 97–106.

75. Buckland, *Book Availability*.

76. Virginia E. Yagello and Gerry Guthrie, "The Effect of Reduced Loan Periods on High Use Items," *College & Research Libraries* 36 (September 1975): 411–414.

77. Buckland, *Book Availability*.

78. Robert Goehlert, "The Effect of Loan Policies on Circulation Recalls," *Journal of Academic Librarianship* 5 (May 1979): 79–82; Jan Baaske, Don Tolliver, and Judy Westerberg, "Overdue Policies: A Comparison of Alternatives," *College & Research Libraries* 35 (September 1974): 354–359.

79. Robert Goehlert, "Book Availability and Delivery Services," *Journal of Academic Librarianship* 4 (November 1978): 368–371.

80. Stayner, "Economic Characteristics."

81. Buckland, "An Operations Research Study"; Robert J. Greene, "The Effectiveness of Browsing," *College & Research Libraries* 38 (July 1977): 313–316; Harold B. Shill, "Open Stacks and Library Performance," *College & Research Libraries* 41 (May 1980): 220–226.

82. Bob Carmack and Trudi Loeber, "The Library Reserve System—Another Look,"

College & Research Libraries 32 (March 1971): 105–109; Peter Marshall, "How Much, How Often?" *College & Research Libraries* 35 (November 1974): 453–456.

83. James R. Martin, "Automation and the Service Attitudes of ARL Circulation Managers," *Journal of Library Automation* 14 (September 1981): 190–194; Malcolm Getz, "More Benefits of Automation," *College & Research Libraries* 49 (November 1988): 534–544; Isobel Jean Mosley, "Cost-Effectiveness Analysis of the Automation of a Circulation System," *Journal of Library Automation* 10 (September 1977): 240–254.

84. Mansbridge, "Availability Studies."

85. Shaw, "Longitudinal Studies."

86. Shill, "Open Stacks"; James Michalko and Toby Heidtmann, "Evaluating Effectiveness of an Electronic Security System," *College & Research Libraries* 39 (July 1978): 263–267; Neal K. Kaske, *A Study of Book Detection System Effectiveness and the Levels of Missing Materials at the University of California, Berkeley* (Washington, D.C.: Educational Resources Information Center, 1978), ED 165 727; Allyne Beach and Kaye Gapen, "Library Book Theft: A Case Study," *College & Research Libraries* 38 (March 1977): 118–128; Larry Greenwood and Harlley McKean, "Effective Measurement and Reduction of Book Loss in an Academic Library," *Journal of Academic Librarianship* 11 (November 1985): 275–283.

87. David F. Kohl, "High Efficiency Inventory through Predictive Data," *Journal of Academic Librarianship* 8 (May 1982): 82–84.

88. Irving Zelkind and Joseph Sprug, "Increased Control through Decreased Controls: A Motivational Approach to a Library Circulation Problem," *College & Research Libraries* 32 (May 1971): 222–226; Ronald A. Hoppe and Edward C. Simmel, "Book Tearing and the Bystander in the University Library," *College & Research Libraries* 30 (May 1969): 247–251; Beach and Gapen, "Library Book Theft"; Dana Weiss, "Book Theft and Book Mutilation in a Large Urban University Library," *College & Research Libraries* 42 (July 1981): 341–347.

89. Mansbridge, "Availability Studies"; Shaw, "Longitudinal Studies."

90. Terry Ellen Ferl and Margaret G. Robinson, "Book Availability at the University of California, Santa Cruz," *College & Research Libraries* 47 (September 1986): 501–508.

91. Gene K. Rinkel and Patricia McCandless, "Application of a Methodology Analyzing User Frustration," *College & Research Libraries* 44 (January 1983): 29–37; Jo Bell Whitlatch and Karen Kieffer, "Service at San Jose State University: Survey of Document Availability," *Journal of Academic Librarianship* 4 (September 1978): 196–199.

92. Anne Brearley Piternick, "Measurement of Journal Availability in a Biomedical Library," *Bulletin of the Medical Library Association* 60 (October 1972): 534–542; Elizabeth Hanson and Judith Serebnick, "Evaluation of the Public Service Functions of Serial File Systems," *College & Research Libraries* 47 (November 1986): 575–586; Marjorie E. Murfin, "Myth of Accessibility: Frustration and Failure in Retrieving Periodicals," *Journal of Academic Librarianship* 6 (March 1980): 6–19.

93. Peter Hernon, "Use of Microformated Government Publications," *Microform Review* 11 (Fall 1982): 237–252.

94. Clyde Hendrick and Marjorie E. Murfin, "Project Library Ripoff: A Survey of Periodical Mutilation in a University Library," *College & Research Libraries* 35 (November 1974): 402–411; Mary Noel Gouke and Marjorie Murfin, "Periodical Mutilation: The Insidious Disease," *Library Journal* 105 (September 15, 1980): 1795–1797; Esther L. Sleep, "Periodical Vandalism: A Chronic Condition?" *Canadian Library Journal* 39 (February 1982): 39–42.

95. C. James Schmidt and Kay Shaffer, "A Cooperative Interlibrary Loan Service for the State-Assisted University Libraries in Ohio," *College & Research Libraries* 32 (May 1971): 197–204; Libby Trudell and James Wolper, "Interlibrary Loan in New England," *College & Research Libraries* 39 (September 1978): 365–371.

96. Richard M. Dougherty, "A Conceptual Framework for Organizing Resource Sharing and Shared Collection Development Programs," *Journal of Academic Librarianship* 14 (November 1988): 287–291.

97. P. Robert Paustian, "Collection Size and Interlibrary Loan in Large Academic Libraries," *Library Research* 3 (1981): 393–400.

98. Thomas J. Waldhart, "The Growth of Interlibrary Loans among ARL University Libraries," *Journal of Academic Librarianship* 10 (September 1984): 204–208.

99. Ingrid T. M. Glasco, "The Impact of the OCLC Interlibrary Loan Subsystem on ARL Libraries" (Ph.D. diss., University of Pittsburgh, 1985).

100. John Budd, "Interlibrary Loan Service: A Study of Turnaround Time," *RQ* 26 (Fall 1986): 75–80; Connie Miller and Patricia Tegler, "An Analysis of Interlibrary Loan and Commercial Document Supply Performance," *Library Quarterly* 58 (1988): 352–366; Edward S. Warner, "The Impact of Interlibrary Access to Periodicals on Subscription Continuation/Cancellation Decision Making," *Journal of the American Society for Information Science* 32 (March 1981): 93–95; Laurie S. Linsley, "Academic Libraries in an Interlibrary Loan Network," *College & Research Libraries* 43 (July 1982): 292–299.

101. *Interlibrary Loan Survey: Report and Data Analysis* (Washington, D.C.: Association of Research Libraries, 1982).

102. William Gray Potter, "Creative Automation Boosts ILL Rates," *American Libraries* 17 (April 1986): 244–246.

103. Warner, "The Impact of Interlibrary Access."

104. Mary Kay Matthew Stansbery, "Attitudes of Selected Graduate Faculty toward the Use of Library Funds to Pay for Electronic Access to Scholarly Journals" (Ph.D. diss., Texas Woman's University, 1986).

Mary W. George

Instructional Services

Three ironies and a quibble surround the topic of this chapter. With 1 percent of the millennium to go, every channel of inquiry is seeping into every other, knowledge is flooding beyond control, and technology is exceeding its own limits. Information sources are seldom easy to identify and often frustrating to locate. Given this tumult, it seems obvious that clientele of academic and research libraries would demand instructional services, that is, systematic explanations of the origin, nature, organization, and retrieval of information. But they do not, and therein lie the ironies.

First of all, almost everyone who has entered—never mind "used"—more than one library concludes from the venture that each is idiosyncratic, not just in layout and collections, but in underlying logic. The same people who go into an unfamiliar airport or grocery with clear expectations of what to do will set foot timorously in a strange library, doubtful they will come away satisfied and uneasy about how to proceed, a condition Richard Saul Wurman calls "the anxiety of not knowing" in his perceptive book, *Information Anxiety.*[1]

In academe this distress is complicated by many other factors, among them pride, peer pressure, embarrassment, confusion, ignorance of the range of possibilities, overconfidence, carelessness, an urge to show off, and a belief that more is better: the same symptoms, interestingly, that justify early sex education. With information anxiety, however—or more specifically with its variant, library anxiety, first examined closely by Constance Mellon—the stimulus is intellectual rather than hormonal, and trepidation rarely lessens with experience.[2]

The second irony comes from scholars and faculty, often themselves widely published experts, who firmly hold that concepts, patterns, and procedures for retrieving recorded knowledge cannot and furthermore should not be taught in college. Why? Because, they claim, these are content-free, rote skills, not disciplines. Or because students should have learned such things in grade school. Or because they themselves gleaned all they need to know the hard way, which is ergo the only right way. Or because the only reliable guide is a mentor or another expert. Yet these same scholars deplore the shallow liberal arts background of today's undergraduates and bemoan their reasoning and writing abilities. It somehow escapes many otherwise shrewd people that critical thinking requires both facility and independence in seeking information, and that these twin crafts must be cogently taught to be successfully learned. Yet many who have mastered these feats think them too mysterious or mundane to teach.

The first two ironies culminate in the third: instructional services exist in academic and research libraries because librarians want them, not because users do. Students, faculty, and scholars demand traditional access services—circulation, reference, interlibrary borrowing, and reserves—and expect online catalogs, national networks, bibliographic databases, and CD-ROM tools. They do not, however, either demand or expect more than simple signage, a descriptive brochure, and occasional tours. Where instructional services have flourished, it is owing to the initiative and energy of professional staff, typically reference librarians, sometimes without designated resources or the approval of administrators. No doubt users who have benefited from these efforts would support programs if they were threatened and miss them if they were cut, but the majority of clientele do not consider instruction an essential library service. This topic is unique in this volume, because it concerns an activity whose claim to being, not to mention legitimacy and importance, is tenuous.

The quibble arises from the term *library research.* Laymen and librarians have no trouble with the phrase; to them, it means the act of seeking information that has been methodically gathered and organized in libraries or, by extension, in archives. Futurists like Philip Young have also applied the term to work done at interactive computer workstations, remote from any physical collection, which allow people to search for, retrieve, and manipulate sources without leaving a terminal.[3]

In ordinary parlance, library research indicates both the place and manner of inquiry, just as field research and laboratory research express location and technique when used in connection with a particular area of investigation. Among specialists, however, library research has a double meaning, which Mary Jo Lynch has contrasted as "research done *in* libraries (bibliographical) and research *about* libraries." She also called "perhaps unfortunate" the name *Research Strategies* for the journal devoted to library instruction.[4]

Jane Robbins-Carter put it more forcefully: "They [the editors] understand doing research to be synonymous with using the library. By selecting the title *Research Strategies* these editors have done a disservice to both library and information science research and bibliographic instruction by perpetuating the obfuscation of the meaning of the word research."[5]

In this essay library research will always denote the popular sense of the locale and process of an information search.

Catchwords

Defining library research is not the only semantic woe besetting instructional services. In the past twenty years, North American terminology for the object or activity of teaching users to become more self-reliant information seekers has included (in alphabetical order since there is no consensus on the exact relationship of one phrase to another): bibliographic education; bibliographic instruction (BI for short), by far the most common term and the one adopted in 1988 as both a subject heading in *Library Literature* and as a separate entry in the *ALA Yearbook of Library and Information Services;* instruction in the use of libraries; library instruction; library orientation; library skills instruction; and library user education. Although there are other variants, these occur most frequently in the literature, as headings in indexes, and as names of professional groups and conferences. The only universal distinction seems to be that orientation is restricted to acquainting people with the building, services, policies, and procedures of a given library. Beyond that—and it is the great beyond that instructional services librarians seek to convey to users in a coherent fashion—there is no agreement on the definitions of these words, despite the attempt by compilers of the *ALA Glossary* to reduce confusion by recognizing just two terms, bibliographic instruction and library use presentation (orientation).[6] Consequently, all of the above will appear more or less interchangeably in this chapter.

One other phrase deserves some attention. Library literacy is not to be confused with the much broader concept of information literacy, the topic of a recent report by a committee of the American Library Association.[7] Jill Fatzer, writing in the *RQ* column "Library Literacy" offers a valuable continuum to describe the audience for instructional services: from "prelibrary literate" (someone who cannot find a book without help) to "semilibrary literate" (someone who can find some materials on his or her own and who can use the *Readers' Guide*) to "library literate" (someone who can carry through a search strategy and evaluate the information identified) to "library fluent" (someone who comprehends the origin and transmission of information and who can transfer that comprehension to new subjects).[8] Although researchers seldom use these labels, the focus of each study is usually apparent, making this scheme a useful way to view the literature. About ninety percent of the published works on BI describe one or more of Fatzer's first three categories; virtually none, except for explorations of how scholars know and communicate, such as Constance Gould's and Mark Handler's interview-based surveys on behalf of the Research Libraries Group, address the fourth and most complex one.[9]

The Stuff of Instruction

Variables and constraints surround library instruction, and these factors dictate both the questions researchers ask and the methodologies they select to answer them. Like other library activities, BI requires an understanding of the unique audience, institution, and community served. But unlike most other endeavors in the field where approaches are few once a goal has been set, there are numerous means for "delivering" instruction to users.

The standard modes or techniques of library instruction are in-person and mediated, and many programs combine both. In-person approaches include orientation tours, single lectures, courses, and tutorials. Mediated instruction involves printed materials such as guides, workbooks, and point-of-use directions, audio-visual presentations, and computer-assisted lessons. The majority of studies attempt to determine the effectiveness of one or more modes, usually relative to a control group receiving no instruction. Hence, the method or content of instruction is typically the independent, manipulated variable, and some measure of learning serves as the dependent variable in the research design.

Constraints affecting user education also have a significant bearing on research motivation and practice. BI almost inevitably engenders organizational conflict because it has a high profile but a negligible priority vis-à-vis collection development, cataloging, automation, and practically any other activity, at least in the eyes of students and faculty. Strained campus budgets in the late 1980s exacerbated the struggle to establish, develop, and justify the resources spent on instruction. The effect on library science research and publication is deleterious and predictable: it is all but impossible for practitioners to remain disinterested in the results of their studies, all the more so if they must produce or succumb, or if their program's funding is in jeopardy. They may attempt a careful design, carry it out conscientiously, and report it accurately with due attention to caveats (and in fact, most instructional literature is clearly written and presented, if frequently unpersuasive), but many researchers substitute learning objectives for research hypotheses and simplistic tests for carefully constructed research instruments. Except for the comparatively few outside researchers and Ph.D. students looking scientifically at library instruction, most studies suffer from a familiarity that breeds weak and sometimes biased conclusions, because they are conducted by practitioners in their local situations.

The Past Is Prolific: The Literature of Instruction

The mass of BI literature is daunting, attested annually by Hannelore Rader's annotated bibliography in *Reference Services Review*, beginning in 1973 and covering the previous year's publications. Major retrospective bibliographies were published by Maureen Krier in 1976, Deborah Lockwood in 1979, Carolyn Kirkendall and Carla Stoffle in 1982, and Tian-Chu Shih in 1986.[10] Krier's and Lockwood's are annotated; the others are not. Arthur Young has written several incisive bibliographic essays.[11] A relative indication of the gross quantity of literature on BI can be found in Stephen Atkins's analysis of articles over the ten-year period, from 1975 to 1984, in the nine most prestigious library and information science journals as identified by David Kohl and Charles Davis.[12] This list did not include *RQ*, which came in tenth in the ranking and which frequently runs research articles on library instruction.

Atkins found that 1.8 percent, or eighty-four, of the articles concerned BI as either a primary or secondary subject. Furthermore, of the fifty-eight categories he traced, only BI showed a bell-shaped curve, with the number of articles peaking between 1979 and 1982, then declining, a pattern not corroborated by Rader in her annual count. Rader, in fact, noted decreases in the number of publications on library instruction in 1982, 1985, and 1987 (respectively 15 percent, 47 percent, and 10 percent fewer than the previous year).[13] The drop-off in Atkins's study is certainly due in part to the founding of *Research Strategies* in 1983, a quarterly that siphoned manuscripts from its parent, the *Journal of Academic Librarianship* and, no doubt, from several of the other journals he reviewed. Unlike Atkins, who examined only nine journals, Rader has been documenting instruction-related publications in all formats and with no set universe. More important in the context of this volume, neither author made any attempt to distinguish research-based literature from the other, more voluminous forms of BI discourse: example, essay, and exhortation.

A relative indication of the net quantity of the research literature on BI can be found in work done by Patricia Feehan and her colleagues. They identified what they termed substantive articles appearing in 1984, in ninety-one library or information science journals.[14] Their total was 2,869 articles, from which they drew a random sample of 520 items. They coded these on the basis of methodology as either research or nonresearch, and found 123 articles (23.6 percent) in the former category. Bluma Peritz used a similar technique to examine articles published in 1975, and found that fully 35 percent of those contributions qualified as research studies.[15]

Although these tallies do not correlate specific topics with the research and nonresearch dichotomy, they do provide a notion of how many research articles on user education to expect in a given period. For instance, Rader records ninety-one entries in her 1987 bibliography under the heading academic libraries; using the Feehan figure of 23.6 percent, approximately twenty-one would have been research-based. That figure is much too high in the case of instruction, no matter how or what one counts. Concern should focus not on the absolute number of research studies but on the rigor and reasoning of those that do appear.

The section on library instruction in David Kohl's Handbook for Library

Management series might have been a helpful tool for sorting out the wheat from the chaff, but it turns out to be much too superficial for the purpose.[16] In an effort to help administrators identify topical research, Kohl provides succinct descriptive abstracts of the problem, sample, method, and findings of eighty-five user education studies, arranged in twenty-five categories and published in thirty-four journals between 1960 and 1983. Although Kohl mentions technique in each of his summaries, he does not specify the larger methodology used by the researcher, and hence there is no way to determine such key components as the hypotheses, sampling procedure, statistical tests, or cautions without going to the full article.

Chroniclers of Instruction

Before reviewing scientifically rigorous studies of library instruction, it is well to acknowledge the excellent historical work that exists. To judge from these contributions, academic librarians have been thinking and writing for well over a hundred years about their obligation to train college students to conduct independent inquiry using diverse, large collections. Johnnie Givens provided an extensive review of this literature in 1974, shortly after the close of the first "new wave" of library instruction activity, dating that era from Patricia Knapp's groundbreaking research at Monteith College.[17] Since Givens's survey, papers delving into the origins of user education have appeared with increasing frequency. Articles by John Mark Tucker, Carolyn Kirkendall and Carla Stoffle, Frances Hopkins, and Peter Hernon as well as speeches by Tucker and Thomas Kirk, have all traced the history of BI and attempted to relate the activities and concerns of the past to those of the present.[18] The historical impulse culminated in 1986 in a collection of seminal contributions, *User Instruction in Academic Libraries: A Century of Selected Readings*.[19]

All this interest and output is hardly surprising, since librarians are no less curious about their antecedents than are other people, and since, if nothing else, they can draw on their knowledge of processes, tools, and sources to conduct exemplary traditional historical research.

Patricia Knapp: The Monteith Classic

For years BI librarians have spoken the name of Patricia Knapp (1914–1972) with reverence, although few who knew her are still active in instruction. This homage is wholly justified on at least three counts. First, Knapp was a thoughtful and articulate visionary in a time of turbulence, the 1960s, when surges in the size and complexity of college collections coincided with surges in social activism on campuses everywhere. Second, she seized an opportunity few researchers have had before or since, the chance to work within and simultaneously to examine the microworld of a new institution, Monteith College, a small undergraduate unit of Wayne State University in Detroit. Lastly, Knapp was forthright about the weaknesses as well as the strengths of her work, an honesty and perspective more instruction practitioners should emulate.

Knapp's dissertation and subsequent book did not concern instruction per se, but her findings about the role of the library in the life of a small liberal arts school (Knox College in Galesburg, Illinois), based largely on correlations of circulation data with student characteristics and on interviews with faculty, clearly influenced her thinking in that direction. As she wrote at the close of *College Teaching and the College Library* "The library is, by definition, a most important storehouse for the accumulated resources of society. Education must produce people with the ability to use it fully."[20]

Monteith was unique at its founding in 1959 in the interdisciplinary emphasis of its curriculum, in the close and continuing relationship between students and faculty, and in the stress it gave to independent learning. Knapp led a project funded by the Office of Education to study the library competence of Monteith students and to design a model program, which she termed the "Way," to coordinate the knowledge and experiences shared in the classroom with those to be found in the library. A central aspect of the effort was the involvement of specially trained graduate students as bibliographical assistants to assist faculty with creating library assignments and undergraduates with completing them. In her 1966 book about this project she describes course-related assignments and the accompanying library instruction offered in all areas of the Monteith curriculum from 1960 to 1962. She also offers the results of her small-sample studies of student performance on tests she designed (1) to measure facility with the subject approach to the card catalog and periodical indexes, (2) to evaluate books using what she called surface clues, (3) to explore annotated bibliographies (guides) to reference materials, and (4) to construct an effective search strategy. She used various statistical techniques to correlate scores on these tests with those on standard psychological and library proficiency tests, background information on the students in the sample, and student response to assignments as gauged by interviews and questionnaires. Knapp also interviewed faculty and reported their reactions at each stage of the program. Her research findings and experience led to the principles she outlined as the "Way," based on ten sequenced library assignments related to course content, to be incorporated in a four-year undergraduate curriculum. The full extent of this plan was never carried out.

From the point of view of research, Knapp's work is rigorous but confusing. Her point of view seems to skip from description to analysis and back again several times. She and her colleagues were bombarded by so many variables—not the least of which were the interpersonal and political dynamics of Monteith itself—during the years of the project's funding that her book can overwhelm almost as much as it inspires. She interrupts the Monteith story with discussions and data analyses of each component of her research, amplified by details in the appendixes that take up fully half the volume, and she waits until the summary chapter to state her general hypotheses and to tie everything together.

In Knapp's defense, it is clear from a statement she makes at the start of the summary chapter of her book that she fully understood the preliminary nature of her work:

> The pilot project phase of the Monteith Library Program was designed as exploratory research. . . . We focussed our attention on the *central* function of the academic library, that of contributing to the instructional program of the institution it serves and we addressed ourselves to basic and fundamental questions about this library function. But these questions were broad and ill-defined. They were to be asked in the context of a "real life" situation, with all the fluidity and intransigence that term implies. We were content, therefore, that our work should be of interest primarily as a demonstration of methodology.[21]

In those terms, and given that no one before had both created and investigated a program on so large a scale, concentrating on the complex relationships among undergraduates, faculty, and information seeking, Knapp's work at Monteith was a complete success, although she was unwilling to call it that in her later writing. Among her numerous subsequent reflections on Monteith is her comment in a speech to library school students in 1965 that "what seemed to me the most important outcome of our work was the discovery of certain general principles....Perhaps discover is the wrong word, for what felt like discoveries were really experiences of recognition."[22] Reading Knapp, despite the difficulties of the narrative flow, is itself a discovery experience.

Bird's Eye Views: Descriptive Multi-Institution Surveys

Recognizing the lack of basic information about what goes on in large academic libraries, the Association of Research Libraries (ARL) has been gathering and distributing internal documents from its members in so-called SPEC kits. Two relatively recent ones have dealt with instruction.[23] While in no way scientific in compilation method or uniform in content, these files serve an important overview function, permitting ARL librarians to share ideas and approaches.

The national clearinghouse for library instruction is the Library Orientation and Instruction Exchange (LOEX), operating since 1972 at Eastern Michigan University in Ypsilanti. Over the years LOEX's directors have not only collected and indexed massive files of information and used them to respond to thousands of queries from BI librarians, they have also organized an annual conference or workshop; edited proceedings; issued *LOEX News;* created the National Bibliographic Instruction Database; written a regular column,

"Dialogue and Debate," originally for the *Journal of Academic Librarianship* and now for *Research Strategies;* and published and spoken extensively about LOEX as a resource.[24] Although LOEX depends on its members for donations of material and hence is neither comprehensive nor current, it has great potential for research. For instance, using the LOEX files investigators can identify which libraries have tried a given technique. They can also draw samples from the data, either to analyze the documents or to contact selected institutions for follow-up studies. Surprisingly few authors seem to have tapped this gold mine in their research designs. One who did was Larry Hardesty for his 1975 survey of slide-tape programs.[25] From time to time the Association of College and Research Libraries (ACRL) publishes a list of state and regional repositories that complement LOEX and can serve the same purposes.[26]

Teresa Mensching, a former director of LOEX, has compiled comparative summary data from two similar LOEX questionnaires, one in 1979 (830 responding institutions) and one in 1987 (834 responding institutions).[27] Although they are almost identical in size, the two samples are independent, and Mensching did not attempt to match data by institution. Among the features she has tracked—giving number and percentage of respondents in order to portray general trends and changes—are enrollment and library type, unit responsible for BI, user education requirements, instructional methods, evaluation techniques, and types of publicity. She has concluded that there has been a decrease in credit courses and term-paper clinics and an increase in the number of institutions requiring or evaluating their instructional efforts. At the end of her descriptive survey she indicates several areas that require further probing. Of these, the most crucial research need is for longitudinal studies of BI at selected institutions.

National questionnaire-based surveys abound in BI, although most share the weakness that their universes or sampling methods are not clearly stated. A typical survey was conducted by E. J. Josey in the early 1960s when he surveyed 500 college and university library administrators about their orientation and instruction programs for freshmen.[28] At that time his 397 respondents indicated that their primary mode was the orientation tour and that they were doing little beyond that. What is notable about Josey's study is that he named institutions in his article when he quoted from replies. Institutions were also identified in reports of a pair of smaller surveys on BI for graduate students conducted by Lloyd Griffin and Jack Clarke, first in the late 1950s and again a decade and a half later.[29]

More common is questionnaire research that focuses on a particular aspect of BI and does not reveal the names of respondents. For instance, Lois Pausch and Jean Koch were interested in the involvement of technical services librarians in instruction, so they surveyed 300 academic libraries having seven or more professional staff and book budgets of at least $100,000. Of the 219 respondents, 140 (64 percent) said that their technical services librarians participate in BI, going on to describe the nature of those positions, the effect of automation on their operation, and the extent of administrative support for instruction.[30]

Peter Hernon conducted a survey of 112 randomly selected institutions regarding evaluation of BI, both how it was being done and librarians' opinions about it. He concluded that many evaluation efforts at the time, the mid-1970s, attempted to "translate informally and subjectively gathered findings into empirical data capable of interpretation."[31] Hernon rightly points out that this is not the way to do research.

For her 1983 dissertation, Carol Ahmad surveyed a random sample of 400 colleges and universities in order to compare their BI programs with the guidelines published by ACRL six years earlier. She concluded that few of the institutions met the guidelines and that most were then providing just orientation tours and course-related lectures for English composition students.[32] Sandra Sadow and Benjamin Beede surveyed law school libraries regarding their instructional services. Two different studies in 1984, one by Frank Goudy and Eugene Moushey and one by Laura Kline with Catherine Rod, examined user education for foreign students.[33] With the exception of Ahmad's dissertation research, none of these studies has a full or rigorous design, but they help answer the perennial question of who's doing what.

Accounts of site visits are another form of large-scale survey research. Allan Dyson combined interviews at ten U.S. and twelve British universities with questionnaire responses from another forty-eight U.S. and Canadian institutions to draw a picture of BI across three countries in the mid-1970s. A few years later Nancy Gwinn looked at libraries that had received instruction grants from the Council on Library Resources. Hannelore Rader described the programs at eleven institutions based on visits she made in the early 1980s.[34]

Mixed Bags: Use, Need, and Opinion Studies

When it comes to information seeking, indistinct boundaries separate what people do, what they desire, and what they think about it all. Beth Shapiro and Philip Marcus attempted to correlate library instruction with user "success" at Michigan State University by surveying a stratified quota sample of over 1,700 library users, asking about frequency of library use, motivation, search strategy, and what action people take when they cannot locate information.[35] Their conclusions were that those who had more exposure to library instruction tended to have a wider range of library use. This research design could be replicated at any institution as a helpful first step in either instruction planning or program assessment.

The opposite tack was taken by John Lubans when he conducted interviews with twenty-seven students at Rensselaer Polytechnic Institute who had previously claimed that they did not use the library. Not surprisingly, Lubans learned from his conversations that most of these students had since become library users, but only as the result of course requirements.[36]

Research on student information use and on the effectiveness of instruction has appeared for half a century, frequently in doctoral dissertations. In the 1930s Peyton Hurt studied graduate student library use at Stanford and Berkeley, and Lulu Reed devised a library knowledge test for high school students.[37]

Colleen Amundson employed questionnaires and interviews of freshmen doing term papers to correlate the reference sources they used with prior library instruction, whether they lived on campus or commuted, and with their particular subculture. She found that the catalog and *Readers' Guide* were the most used sources and librarians the least used. Of particular interest is her investigation of whether students made choices based on relative expenditure of effort and her conclusion that they were not enough aware of options to make such choices.[38]

Sanford McDowell was able to reject his principal hypothesis that a sample of freshmen at the University of Michigan would fail to demonstrate average knowledge and skill on the *Library Orientation Test for College Freshmen*, usually referred to as the Feagley test. He also attempted to correlate scores on that test with students' perceptions about the library instruction they had in high school.[39]

Morell Boone examined motivation of students and conducted an experiment to determine the characteristics of those who spent relatively more time and effort seeking information. He concluded that students who were either internally oriented with high perceived value or who were, conversely, externally oriented with a low perceived value score took longer and expended more energy on their information searches than did others.[40]

Kathleen Dunn also worked with motivation, using a questionnaire with a stratified random sample of undergraduates. She defined the major motivations behind information seeking as professional success, self-approval, self-extension, success in college, approval of others, and intellectual stimulation. The five kinds of sources students reported using were their own materials, experts, libraries, family, and friends. Dunn used factor analysis and correlation techniques to analyze her data.[41]

Larry Miller's 1983 dissertation concerned the relationship between library instruction and common academic variables. He conducted an experiment involving random assignment of communications students. The treatment group received several BI lessons and the control group had research guidance only from the professor. Miller used an identical inventory-type instrument as both a pretest and posttest, then correlated scores with students' grade points in the course, with their semester grade point, with continued enrollment, and with attrition. The only significant correlation was that the experimental group tested higher on the posttest, perhaps an indication that the search skills taught were not essential to success or continuation in college.[42]

Jacqueline Mancall's dissertation and resulting book, written with Carl Drott, are landmarks in the use of bibliography analysis as a research method. Although she studied the sources cited by high school students, relating these to data obtained on questionnaires completed by the same students and their teachers and to information from interviews with librarians, her research design can and should be duplicated at the college level because it provides evidence of use based on product.[43]

One attempt to do so was Judy Reynolds's investigation of the bibliographies of 646 randomly selected master's theses from San Jose State University. She looked in particular at format choice (books, articles, miscellaneous) and at which indexes covered the articles used by students in various fields. Her most significant finding was students' lack of concern for the currency of sources, even in the sciences, and she urged replication of her study at other institutions.[44]

Not a dissertation but a major use study is David King and John Ory's article about three groups of students at the University of Illinois at Urbana-Champaign. The group receiving BI from librarians used more indexes, articles, microforms, and other media as sources than did the group instructed in research by teaching assistants. Both performed better, and showed more confidence in information seeking, than did the control group.[45]

Faculty: Inscrutable, Suspicious, or Supportive

Faculty are an intriguing faction to examine: always ready to discuss their own research needs, generally willing to specify what their students should know about information seeking, and yet hard to pin down about their own actual use patterns. The best background for anyone contemplating faculty as both model and motivator for library instruction is to read two essays, one by Stephen Stoan on the distinction between research skills and library skills and the other by Constance McCarthy on what she aptly terms "the faculty problem."[46] Stoan's essay helps one appreciate the role of the scholar in the creation of knowledge, while McCarthy's explains why these same people can be so difficult to deal with.

Research studies concerning faculty have almost all involved survey techniques or interviews. Foremost among them is Margaret Stieg's descriptive work on historians, a key article for BI because it documents use patterns and preferences of a prominent group of scholars, throwing light on their research techniques and showing areas where they—and presumably their graduate students—would benefit from instruction.

Stieg sent a questionnaire to 767 people in the field, drawing their names from a major directory and obtaining almost a 50 percent response rate. She asked these historians to rank their current use of various physical formats of sources and to identify the two most and two least convenient ones. She also had them rank their methods of discovering relevant published information, specify which indexes they used, and indicate means by which they accidentally found useful information. Finally she inquired about their opinions on the importance of currency of bibliographic control and on the effect of foreign language sources on their research. Stieg summarized her findings in tables, several of which compare her results with a similar British survey. In addition she found her study confirmed by two earlier citation studies. Nothing in her conclusions is surprising to anyone who has worked closely with historians: they work independently, prefer books and periodicals over other formats, and rely on the *Readers' Guide, America: History and Life*, and *Historical Abstracts* far more than on other indexes. "Both historians and librarians have to feel embarrassment over the picture that emerges," according to Stieg, and "the primary responsibility for solving the problem must...be taken by the librarian," a clear call for rethinking instructional services for this group. No other research on faculty library use approaches this article in scope and clarity. It should be undertaken in other disciplines without delay.[47]

Several researchers have looked at faculty attitudes toward library instruction. In his dissertation based on faculty interviews, Larry Hardesty attempted to devise a scale to measure professors' views of the role of the college library, including instruction. Susan Edwards surveyed economics and history faculty at the University of Colorado, which had a very active user education program at the time, for their opinions about the place of BI, who should offer it, and how they themselves learned the library research tools of their field. John Tucker, as part of the evaluation of the Wabash College BI effort, queried faculty, students, and library reference assistants who had participated in the program regarding their retrospective view of it.[48]

A faculty opinion survey by Joy Thomas and Pat Ensor at the University of California, Long Beach,and one by Rae Haws, Lorna Peterson, and Diana Shonrock at Iowa State University are both typical, attempting to document beliefs about student information-gathering skills and to relate these beliefs to other factors. The Iowa State study was also intended to elicit comments from faculty on whether the required freshman library skills course should be continued in its same form.[49]

In an innovative but limited study, Lyn Thaxton conducted detailed, semistructured interviews with ten faculty members representing different areas of psychology, asking them about the validity of William Garvey's communication model for the field, then had fifty-one psychology graduate students complete a questionnaire about the frequency of their use of various sources. Results are presented by whether students had or had not received instruction. Unfortunately, while the idea of comparing faculty views of their discipline with graduate student research practice is promising, Thaxton's sample is too small for generalizations.[50]

Teacher Perpetuation

Understandably, interest has been keen in how teachers and future teachers find information and regard library instruction. In the early sixties, Ralph Perkins gave standardized library knowledge tests to over 4,000 college seniors who were student-teaching at sixty-nine colleges. He used their scores to rank colleges (anonymously, however) by the performance of their seniors, concluding that "there can be no substitute for a required and meaningful course, with practical applications, in library instruction."[51]

Camila Alire also concentrated on teacher training in her dissertation on the attitudes and opinions of doctoral students in education regarding library research expertise and how it should be acquired. To gather data she sent questionnaires to a proportional stratified sample drawn from the entire country. Responses indicated that these students, many of whom have now become school administrators and education professors, believed knowledge about libraries and information seeking to be important, but felt their own abilities were poor and wanted a graduate-level library research methods course.[52]

Angie LeClercq queried high school teachers about the library use, needs, and sophistication of their students in an attempt to design a library outreach program at the University of Tennessee, Knoxville, to ease the transition of students to college.[53] Asking the same sort of questions of all elementary education professors in Ohio and correlating their responses with variables such as academic rank, years of college teaching experience, and the nature of their institutions, Nancyanne O'Hanlon concluded that "teacher-education faculty support teaching of the library research process [to undergraduates majoring in elementary education], but apparently do not view the development of library skills as necessarily related to the development of critical thinking skills."[54] Hers is an especially clear research design and presentation of findings.

Portrayals

Related to these opinion surveys are two studies using content analysis as a methodology to examine the portrayal of librarians, libraries, and the library research process in books intended for college students. Michael Freeman looked closely at sixteen study guides and concluded that "these publications do not offer a fruitful or sophisticated approach to library research and make serious omissions in their recommendations of two important types of reference tools, indexes and abstracts."[55]

Virginia Tiefel conducted the same sort of inquiry with twenty-five freshman English textbooks published between 1952 and 1980. In particular she noted the attitudes each author conveyed about libraries and librarians, the specific reference works each discussed, and their relative emphasis on primary over secondary sources, indicating her findings as the percentage of pages covering each topic.[56]

As one would expect, both Freeman's and Tiefel's results were disheartening in the extreme. There has been little improvement in the interim, although it is only fair to note that two recent titles from Oxford University Press do a much better job describing the search process than do any of their predecessors. These are Thomas Mann's *Guide to Library Research Methods* and David Beasley's *How To Use a Research Library*.[57]

Sampling users for their awareness of library services addresses another question. Jerold Nelson surveyed randomly selected faculty at six California State campuses concerning reference services generally, but with a specific item about their awareness of BI; 74 percent of the respondents indicated they knew the library offered such a service. Mollie Sandock telephoned a stratified random sample of University of Chicago students to ask what they believed were the services offered by the Regenstein Library reference department, including orientation tours.[58] Neither method has appeared again in the literature for over a decade, but both deserve to be considered by anyone curious about their library's public service image.

Evaluation: The Perilous Side of Instruction

No component of library instruction is as misunderstood and mishandled as evaluation. The only precept everyone agrees on is that it is somehow good to evaluate BI. To judge from the literature, evaluation motives, methodology, and interpretation all vary widely—and are sometimes absent—from study to study, a situation that besets educational evaluation generally but which in BI is deplorable nonetheless. The main difficulty is that instruction librarians tend to assume that evaluation equals research and vice versa, and they then proceed to describe and assess their own efforts in their own way and for their own purposes. In short, their inquiries are often imperfectly conceived and poorly conducted.

Practicing instruction librarians are seldom disinterested parties in evaluation. They often embark on it to justify their work to administrators or funding agencies. In so doing they test program objectives instead of hypotheses and ignore the many factors, particularly learning from other sources, that can contaminate results. Another weakness that appears time and again in published articles is the ad hoc and afterthought nature of the research design. Lastly, data presentation and analysis are often either unduly primitive or unduly complex for the questions at hand, with the most common statistics being simple percentages of responses in each category on a questionnaire or change in raw scores in a pretest-posttest design. A prototypical evaluation statement in a descriptive article runs, "In [year], X percent of attendees who completed evaluation forms indicated that the sessions had increased their knowledge of the sources and services of the libraries." Numerous writers have pointed to these fallacies, like Richard Werking who commented that "there seems to be too great a concern with statistically 'proving' certain impacts [of BI] to ourselves and others."[59]

Rare indeed are the BI authors who undertake the classic experimental steps of problem statement; literature review; hypotheses; pilot testing of instruments for validity and reliability; designation of control group; determination of appropriate sample size and randomization method for both selection and assignment of subjects; discussion of conditions, treatments, treatment intervals, and sources of bias; choice and application of statistical tests; and separate confirmation or rejection of each original hypothesis.[60] Rarer yet are investigators who will commit their previous mistakes to print and explain how and why they reworked their research design. Virginia Tiefel is one who has shared what she and her colleagues at Ohio State University learned the hard way about evaluation techniques; anyone attempting to review a BI program should be grateful for her candor.[61] On the other hand, BI investigators almost always thoroughly describe their situation and concerns, summarize their findings, and extrapolate new research questions from them. Not every problem requires, or deserves, full experimental design, but it is good to recall the possible components as one examines the evidence of research activity.

Neophytes can use several clear presentations of evaluation techniques for library instruction to complement the standard texts on research methods and statistics. In 1983 the ACRL Bibliographic Instruction Section (BIS) issued the excellent *Evaluating Bibliographic Instruction.* No one should undertake any type of BI evaluation project until they have mastered everything in this manual. Other worthwhile overviews of evaluation techniques are by Richard Werking, James Rice, and Janet Freedman and Harold Bantly.[62]

One key argument for what should be examined comes from Thomas Kirk, who defines evaluation as "systematic collection of data to determine as precisely as possible the cause and effect relationships amongst student backgrounds, bibliographic instruction programs, library use, and student attitudes toward the library," and who stresses a fourfold object of evaluation: knowledge, products, processes, and attitudes. Jill Fatzer advocates performance measures.[63]

Better than What?

The central question in any analytical or experimental research is always, does it matter? Patricia Breivik's dissertation involving basic skills students at Brooklyn College of the City University of New York rivals Patricia Knapp's Monteith work in its impact on BI. Breivik determined that for these students, entering college under an open admissions plan in the early 1970s, no library instruction or just an orientation tour (for the control group) led to more improvement on homework assignments requiring information seeking than did traditional BI, meaning orientation plus an introduction to the card catalog and periodical indexes. Although she also found that students in a second treatment group who had weekly sessions on retrieval and evaluation skills improved more than did the control group, the discovery that no instruction was better than what was then the usual approach shook the world of BI for quite some time.[64]

Less sensational were Janet Hansen's essentially similar findings, no doubt because she did not publish and speak about her research. In a five-group experiment with average college students and a pretest-posttest design, Hansen concluded that there was no significant difference in test score improvement between the control group and students presented with a standard BI lecture.[65]

Over a decade later, Janice Bolt conducted a study, using a causal-comparative design, with undergraduates who had failed basic competency tests and were taking a course in study and reference skills. She matched their subsequent academic achievement, grades, retention, and graduation rates with those of a control group who had passed the same initial screening tests. She found no difference for these variables.[66]

About the same time, Marsha Broadway looked closely at the distinction between reference and research inquiries and devised a model experiment to determine if effective question formation skills can be taught to students. Her findings were positive. Students in a treatment group who received instruction on query formation and presentation as part of a required BI course improved significantly more from pretest to posttest than did members of her control group. Broadway did a small follow-up study some weeks later and found that students in the treatment group had retained the knowledge and skills they learned.[67]

Donna Corlett attempted to predict grade point averages of college freshmen using *Library Orientation Test* scores, study skills test scores, and sex as variables in a multiple regression equation. She concluded from a sample of eighty-one students that the Feagley test can validly forecast success in college and that women would have a somewhat higher grade point average than men. Corlett did not, however, verify her predictive technique with any follow-up study of these students.[68]

Similar in intent but inferior in design to these dissertations are the plethora of articles examining a single BI technique. Workbook effectiveness in particular has been studied, with and without enhancements such as structured assignments.[69] Of particular interest are aspects of the research design in several articles. In the early 1970s at Brigham Young University, Marvin Wiggins and his colleagues conducted experiments based on principles of instructional psychology. They analyzed how experts (librarians) performed tasks such as using the subject card catalog and then wrote test questions on that basis. Wiggins also broke ground at the time by requiring both traditional pencil-and-paper tests, what he called simulations, and equivalent hands-on demonstrations of student learning.[70] Susan Ware and Deena Morganti have used evaluation methodology to study the involvement of librarians to determine minimum competency levels for student posttest scores after completing a workbook.[71]

Which Works Best

Practitioners of BI are especially fond of studies that contrast different ways to impart the same information, usually time-honored BI lecture versus another approach. Interestingly, although Earlham College's curriculum, frequently cited as the national standard for course-related BI, has never been formally and fully assessed, Thomas Kirk's comparison of lecture plus demonstration against guided exercise in Earlham's general biology sequence is the model for this type of evaluation.[72] Kirk judged student learning from essays and analysis of the accompanying bibliographies, from two tests during the second term, and from both a library instruction and a whole-course evaluation completed by students at the end of the year. He concluded there was virtually no difference in student performance or attitude between the two methods.

Patricia Donegan, Ralph Domas, and John Deosdade, comparing the lecture and tutorial (term-paper counseling) approaches, likewise found no significant distinction in student grasp of basic search strategy.[73] Their work is especially noteworthy for its detailed discussion of test design.

Thomas Surprenant's dissertation and its offspring are exemplary both for his near-perfect research design using the Solomon four-group technique to compare lecture and programmed instruction, and for the grounding he gave his work in the learning theory of Robert Gagné.[74] Susan Ware conducted various statistical analyses of the posttest-only scores of 300 students who took the same course but were randomly assigned to one of three treatments: a basic library skills lecture, a workbook, or "informal" instruction—meaning ordinary interaction with a reference librarian. Ware discovered that the lecture and workbook treatments produced similar minimum competence, but that the lecture led to significantly better mastery of higher concepts.[75] Patricia Kenney and Judith McArthur came to a different conclusion in their study. They found that the workbook was superior to the lecture for teaching low- to medium-level cognitive skills, although they did not use either random assignment or a control group.[76]

Now out of vogue, computer-assisted instruction has been compared with other methods. Mitsuko Williams and Elisabeth Davis designed an experiment using PLATO software in which the treatment group received a reference and bibliography lesson and the control group merely information on library services. Students in both groups took an identical test and attitude survey afterwards. The results indicated a strong preference for one-to-one instruction, whether with a person or a terminal. Also using PLATO, Kathleen Johnson and Barbara Plake designed a card catalog lesson and divided subjects into four groups: control, PLATO, personal tutorial, and tour-only. The control and tour-only groups performed similarly on a catalog skills test, as did the PLATO and tutorial groups, the latter two at a significantly higher level than the former two. The small size of the groups and the fact that this study was never replicated are two deficiencies.[77]

Denise Madland and Marian Smith performed a three-group nonrandom experiment involving a lecture group, a computer-assisted group, and a control group, with posttest only. Although the design was flawed, there may be something worth pursuing in their findings that posttest scores were highest for the lecture group, but that students preferred the computer.[78]

A well-executed comparison, not of mode but of content, between tool-based and strategy-based lectures was conducted by David Kohl and Lizabeth Wilson. They had librarians and writing instructors independently rate the bibliographies of term papers done by students in both educational opportunity and regular sections. Criteria were the appropriateness, age, and quality of sources students cited. Statistical tests compared the consistency of raters, the relationship of tool-based versus strategy-based lectures to the quality of student bibliographies, and the correlation between the quality of bibliographies and ultimate course grades. Kohl and Wilson found that librarians and instructors made, on the whole, similar judgments about items cited by students, that students who attended the strategy-based lecture created significantly better bibliographies than those who heard the more common tool-based presentation, but that there was no significant relationship between bibliography ratings and course grades.[79] This study should inspire other researchers to focus on lecture content and correlate different approaches with student performance.

Long Run

Few investigators have attempted to document the long-term effects of library instruction. Larry Miller's and Janice Bolt's dissertations, discussed earlier, both include retention in college among the dependent variables, and Bolt also looked at the graduation rate of her subjects. Other studies have been done by Roland Person, looking at how students "appreciate" BI over time; Larry Hardesty, surveying the Depauw University graduates of the classes of 1977 and 1980 where none of the former but some of the latter had had BI as freshmen; and John Selegean and his colleagues who used matched pairs of students who had and had not taken the "Biblio Strategy" course at the University of California, Irvine.[80] These studies all report significant, positive effects of instruction over time, but their research designs do not address the key question of how instruction affects the individual's concepts and information-seeking behavior beyond college.

The only researcher so far who has tried to track subjects is Carol Kuhlthau, who repeated in-depth interviews with four of her former high school students following their graduation from college.

Kuhlthau's interest was specifically in each person's mental picture of the search process, not with whether or not they experienced a particular sort of instruction. Her before-and-after-college transcriptions for each student, together with flowcharts of the search process the students sketched at each point, make fascinating reading and provide a model for how to design a longitudinal case study.[81]

Bosom Buddies: BI and Online Searching

No development since open stacks has changed how users conduct their business as much as the online public access catalog (OPAC). The salient difference between open stacks and OPAC is that whereas users received no guidance to the former beyond a chart or map, OPAC users have been bombarded with brochures, help screens, and training sessions. Public service librarians, working closely with programmers, have influenced both the logic of OPAC commands and the layout of screen displays, input they did not enjoy in the 3x5–card era. Their vested interest in success, bolstered by the quick realization that users were not fully exploiting OPACs and the exciting possibility of tracking searches via software, yielded a spate of research. Northwestern University, home of NOTIS, has been the leader in this area.[82]

Brian Nielsen and Betsy Baker have written extensively on their experiment with transaction logs, unobtrusive "spying" on students' searches in an effort to describe and understand query formulation and to determine whether classroom instruction or a printed brochure is more effective in teaching OPAC concepts and commands. In a random sample of ninety freshmen assigned to three groups, students performed significantly better on tests immediately following in-person OPAC presentations than they did after reading a brochure; those who received neither sort of instruction performed worst of all.[83]

Ron Blazek and Dania Bilal analyzed questionnaires returned by sixty-five OPAC users at Florida State University, asking about the problems they were encountering. After correlating responses with user characteristics, field, and previous experience searching the online catalog, they concluded that there is a need for both point-of-use instruction, reference staff explaining commands and displays to users on an ad hoc basis, and formal instruction in OPAC scope and search procedures.[84]

Although she did not state her findings in BI terms, Karen Markey's superbly conducted research on what types of OPAC assistance users had actually sought is a touchstone in this area of inquiry. She combined surveys, transaction logs, and small-group interviews of users at six libraries and discovered that people preferred assistance from the screen itself, such as informative error messages and multiple-dialog modes. Of particular merit in Markey's research design was her inclusion in her samples of both library staff and nonusers of OPACs. And of particular interest in her findings was the retention difficulty that infrequent OPAC users reported having over and over again, clearly a matter that deserves its own careful study.[85]

An extremely promising technique for revealing users' preconceptions and logic is protocol analysis, in which subjects verbalize all their thoughts as they conduct a search. The best description of this method is by Peter Ingwersen who recorded the protocols of a small sample of librarians and users on tape as they went about traditional library research in a Danish public library. Patricia Sullivan and Peggy Seiden applied protocol analysis to OPAC searching, asking thirteen volunteers to answer five questions using the online catalog. They videotaped their efforts, then categorized the users' misunderstandings about the database and its structure, commands, and features, pointing out how helpful such a study can be for BI design. In a more theoretical discussion of protocol analysis, but one that can easily be extrapolated to the OPAC situation, Diane Nahl-Jakobovits and Leon Jakobovits have advocated the procedure for investigating any reasoning process.[86]

Closely related to OPAC research are studies focusing on instruction for end-users of bibliographic databases. Although BRS, DIALOG, and their like have been around much longer than online catalogs, virtually all searches were done by highly skilled mediators until this decade. Now that more and more institutions are training their clientele to perform successful searches on their own, attempts to assess that activity are beginning to appear. The most interesting research to date was reported by Sara Penhole and Nancy Taylor. They compared the manual and online search results of Earlham College science students in terms of both recall and precision and then compared their findings with the same online searches performed by librarians.[87]

Rowena Swanson surveyed the end-user training programs of several libraries and database vendors in terms of the documentation, teaching, resources, and evaluation they provided.[88] Charlene York and her colleagues at Bowling Green State University interviewed 117 people to determine whether they understood the distinctions among OPAC, OCLC (to which they had direct access), and other databases such as InfoTrac and NewsBank Electronic Index and how they approached each as part of their search process. The basic finding, that automation attracts users, is hardly earthshaking, but the design of this experiment, with modifications to expand the sample, deserves to be emulated, especially as CD-ROMs become more prominent.[89] Only when BI librarians fully understand users' misconceptions about various computerized tools can they design instruction to clarify the nature and scope of each.

Professional Concern: Studies of Those Who Teach

No sooner did BI become a service imperative, to purloin the title of Margaret Monroe's festschrift, than researchers started to treat its practitioners as objects of investigation. Surveys of library schools by Sue Galloway, Esther Dyer, Maureen Pastine and Karen Seibert, Robert Brundin, and Mary Ellen Larson and Ellen Meltzer all attempted to determine whether and how instruction topics were being covered in the M.L.S. curriculum.[90] As one would expect, the situation shifts from school to school over time.

Joy Thomas both surveyed library schools and analyzed questionnaire responses from one hundred science librarians in California about their BI involvement and preparation for it.[91]

In a superbly designed study dealing with how academic librarians learn what they know, Ronald Powell analyzed questionnaires from 349 professionals. The respondents were asked to rate fifty-six areas in terms of importance to professional work. Bibliographic/library instruction was one of these, and it emerged respectably in the composite result as the nineteenth most important area. Other topics central to instruction were high on the list as well: bibliographic tools and oral communication skills tied for first place; specialized reference sources came in fourth; search strategy was sixth; subject field knowledge was seventh; and structure of subject literature (which presumably includes expert communication) ranked eighteenth. Teaching methods, however, counted only twenty-sixth. Not surprisingly, more respondents said that they had acquired their knowledge about bibliographic/library instruction on the job than any other way. To the question about how the different knowledge bases can best be acquired, there was a near tie for BI between on the job and library school, with continuing education and staff development also ranking as relatively strong preferences.[92]

Two excellent articles by Ron Blazek treat the administration of instruction. In one he tested the hypothesis that a "supportive attitude toward bibliographic instruction is a function of [a staff member's] direct proximity to managerial responsibility." He rejected this hypothesis after surveying a randomly selected group of top administrators, BI coordinators, and heads of reference from ARL libraries and performing a chi square test on their scored responses to ten value statements. His second study, an extension of the first, examined the organization of BI in the same libraries. The independent variable was whether each library's program was run by a systemwide BI coordinator or by the head of reference, and the dependent variables were such factors as staff involvement, groups served, and modes of BI. Blazek concluded that there is "a definite link between the presence of a bibliographic instruction coordinator and the existence of certain conditions associated with effective programs."[93]

Underpinnings: Theoretical and Methodological Contributions

A telling sign of the importance to the BI movement of concept learning and models is that there have been two collections with that focus, one edited by Cerise Oberman and Katina Strauch and the other edited by Mary Reichel and Mary Ann Ramey.[94] Numerous articles and monographs also propose conceptual frameworks; the best and most enduring are by Thelma Freides, Elizabeth Frick, John MacGregor and Raymond McInnis, and Pamela Kobelski and Mary Reichel.[95] Learning theory per se is reviewed for its relevance to BI by Harold Tuckett and Carla Stoffle, by Rao Aluri and Mary Reichel, and Constance Mellon and Kathryn Pagles.[96]

Two theorists' cited repeatedly are Jerome Bruner and Robert Gagné. Constance Miller has described Gagné's work in terms of BI, Mary Reichel has done the same for Bruner, and Janet Hanson has discussed the thought of both men.[97] Betsy Baker suggested a specific conceptual framework for online catalog instruction, and Bruce Morton devised a concept-based approach to introduce history students to federal documents. He persuasively argues that "librarians would better serve themselves and those whom they wish to educate by focusing on the discipline and its information requirements rather than on the reference titles that are the product of those requirements."[98] Although the connection between critical thinking and BI has always been self-evident to librarians, it took Sandra Bodi to articulate the relationship, bringing William G. Perry's work on intellectual and ethical development to bear on library instruction.[99]

All of these writers found that rote learning of reference tools or search strategies, even with reinforcing exercises, is not an effective teaching method, and that users need clear mental constructs about information storage and retrieval in order to organize facts about titles and procedures. Their thinking needs to be molded into practice and carefully tested by future research.

Only two truly new theories pertaining to instruction have come from research rather than from pure reasoning. Constance Mellon recognized library anxiety from a qualitative study using students' research logs. Carol Kuhlthau's model of the information search process ties together users' thoughts and feelings with their search behavior from start to finish of a project.[100] Kuhlthau developed her model from close study, using several instruments, of college-bound high school students as they engaged in research for term papers. She also validated the model in a study involving another sample of high school students, undergraduates, and adult independent learners.[101]

Not a theory, but an exceedingly helpful way to chart the same factors Kuhlthau examined, is the scheme offered by Leon Jakobovits and Diane Nahl-Jakobovits with affective, cognitive, and psychomotor skills above the columns and internalizing, interacting, and orienting functions marking the rows. Although their taxonomy does not document process, it does instantly show which skills a person lacks and can be profitably used by BI planners as part of either the needs assessment or evaluation step.[102]

Several research methodologies have already been noted that have a particular application to instruction, among them Mancall's analysis of student bibliographies, Ingwersen's verbal protocol technique, and Kuhlthau's longitudinal case study approach. The Delphi method of eliciting opinions from leaders in the field in a series of more and more focused rounds was employed uniquely by Theophil Otto to predict the key issues in academic librarianship, including instruction, for the next century. The pilot work conducted by Philip Clark and James Benson defines the individual user as the optimum unit of analysis for circulation and reference research.[103] All of these designs deserve consideration and elaboration by other investigators.

Overcast

One conclusion from this survey of research on library instruction is that these studies, many of which are imperfect even though each does contribute some insight, do not represent the thousands of poor BI research attempts and that we should lament the weak rather than honor the strong. To make matters worse, there is no mention whatsoever of the need for research on instruction in either of the two major reference textbooks, Katz's *Introduction to Reference Work* or Stevens and Smith's *Reference Work in the University Library*, both of which devote a few pages to BI as a standard service.[104]

What is clear is that the best BI research has been conducted by investigators who have doctoral training; that *College & Research Libraries* carries more research articles in the area than any other journal; and that the principal flaw in design of the studies omitted here is either vague (or absent) research questions or a mismatch between inquiry and approach—usually an attempt to assess a program using quantitative methods alone when qualitative ones are indicated.

Guideposts and Lifelines

The existence or imminent arrival of half a dozen competing research agendas confuses matters exceedingly. No two lists of topics have the same method of compilation, purpose, or categories, so comparing them leads to madness. First in this decade came the research agenda issued in 1980 by the ACRL Bibliographic Instruction Section's Research Committee, which neatly arranges topics under three headings: library skills, defining needs, and measuring actual levels; design and implementation of BI programs; and management aspects.[105] Everything in this brief document is still valid and anyone searching for a research area should refer to it, but it does not deal with concept formation and information seeking as process, ideas which have come to the forefront more recently.

The first BI Think Tank was held as a preconference in San Francisco in 1981, a retreat involving seven librarians who wrote a statement that has guided instruction throughout this decade. They strongly advocated research activity and publication as essential to the development of the movement.[106] *Bibliographic Instruction: The Second Generation* (Libraries Unlimited, 1987) is a direct result of the Think Tank, a collection of articles touching virtually all the BI concerns of the 1980s. The second Think Tank occurred July 21 through 23, 1989, in Dallas.

Other research agendas have come from Cuadra Associates in 1982, the Council on Library Resources in 1985, the Association of Research Libraries in 1987, the U.S. Office of Education in 1988, and the ACRL Research Committee in 1990.[107] Each of these documents mentions research on instruction in one way or another, but trying to pull out commonalities regarding any topic, let alone one as diffuse as user education, is a big chore, one Bonnie Gratch has helpfully undertaken.[108]

To complicate matters still more, the Bibliographic Instruction Section's own Research Committee has been trying to define its role. Thomas Kirk headed a task force in 1988 and 1989 that was charged to recommend whether the section should continue to have a separate research group and, if so, what its members should do. After close examination and debate of all sides of the issue, the task force has recommended to the BIS Executive Committee that, among other things, the Research Committee be disbanded, that all units within the section should in the future need to conduct their own research in support of projects, that program planning committees should compile bibliographies to distribute at sessions they sponsor, and that a research discussion group be formed within the section.[109] The rationale for these beliefs is excellent and affords an extremely useful classification of research and the agents who should conduct it: "pure" inquiry is never appropriate for a professional organization to engage in on its own; highly specific applied research might be done by an ad hoc group; and surveys of current practice or opinion and literature reviews can and should be carried out in support of committee projects or programs.

Gleaning guidance is difficult when the library world is awash in agendas. Even if there were only one such document, it would have limited value except perhaps to funding agencies or to graduate students too inexperienced to discover topics on their own. Rather than rely on anybody else's agenda, experienced researchers prefer to tackle a problem that strikes them as universal, wrestle it into specific questions, and apply rigorous methodologies. The problem may not appear on an official list; but if it fascinates a researcher who can imagine its relevance to other problems or situations, that is sufficient. "Do what makes you smile."[110]

In addition to an ACRL research discussion group to purvey mutual aid and comfort, novice BI researchers might be helped by the creation of a network of veteran investigators willing to critique their research designs before they launch a study. Both the Library Instruction Round Table and the Library Research Round Table should be involved with ACRL in such a project. A second idea would be to create a small database, on the order of a hundred items that would cite and code the best BI research studies by topic and methodology, perhaps going back to 1980, with a few excellent examples added each year. This model-research database could be made available at a nominal charge on floppy disk by ACRL, LOEX, or some other organization willing to sponsor what would be initially a labor-intensive project but whose updates could be easily done. A good classification scheme, with some refinement, would be that used by Feehan and her colleagues in their analysis of one year's research literature.[111]

The Ultimate Question: What Lasts and Grows

One overarching issue demands urgent and special attention in the 1990s: the transferability of information-seeking skills—whether of tools or techniques, concepts or processes—across the dimensions of time, place, level, and discipline in people's lives. Only when BI researchers relate their findings to an individual's lifelong need to identify, locate, and verify information will they contribute useful knowledge to society. To return to Jill Fatzer's continuum, the prelibrary literate person, whether child or adult, needs to make steady progress throughout life toward the condition of library fluency. The BI experience in kindergarten should be the basis for continual growth and learning for each person in a smooth crescendo as new subjects, sources and collections, and information needs arise. Research methodologies that focus on cognitive development, long-term learning retention, and creativity should supplement traditional data-gathering techniques that take snapshots but not videos. Fortunately, the question of transferability does not limit the range of valuable BI research problems; it just adds a new facet to any inquiry.

Notes

1. Richard Saul Wurman, *Information Anxiety* (New York: Doubleday, 1989), p. 41.

2. Constance A. Mellon, "Library Anxiety: A Grounded Theory and Its Development," *College & Research Libraries* 47 (March 1986): 160–165.

3. Philip H. Young, "Library Research in the Future: A Prognostication," *College & Research Libraries* 50 (January 1989): 7–10.

4. Mary Jo Lynch, "Research and Librarianship: An Uneasy Connection," *Library Trends* 34 (Spring 1984): 368, 370.

5. Jane Robbins-Carter, "Editorial," *Library & Information Science Research* 6 (January-March 1984): 1.

6. *ALA Glossary of Library and Information Science*, ed. Heartsill Young (Chicago: American Library Assn. 1983),pp. 22, 132.

7. American Library Association, Presidential Committee on Information Literacy, *Final Report* (Chicago: American Library Association, 1989); Patricia Senn Breivik and E. Gordon Gee, *Information Literacy: Revolution in the Library* (New York: American Council on Education, Macmillan, 1989).

8. Jill B. Fatzer, "Library Literacy," *RQ* 26 (Spring 1987): 313–314.

9. Constance C. Gould, *Information Needs in the Humanities: An Assessment* (Stanford, Calif.: Research Libraries Group, 1988); Constance C. Gould and Mark Handler, *Information Needs in the Social Sciences: An Assessment* (Mountain View, Calif.: Research Libraries Group, 1989).

10. Hannelore B. Rader, "Library Orientation and Instruction - [coverage year]," *Reference Services Review* 2- (1973-). Issue and pagination vary; Maureen Krier, "Bibliographic Instruction: A Checklist of the Literature, 1931–1975," *Reference Services Review* 4, no. 1 (1976): 7–31; Deborah L. Lockwood, *Library Instruction: A Bibliography* (Westport, Ct.: Greenwood, 1979); Carolyn A. Kirkendall and Carla J. Stoffle, "Instruction," in *The Service Imperative for Libraries: Essays in Honor of Margaret E. Monroe*, ed. Gail A. Schlachter (Littleton, Colo.: Libraries Unlimited, 1982), 68–93; Tian-Chu Shih, *Library Instruction: A Bibliography, 1975 through 1985* (Jefferson, N.C.: McFarland, 1986).

11. Arthur P. Young, "Research on Library-User Education: A Review Essay," in *Educating the Library User*, ed. John Lubans (New York: Bowker, 1974), 1–15; Arthur P. Young and Exir B. Brennan, "Bibliographic Instruction: A Review of Research and Applications," in *Progress in Educating the Library User*, ed. John Lubans (New York: Bowker, 1978), 13–28; Arthur P. Young, "And Gladly Teach: Bibliographic Instruction and the Library," *Advances in Librarianship* 10 (1980): 63–88.

12. Stephen E. Atkins, "Subject Trends in Library and Information Science Research, 1975–1984," *Library Trends* 36 (Spring 1988): 633–658; David F. Kohl and Charles H. Davis, "Ratings of Journals by ARL Library Directors and Deans of Library and Information Science Schools," *College & Research Libraries* 46 (January 1985): 40–47.

13. Hannelore B. Rader, "Library Orientation and Instruction—1982," *Reference Services Review* 11, no. 2 (1983): 57; "Library Orientation and Instruction—1985," *Reference Services Review* 14, no. 2 (1986): 59; "Library Orientation and Instruction—1987," *Reference Services Review* 16, no. 3 (1988): 57.

14. Patricia E. Feehan et al., "Library and Information Science Research: An Analysis of the 1984 Journal Literature," *Library & Information Science Research* 9 (July-September 1987): 173–185.

15. Bluma Cheila Peritz, "Research in Library Science as Reflected in the Core Journals of the Profession: A Quantitative Analysis (1950–1974)" (Ph.D. diss., University of California, Berkeley, 1977); *Dissertation Abstracts International* 39 (August 1978): 523–524A.

16. David F. Kohl, "Library Instruction," in *Reference Services and Library Instruction: A Handbook for Library Management* (Santa Barbara, Calif.: ABC-Clio, 1985), pp. 227–257.

17. Johnnie Givens, "The Use of Resources in the Learning Experience," *Advances in Librarianship* 4 (1974): 149–174.

18. John Mark Tucker, "User Education in Academic Libraries: A Century in Retrospect," *Library Trends* 29 (Summer 1980): 9–27; John Mark Tucker, "Emerson's Library Legacy: Concepts of Bibliographic Instruction," in *Increasing the Teaching Role of Academic Libraries,* ed. Thomas G. Kirk, New Directions for Teaching and Learning, no. 18 (San Francisco: Jossey-Bass, 1984), pp. 15–24; Kirkendall and Stoffle, "Instruction," pp. 42–93; Frances L. Hopkins, "User Instruction in the College Library: Origins, Prospects, and a Practical Program," in *College Librarianship,* ed. William Miller and D. S. Rockwood (Metuchen, N.J.: Scarecrow, 1981), pp. 173–204; Frances L. Hopkins, "A Century of Bibliographic Instruction: The Historical Claim to Professional and Academic Legitimacy," *College & Research Libraries* 43 (May 1982): 192–198; Peter Hernon, "Instruction in the Use of Academic Libraries: A Preliminary Study of the Early Years Based on Selective Extant Materials," *Journal of Library History* 17 (Winter 1982): 16–38; John Mark Tucker, "The Origins of Bibliographic Instruction in Academic Libraries, 1876–1914," in *New Horizons for Academic Libraries,* ed. Robert D. Stueart and Richard D. Johnson, papers presented at the First National Conference of the Association of College and Research Libraries, Boston, Massachusetts, November 8–11, 1978 (New York: K. G. Saur, 1979), pp. 268–276; Thomas Kirk, "Past, Present, and Future of Library Instruction," *Southeastern Librarian* 27 (Spring 1977): 15–18.

19. *User Instruction in Academic Libraries: A Century of Selected Readings,* comp. Larry L. Hardesty, John P. Schmitt, and John Mark Tucker (Metuchen, N.J.: Scarecrow, 1986).

20. Patricia B. Knapp, "The Role of the Library of a Given College in Implementing the Course and Non-Course Objectives of That College" (Ph.D. diss., University of Chicago, 1958); Patricia B. Knapp, *College Teaching and the College Library,* ACRL Monograph, no. 23 (Chicago: American Library Assn., 1959), p. 97.

21. Patricia B. Knapp, *The Monteith College Library Experiment* (Metuchen, N.J.: Scarecrow, 1966), p. 130.

22. Patricia B. Knapp, "The Meaning of the Monteith College Library Program for Library Education," *Journal of Education for Librarianship* 6 (Fall 1965): 121.

23. *User Instructions for Online Catalogs in ARL Libraries,* SPEC kit no. 93 (Washington, D.C.: Systems and Procedures Exchange Center, Office of Management Studies, 1983); *SPEC Kit on Bibliographic Instruction in ARL Libraries,* no. 121, comp. Carol F. Ahmad (Washington, D.C.: ARL Office of Management Studies, 1986).

24. *LOEX News* (quarterly newsletter of the Library Orientation and Instruction Exchange) (Ypsilanti, Mich.: Eastern Michigan University Library, 1974-).

25. Larry L. Hardesty, *Use of Slide-Tape Presentations in Academic Libraries* (New York: Jeffrey Norton, 1978). The 1975 survey is also reported in Larry L. Hardesty, "Use of Slide-Tape Presentations in Academic Libraries: A State-of-the-Art Survey," *Journal of Academic Librarianship* 3 (July 1977): 137–140.

26. *Library Instruction Clearinghouses 1986: A Directory* (Chicago: Association of College and Research Libraries, 1986).

27. Teresa B. Mensching, "Trends in Bibliographic Instruction in the 1980s: A Comparison of Data from Two Surveys," *Research Strategies* 7 (Winter 1989): 4–13.

28. E. J. Josey, "The Role of the College Library Staff in Instruction in the Use of the Library," *College & Research Libraries* 23 (November 1962): 492–498.

29. Lloyd W. Griffin and Jack A. Clarke, "Orientation and Instruction of the Graduate Student by University Libraries: A Survey," *College & Research Libraries* 19 (November 1958): 451–454; "Orientation and Instruction of Graduate Students in the Use of the University Library: A Survey," *College & Research Libraries* 33 (November 1972): 467–472.

30. Lois M. Pausch and Jean Koch, "Technical Services Librarians in Library Instruction," *Libri* 31 (September 1981): 198–204.

31. Peter Hernon, "Library Lectures and Their Evaluation: A Survey," *Journal of Academic Librarianship* 1 (July 1975): 14–18.

32. Carol Fulton Ahmad, "A Comparison of the Profiles of Freshman Library Use Instruction Programs in Four Types of Academic Institutions in the United States to the ACRL Guidelines" (Ph.D. diss., Oklahoma State University, 1983); *Dissertation Abstracts International* 44 (April 1984): 2916–2917A; Bibliographic Instruction Task Force, Association of College and Research Libraries, "Guidelines for Bibliographic Instruction in Academic Libraries," *College & Research Libraries News* 38 (April 1977): 92.

33. Sandra Sadow and Benjamin R. Beede, "Library Instruction in American Law Schools," *Law Library Journal* 68 (February 1975): 27–32; Frank W. Goudy and Eugene Moushey, "Library Instruction and Foreign Students: A Survey of Opinions and Practices among Selected Libraries," in *Library Instruction and Reference Services,* ed. Bill Katz and Ruth A. Fraley (New York: Haworth Pr., 1984), pp. 215–226; originally published in *Reference Librarian* 10 (Spring–Summer 1984): 215–226; Laura S. Kline and Catherine M. Rod, "Library Orientation Programs for Foreign Students: A Survey," *RQ* 24 (Winter 1984): 210–213.

34. Allan J. Dyson, "Organising [sic] Undergraduate Library Instruction: The English and American Experience," *Journal of Academic Librarianship* 1 (March 1975): 9–13; Nancy E. Gwinn, "Academic Libraries and Undergraduate Education: The CLR Experience," *College & Research Libraries* 41 (January 1980): 5–16; reprinted

in *User Instruction in Academic Libraries: A Century of Selected Readings,* comp. Larry L. Hardesty, John P. Schmitt, and John Mark Tucker (Metuchen, N.J.: Scarecrow, 1986), pp. 275–301; Hannelore B. Rader, "Bibliographic Instruction in Academic Libraries," in *Increasing the Teaching Role of Academic Libraries,* ed. Thomas G. Kirk, New Directions for Teaching and Learning, no. 18 (San Francisco: Jossey-Bass, 1984), pp. 63–78.

35. Beth J. Shapiro and Philip M. Marcus, "Library Use, Library Instruction, and User Success," *Research Strategies* 5 (Spring 1987): 60–69.

36. John Lubans, "Nonuse of an Academic Library," *College & Research Libraries* 32 (September 1971): 362–367.

37. Peyton Hurt, "The Need of College and University Instruction in Use of the Library," *Library Quarterly* 4 (July 1934): 436–448; Lulu Ruth Reed, "A Test of Students' Competence to Use the Library," *Library Quarterly* 8 (April 1938): 236–283. This is her University of Chicago dissertation published in full.

38. Colleen Coghlan Amundson, "Relationship between University Freshmen's Information-Gathering Techniques and Selected Environmental Factors" (Ph.D. diss., University of Minnesota, 1971); *Dissertation Abstracts International* 32 (November 1971): 2718A. Critiqued by Thomas Kirk, "Bibliographic Instruction—A Review of Research," in *Evaluating Library Use Instruction,* ed. Richard J. Beeler, papers presented at the University of Denver Conference on the Evaluation of Library Instruction, December 13–14, 1973, Library Orientation Series, no. 4 (Ann Arbor, Mich.: Pierian Press, 1975), 7–8.

39. Sanford McDowell, "A Study of the Library Skills of Selected College Freshmen as Related to High School Library Orientation" (Ph.D. diss., University of Michigan, 1977); *Dissertation Abstracts International* 38 (December 1977): 3192A; Ethel M. Feagley et al., *A Library Orientation Test for College Freshmen* (New York: Teachers College Pr., 1950–1961.)

40. Morell D. Boone, "Motivation and the Library Learner," in *Bibliographic Instruction and the Learning Process: Theory, Style and Motivation,* ed. Carolyn A. Kirkendall, papers presented at the Twelfth Annual Library Instruction Conference, Eastern Michigan University, May 6 and 7, 1982, Library Orientation Series, no. 14 (Ann Arbor, Mich.: Pierian Press, 1984), pp. 37–47. Based on his dissertation, "Expectancies and Values as Predictors of Motivation of Pre-Decisional Information Search" (Ph.D. diss., Syracuse University, 1980); *Dissertation Abstracts International* 42 (August 1981): 435A.

41. Kathleen Elisabeth Kelpien Dunn, "Psychological Needs and Source Linkages in Undergraduate Information-Seeking Behavior: A Factor Analytic and Multiple Correlation Study" (Ed.D. diss., University of Southern California, 1984); *Dissertation Abstracts International* 45 (January 1985): 1900A.

42. Larry Alan Miller, "Course Integrated and Related Bibliographic Instruction: A Study of Effects on College Students' Academic Indicators" (Ed.D. diss., Loyola University of Chicago, 1983); *Dissertation Abstracts International* 43 (May 1983): 3522A.

43. Jacqueline Cooper Mancall, "Resources Used by High School Students in Preparing Independent Study Projects: A Bibliometric Approach" (Ph.D. diss., Drexel University, 1978); *Dissertation Abstracts International* 39 (March 1979): 5193A;

Jacqueline C. Mancall and M. Carl Drott, *Measuring Student Information Use: A Guide for School Library Media Specialists* (Littleton, Colo.: Libraries Unlimited, 1983).

44. Judy Reynolds, "Master's Candidates' Research Skills," *Research Strategies* 5 (Spring 1987): 78–89.

45. David N. King and John C. Ory, "Effects of Library Instruction on Student Research: A Case Study," *College & Research Libraries* 42 (January 1981): 31–41.

46. Stephen K. Stoan, "Research and Library Skills: An Analysis and Interpretation," *College & Research Libraries* 45 (March 1984): 99–109; Constance McCarthy, "The Faculty Problem," *Journal of Academic Librarianship* 11 (July 1985): 142–145.

47. Margaret F. Stieg, "The Information Needs of Historians," *College & Research Libraries* 42 (November 1981): 549–560; quote appears on 558.

48. Larry Lynn Hardesty, "The Development of a Set of Scales to Measure the Attitudes of Classroom Instructors toward the Undergraduate Educational Role of the Academic Library" (Ph.D. diss., Indiana University, 1982); *Dissertation Abstracts International* 43 (June 1983): 3742A; Susan E. Edwards, "Faculty Involvement in the University of Colorado Program," in *Faculty Involvement in Library Instruction: Their Views on Participation and Support of Academic Library Use Instruction,* ed. Hannelore B. Rader, papers and summaries from the Fifth Annual Conference on Library Orientation for Academic Libraries, May 15–17, 1975, Library Orientation Series, no. 6 (Ann Arbor, Mich.: Pierian Press, 1976), pp. 7–22; John M. Tucker, "An Experiment in Bibliographic Instruction at Wabash College," *College & Research Libraries* 38 (May 1977): 203–209.

49. Joy Thomas and Pat Ensor, "The University Faculty and Library Instruction," *RQ* 23 (Summer 1984): 431–437; Rae Haws, Lorna Peterson, and Diana Shonrock, "Survey of Faculty Attitudes towards a Basic Library Skills Course," *College & Research Libraries News* 50 (March 1989): 201–203.

50. Lyn Thaxton, "Dissemination and Use of Information by Psychology Faculty and Graduate Students: Implications for Bibliographic Instruction," *Research Strategies* 3 (Summer 1985): 116–124.

51. Ralph Perkins, *The Prospective Teacher's Knowledge of Library Fundamentals: A Study of the Responses Made by 4,170 College Seniors to Tests Designed to Measure Familiarity with Libraries* (New York: Scarecrow, 1965), p. 197.

52. Camila Ann Alire, "A Nationwide Survey of Education Doctoral Students' Attitudes Regarding the Importance of the Library and the Need for Bibliographic Instruction" (Ph.D. diss., University of Northern Colorado, 1984); *Dissertation Abstracts International* 45 (September 1984): 673A.

53. Angie LeClercq, "The Academic Library/High School Library Connection: Needs Assessment and Proposed Model," *Journal of Academic Librarianship* 12 (March 1986): 12–18.

54. Nancyanne O'Hanlon, "Library Skills, Critical Thinking, and the Teacher-Training Curriculum," *College & Research Libraries* 48 (January 1987): 17–26; see also her review article, "Up the Down Staircase: Establishing Library Instruction Programs for Teachers," *RQ* 27 (Summer 1988): 528–534.

55. Michael S. Freeman, "Published Study Guides: What They Say About

Libraries," *Journal of Academic Librarianship* 5 (November 1979): 252–255; quote appears on 254.

56. Virginia Tiefel, "Libraries and Librarians as Depicted in Freshman English Textbooks," *College English* 44 (September 1982): 494–504.

57. Thomas Mann, *A Guide to Library Research Methods* (New York: Oxford Univ. Pr., 1987); David Beasley, *How to Use a Research Library* (New York: Oxford Univ. Pr., 1988).

58. Jerold Nelson, "Faculty Awareness and Attitudes toward Academic Library Reference Services: A Measure of Communication," *College & Research Libraries* 34 (September 1973): 268–275; Mollie Sandock, "A Study of University Students' Awareness of Reference Services," *RQ* 16 (Summer 1977): 284–296.

59. Richard Hume Werking, "The Place of Evaluation in Bibliographic Education," in *Proceedings from [the] Southeastern Conference on Approaches to Bibliographic Instruction,* March 16–17, 1978, ed. Cerise Oberman-Soroka (Charleston, S.C.: College of Charleston, 1978), p. 109. For other severe warnings, see Ellen Altman, "Assessment of Reference Services," in *The Service Imperative for Libraries: Essays in Honor of Margaret E. Monroe,* ed. Gail A. Schlachter (Littleton, Colo.: Libraries Unlimited, 1982), pp. 177–180; James Benson, "Bibliographic Education: A Radical Assessment," in *Proceedings from the 2nd Southeastern Conference on Approaches to Bibliographic Instruction,* March 22–23, 1979, ed. Cerise Oberman-Soroka (Charleston, S.C.: College of Charleston, 1980), pp. 53–68; and Mary Biggs, "Learning from Our Mistakes," in *Teaching Library Use Competence: Bridging the Gap from High School to College,* ed. Carolyn A. Kirkendall, papers presented at the Eleventh Annual Library Instruction Conference, May 7–8, 1981, Library Orientation Series, no.13 (Ann Arbor, Mich.: Pierian Pr., 1982), pp. 13–22.

60. A particularly good discussion of test creation is by Larry Hardesty, Nicholas P. Lovrich, and James Mannon, "Evaluating Library-Use Instruction," *College & Research Libraries* 40 (July 1979): 309–317.

61. Virginia Tiefel, "Evaluating a Library User Education Program: A Decade of Experience," *College & Research Libraries* 50 (March 1989): 249–259.

62. Bibliographic Instruction Section, Association of College and Research Libraries, *Evaluating Bibliographic Instruction: A Handbook* (Chicago: American Library Assn., 1983); Richard Hume Werking, "Evaluating Bibliographic Education: A Review and Critique," *Library Trends* 29 (Summer 1980): 153–172; James Rice, "Testing and Evaluation," in *Teaching Library Use: A Guide for Library Instruction,* Contributions in Librarianship and Information Science, no. 37 (Westport, Conn.: Greenwood, 1981), pp. 97–129; Janet Freedman and Harold Bantly, "Techniques of Program Evaluation," in *Teaching Librarians to Teach: On-the-Job Training for Bibliographic Instruction Librarians,* ed. Alice S. Clark and Kay F. Jones (Metuchen, N.J.: Scarecrow, 1986), pp. 188–204.

63. Thomas Kirk, "Bibliographic Instruction — A Review of Research," in *Evaluating Library Use Instruction,* ed. Richard J. Beeler, papers presented at the University of Denver Conference on the Evaluation of Library Instruction, December 13–14, 1973, Library Orientation Series, no. 4 (Ann Arbor, Mich.: Pierian Pr., 1975), pp. 1–29; Jill B. Fatzer, "Evaluation of Library User Instruction," *RQ* 27 (Fall 1987): 41–43.

64. Patricia Senn Breivik, "Effects of Library-Based Instruction in the Academic Success of Disadvantaged College Freshmen" (D.L.S. diss., Columbia University, 1974); *Dissertation Abstracts International* 36 (August 1975): 585A; published as *Open Admissions and the Academic Library* (Chicago: American Library Assn., 1977) and summarized in "Effects of Library-Based Instruction in the Academic Success of Disadvantaged Undergraduates," in *Academic Library Instruction: Objectives, Programs, and Faculty Involvement,* ed. Hannelore B. Rader, papers of the Fourth Annual Conference on Library Orientation for Academic Libraries, May 9–11, 1974, Library Orientation Series, no. 5 (Ann Arbor, Mich.: Pierian Pr., 1975), pp. 45–55.

65. Janet Hopkins Hansen, "A Comparative Study of Programmed Text and Audiovisual Modular Programs for Library Orientation Instruction" (Ph.D. diss., Catholic University, 1975); *Dissertation Abstracts International* 36 (July 1975): 41A.

66. Janice Ann Havlicek Bolt, "A Study of the Effects of a Bibliographic Instruction Course on Achievement and Retention of College Students" (Ph.D. diss., Florida State University, 1986); *Dissertation Abstracts International* 47 (June 1987): 4219A.

67. Marsha Denise Broadway, "Self-Directed Instruction in Query Formation and Presentation for College Students" (Ph.D. diss., Florida State University, 1985); *Dissertation Abstracts International* 46 (March 1986): 2472A.

68. Donna Corlett, "Library Skills, Study Habits and Attitudes, and Sex as Related to Academic Achievement," *Educational and Psychological Measurement* 34 (Winter 1974): 967–969.

69. Shelley Phipps and Ruth Dickstein, "The Library Skills Program at the University of Arizona: Testing, Evaluation, and Critique," *Journal of Academic Librarianship* 5 (September 1979): 205–214; Maria R. Sugrañes and James A. Neal, "Evaluation of a Self-Paced Bibliographic Instruction Course," *College & Research Libraries* 44 (November 1983): 444–457.

70. Marvin E. Wiggins, "The Development of Library Use Instructional Programs," *College & Research Libraries* 33 (November 1972): 473–479; Marvin E. Wiggins and D. Stewart Low, "Use of an Instructional Psychology Model for Development of Library-Use Instructional Programs," *Drexel Library Quarterly* 8 (July 1972): 269–279; Marvin E. Wiggins, "Evaluation in the Instructional Psychology Model," in *Evaluating Library Use Instruction,* ed. Richard J. Beeler, papers presented at the University of Denver Conference on the Evaluation of Library Instruction, December 13–14, 1973, Library Orientation Series, no. 4 (Ann Arbor, Mich.: Pierian Pr., 1975), pp. 89–97.

71. Susan A. Ware and Deena J. Morganti, "A Competency-Based Approach to Assessing Workbook Effectiveness," *Research Strategies* 4 (Winter 1986): 4–10.

72. James R. Kennedy, Thomas G. Kirk, and Gwendolyn A. Weaver, "Course-Related Library Instruction: A Case Study of the English and Biology Departments at Earlham College," *Drexel Library Quarterly* 7 (July and October 1971): 277–297; Thomas G. Kirk, "A Comparison of Two Methods of Library Instruction for Students in Introductory Biology," *College & Research Libraries* 32 (November 1971): 465–474.

73. Patricia Morris Donegan, Ralph E. Domas, and John R. Deosdade, "The Comparable Effects of Term Paper Counseling and Group Instruction Sessions," *College & Research Libraries* 50 (March 1989): 195–205.

74. Thomas Terry Surprenant, "A Comparison of Lecture and Programmed Instruction in the Teaching of Basic Catalog Card and Bibliographic Index Information" (Ph.D. diss., University of Wisconsin–Madison, 1979); *Dissertation Abstracts International* 40 (December 1979): 2957A; "A Comparison of Lecture and Programmed Instruction in the Teaching of Basic Catalog Card and Bibliographic Information—Results of a Pretest," in *Proceedings from [the] Southeastern Conference on Approaches to Bibliographic Instruction,* March 16–17, 1978, ed. Cerise Oberman-Soroka (Charleston, S.C.: College of Charleston, 1978), pp. 54–66; "Learning Theory, Lecture, and Programmed Instruction Text: An Experiment in Bibliographic Instruction," *College & Research Libraries* 43 (January 1982): 31–37.

75. Susan A. Ware, "A Statistical Evaluation of Basic Library Skills Instruction," *Research Strategies* 1 (Summer 1983): 118–124.

76. Patricia Ann Kenney and Judith N. McArthur, "Designing and Evaluating a Programmed Instruction Text," *College & Research Libraries* 45 (January 1984): 35–42.

77. Mitsuko Williams and Elisabeth B. Davis, "Evaluation of PLATO Library Instructional Lessons," *Journal of Academic Librarianship* 5 (March 1979): 14–19; Kathleen A. Johnson and Barbara S. Plake, "Evaluation of PLATO Library Instructional Lessons: Another View," *Journal of Academic Librarianship* 6 (July 1980): 154–158.

78. Denise Madland and Marian A. Smith, "Computer-Assisted Instruction for Teaching Conceptual Library Skills to Remedial Students," *Research Strategies* 6 (Spring 1988): 52–64.

79. David F. Kohl and Lizabeth A. Wilson, "Effectiveness of Course-Integrated Bibliographic Instruction in Improving Coursework," *RQ* 26 (Winter 1986): 206–211.

80. Roland Person, "Long-Term Evaluation of Bibliographic Instruction: Lasting Encouragement," *College & Research Libraries* 42 (January 1981): 19–25; Larry Hardesty, "Library-Use Instruction: Assessment of the Long-Term Effects," *College & Research Libraries* 43 (January 1982): 38–46; John Cornell Selegean, Martha Lou Thomas, and Marie Louise Richman, "Long-Range Effectiveness of Library Use Instruction," *College & Research Libraries* 44 (November 1983): 476–480.

81. Carol Collier Kuhlthau, "Longitudinal Case Studies of the Information Search Process of Users in Libraries," *Library & Information Science Research* 10 (July-September 1988): 257–304.

82. Betsy Baker and Brian Nielsen, "Educating the Online Catalog User: Experiences and Plans at Northwestern University Library," *Research Strategies* 1 (Fall 1983): 155–166.

83. Brian Nielsen et al., *Educating the Online Catalog User: A Model for Instructional Development and Education,* ERIC document, 1985, ED 261 679; Brian Nielsen, "What They Say and What They Do: Assessing Online Catalog Use Instruction through Transaction Monitoring," *Information Technology and Libraries* 5 (March 1986): 28–34; Brian Nielsen and Betsy Baker, "Educating the Online Catalog User: A Model Evaluation Study," *Library Trends* 35 (Spring 1987): 571–585.

84. Ron Blazek and Dania Bilal, "Problems with OPAC: A Case Study of an Academic Research Library," *RQ* 28 (Winter 1988): 169–178.

85. Karen Markey, "Offline and Online User Assistance for Online Catalog Searches," *Online* 8 (May 1984): 54–66.

86. Peter Ingwersen, "Search Procedures in the Library - Analysed from the Cognitive Point of View," *Journal of Documentation* 38 (September 1982): 165–191; Patricia Sullivan and Peggy Seiden, "Educating Online Catalog Users: The Protocol Assessment of Needs," *Library Hi Tech* 3 (2) (1985): 11–19; Diane Nahl-Jakobovits and Leon A. Jakobovits, "Problem Solving, Creative Librarianship, and Search Behavior," *College & Research Libraries* 49 (September 1988): 400–408.

87. Sara J. Penhole and Nancy Taylor, "Integrating End-User Searching into a Bibliographic Instruction Program," *RQ* 26 (Winter 1986): 212–220.

88. Rowena Weiss Swanson, "An Assessment of Online Instruction Methodologies," *Online* 6 (January 1982): 38–53.

89. Charlene C. York et al., "Computerized Reference Sources: One-Stop Shopping or Part of a Search Strategy?" *Research Strategies* 6 (Winter 1988): 8–17.

90. Sue Galloway, "Nobody Is Teaching the Teachers," *Booklegger Magazine* 3 (January-February 1976): 29–31; Esther Dyer, "Formal Library Science Courses on Library Instruction," *Journal of Education for Librarianship* 18 (Spring 1978): 359–361; Maureen Pastine and Karen Seibert, "Update on the Status of Bibliographic Instruction in Library School Programs," *Journal of Education for Librarianship* 21 (Fall 1980): 169–171; Robert E. Brundin, "Education for Instructional Librarians: Development and Overview," *Journal of Education for Library and Information Science* 25 (Winter 1985): 177–189; Mary Ellen Larson and Ellen Meltzer, "Education for Bibliographic Instruction," *Journal of Education for Library and Information Science* 28 (Summer 1987): 9–16.

91. Joy Thomas, "Bibliographic Instruction in the Sciences: A Profile," *College & Research Libraries* 49 (May 1988): 252–262.

92. Ronald R. Powell, "Sources of Professional Knowledge for Academic Librarians," *College & Research Libraries* 49 (July 1988): 332–340.

93. Ron Blazek, "The Administrative Climate for Bibliographic Instruction in Large Academic Libraries," in *Library Instruction and Reference Services*, ed. Bill Katz and Ruth A. Fraley (New York: Haworth Pr., 1984), pp. 161–179 (quote on 164); originally published in *Reference Librarian* 10 (Spring-Summer 1984): 161–179; Ron Blazek, "Effective Bibliographic Instruction Programs: A Comparison of Coordinators and Reference Heads in ARL Libraries," *RQ* 24 (Summer 1985): 433–441.

94. *Theories of Bibliographic Education: Designs for Teaching*, ed. Cerise Oberman and Katina Strauch (New York: Bowker, 1982); *Conceptual Frameworks for Bibliographic Education: Theory into Practice*, ed. Mary Reichel and Mary Ann Ramey (Littleton, Colo.: Libraries Unlimited, 1987).

95. Thelma Freides, *Literature and Bibliography of the Social Sciences* (Los Angeles: Melville, 1973); Elizabeth Frick, "Information Structure and Bibliographic Instruction," *Journal of Academic Librarianship* 1 (September 1975): 12–14; reprinted in *User Instruction in Academic Libraries: A Century of Selected Readings*, comp. Larry L. Hardesty, John P. Schmitt, and John Mark Tucker (Metuchen, N.J.: Scarecrow, 1986), pp. 266–275; John MacGregor and Raymond G. McInnis, "Integrating Classroom Instruction and Library Research: The Cognitive Functions of Bibliographic Network

Structures," *Journal of Higher Education* 48 (January-February 1977): 17–38. McInnis's book, without a doubt the most complex treatise in the BI literature, is an exhaustive discussion of the same ideas: Raymond G. McInnis, *New Perspectives for Reference Service in Academic Libraries* (Westport, Conn.: Greenwood, 1978). See also his article, "Mental Maps and Metaphors in Academic Libraries," in *Library Instruction and Reference Services,* ed. Bill Katz and Ruth A. Fraley (New York: Haworth Pr., 1984), pp. 109–120; originally published in *Reference Librarian* 10 (Spring-Summer 1984), 109–120; Pamela Kobelski and Mary Reichel, "Conceptual Frameworks for Bibliographic Instruction," *Journal of Academic Librarianship* 7 (May 1981): 73–77.

96. Harold W. Tuckett and Carla J. Stoffle, "Learning Theory and the Self-Reliant Library User," *RQ* 24 (Fall 1984): 58–66; Rao Aluri and Mary Reichel, "Learning Theories and Bibliographic Instruction," in *Bibliographic Instruction and the Learning Process: Theory, Style and Motivation,* ed. Carolyn A. Kirkendall, papers presented at the Twelfth Annual Library Instruction Conference, Eastern Michigan University, May 6 and 7, 1982, Library Orientation Series, no. 14 (Ann Arbor, Mich.: Pierian Pr., 1984), pp. 15–27; Constance A. Mellon and Kathryn E. Pagles, "Bibliographic Instruction and Learning Theory," in *Bibliographic Instruction: The Second Generation,* ed. Constance A. Mellon (Littleton, Colo.: Libraries Unlimited, 1987), pp. 134–142.

97. Constance R. Miller, "Scientific Literature as Hierarchy: Library Instruction and Robert M. Gagné," *College & Research Libraries* 43 (September 1982): 385–390; Mary Reichel, "Preparing to Teach: Bruner's Theory of Instruction and Bibliographic Education," in *Teaching Librarians to Teach: On-the-Job Training for Bibliographic Instruction Librarians,* ed. Alice S. Clark and Kay F. Jones (Metuchen, N.J.: Scarecrow, 1986), 20–31; Janet R. Hanson, "Teaching Information Sources in Business Studies: An Application of the Theories of J. Bruner and R. M. Gagné," *Journal of Librarianship* 17 (July 1985): 185–199.

98. Betsy K. Baker, "A Conceptual Framework for Teaching Online Catalog Use," *Journal of Academic Librarianship* 12 (May 1986): 90–96; Bruce Morton, "U.S. Government Documents as History: The Intersection of Pedagogy and Librarianship," *RQ* 24 (Summer 1985): 474–481; quote appears on 477.

99. Sonia Bodi, "Critical Thinking and Bibliographic Instruction: The Relationship," *Journal of Academic Librarianship* 14 (July 1988): 150–153.

100. Constance A. Mellon, "Library Anxiety: A Grounded Theory and Its Development," *College & Research Libraries* 47 (March 1986): 160–165; "Attitudes: The Forgotten Dimension in Library Instruction," *Library Journal* 113 (September 1, 1988): 137–139; "Incorporating Bibliographic Instruction into Education for Librarianship," *Journal of Education for Library and Information Science* 26 (Winter 1986): 187–189; Bobbie L. Collins, Constance A. Mellon, and Sally B. Young, "The Needs and Feelings of Beginning Researchers," in *Bibliographic Instruction: The Second Generation,* ed. Constance A. Mellon (Littleton, Colo.: Libraries Unlimited, 1987), pp. 73–84; Carol Collier Kuhlthau, "Developing a Model of the Library Search Process: Cognitive and Affective Aspects," *RQ* 28 (Winter 1988): 232–242.

101. Carol C. Kuhlthau et al., "Validating a Model of the Search Process: A Comparison of Academic, Public and School Library Users," *Library and Information Science Research* 12 (January-March 1990): 5–31.

102. Leon A. Jakobovits and Diane Nahl-Jakobovits, "Learning the Library: Taxonomy of Skills and Errors," *College & Research Libraries* 48 (May 1987): 203–214.

103. Theophil M. Otto, "The Academic Librarian of the Twenty-first Century," *Journal of Academic Librarianship* 8 (May 1982): 85–88; Philip M. Clark and James Benson, "Linkages between Library Uses through the Study of Individual Patron Behavior," *RQ* 24 (Summer 1985): 417–426.

104. William A. Katz, *Reference Services and Reference Processes,* vol. 2 of *Introduction to Reference Work,* 5th ed. (New York: McGraw-Hill, 1987), pp. 175–185; Rolland E. Stevens and Linda C. Smith, *Reference Work in the University Library* (Littleton, Colo.: Libraries Unlimited, 1986), pp. 52–56.

105. Bibliographic Instruction Section, Association of College and Research Libraries, "Research Agenda for Bibliographic Instruction," *College & Research Libraries News* 41 (April 1980): 94–95.

106. Bibliographic Instruction Section, Association of College and Research Libraries, "Think Tank Recommendations for Bibliographic Instruction," *College & Research Libraries News* 42 (December 1981): 394–398; "Reactions to the Think Tank Recommendations: A Symposium," *Journal of Academic Librarianship* 9 (March 1983): 4–14.

107. *A Library and Information Science Research Agenda for the 1980s: Final Report* (Santa Monica, Calif.: Cuadra Associates, 1982); reprinted as part of Charles Martell's editorial, "Developing a Research Perspective," *College & Research Libraries News* 49 (September 1988): 384; "Research Questions of Interest to ARL," *College & Research Libraries News* 49 (September 1988): 467–468, 470; *Rethinking the Library in the Information Age: A Summary of Issues in Library Research,* vol. 1 (Washington, D.C.: U.S. Department of Education, Office of Educational Research and Improvement, Office of Library Programs, 1988); "ACRL Research Agenda," *College & Research Libraries News* 51 (April 1990): 317, 319.

108. Bonnie Gratch, "Relating Research Agendas," *College & Research Libraries News* 50 (May 1989): 407–409.

109. Research Task Force, Bibliographic Instruction Section, Association of College and Research Libraries, "Final Report" [draft, March 17, 1989].

110. A favorite saying of Professor Herb Kells of the Rutgers University School of Communication, Information and Library Studies.

111. Patricia E. Feehan et al., "Library and Information Science Research: An Analysis of the 1984 Journal Literature," *Library & Information Science Research* 9 (July-September 1987): 183–184.

Paul Metz

Bibliometrics: Library Use and Citation Studies

What kinds of materials are of the greatest use to scholars and researchers? How much less useful do materials become with age? Is this aging a uniform process, or does it vary according to discipline? What can we infer about a discipline from studying the materials its practitioners use? What can we infer about its relationship to other disciplines?

These and similar questions set the agenda for work in the broad area of "bibliometrics," a term coined in 1969 by Alan Pritchard. He defined it as "The application of mathematics and statistical methods to books and other media of communication."[1] In the past twenty years, the science of book measuring has become an increasingly powerful means by which both students of science and library or information scientists could quantify and test their arguments.

The power of computerized analysis and in particular the availability of computerized citation databases have been essential to most bibliometric work. Without the citation data bases developed in the 1960s by Eugene Garfield and the Institute for Scientific Information of which he is founder and president, much bibliometric literature simply would not exist. Garfield and his contemporaries, such as Derek de Solla Price, may be credited with applying the fundamental insight that because there is an intuitively evident subject relationship between citing document and cited documented—often reflecting an intellectual debt—the analysis of patterns of citation could be used to construct a sociometry of research.[2] Not everyone agrees, however, about the face validity of citations as an index of intellectual indebtedness, and it is clearly true that citing practices reflect a variety of motives, including the purely ceremonial.[3]

The first citation studies counted either the number of references (unique documents cited) or citations (all, including duplicates such as ibid. and op. cit.) in the documents under study. These data were used to support arguments about the intellectual relationships among individuals or fields. More recent elaborations, such as co-citation analysis and bibliographic coupling (defined later in this chapter) have helped analysts to construct ever more complex and sophisticated maps of intellectual dependence.

Most bibliometricians are scholars of science with a limited interest in librarianship. This chapter covers only those aspects of these scholars' work that have implications for library science or library policy. As a result, many interesting reports important to science studies are excluded. Some examples of valuable bibliometric work outside the scope of this chapter include studies of networks of influence among individual scientists; debates over whether science progresses as a corporate enterprise to which even lesser lights contribute something; and efforts to fit a variety of bibliometric distributions to a small number of frequently occurring curves.[4] Citation counts have been used to measure the scientific productivity of nations as well as of individuals, and these studies, too, will be outside our scope.

The books and articles reviewed here were identified by searching *Library Literature* for articles on "circulation analysis" or "citation analysis"; by an online search of the LISA database (covering 1969 to 1988) for articles on "citation analysis" or "circulation" in several key library science journals that publish bibliometric studies; by browsing other key journals; and from the author's files. The large number of bibliometric studies required that only major studies be reviewed in any depth. Even among these, studies with policy implications for library practice have been emphasized.

The organizing principle for this chapter is topic, not methodology. The review encompasses citation studies as well as studies of the use of library collections. Studies of library use have been rarer than citation studies, partly because of their greater expense. But since the publication of Fussler and Simon's classic in 1961, a number of studies have examined circulation as well as in-house use of library collections to cast considerable light on the ways in which scholarly and scientific literatures are used.[5] Although circulation studies are not always considered to be bibliometric, they satisfy Pritchard's definition and are true to the word's roots. To define only citation studies as bibliometric would be too narrow and would perpetuate an unfortunate dichotomy. In answering many questions about the scholarly or scientific use of materials, both circulation studies and other techniques of analyzing library use can enter a profitable dialogue with citation studies. Both library science and science studies can profit from a closer exchange between their complementary work using these different techniques. One goal of this chapter is to promote such an exchange.

This review examines what both citation and library use studies have found out about the characteristics that make materials more or less desirable to researchers, including the effects of age; about the skewed distribution of use over the entire population of publications; about different kinds of use, especially within the library; and about individual disciplines or the relationships among disciplines. The concluding section suggests future directions for bibliometric research, especially as these may be influenced by technological advances.

Obsolescence

The popular notion that older books and journals will generally be less useful than more recent contributions reflects a perception of continuous progress in scholarship and research. Both library use and citation studies have generally supported the theory of literature decay. However, the large literature on obsolescence has refined the commonsense notion in significant ways. Research has shown that the rate of obsolescence is slower than may be popularly supposed, once careful methodological controls have been applied; in many cases obsolescence curves begin rapidly but then slow down and are very long-tailed; and obsolescence is not a uniform progression but is subject to many variations, particularly by subject.

Although somewhat dated, Line and Sandison's overview of obsolescence remains the best starting point for readers desiring a cogent analysis of the issues.[6] Among their other insights, Line and Sandison clearly lay out the critical distinction between synchronous studies "which are made on records of use or references at one point in time and compare the uses against the age distribution of the materials used or cited" and diachronous studies which "follow the use of particular items through successive observations at different dates."

Diachronous studies are more cumbersome and expensive to perform, when data are available at all. But they have served as a useful corrective to the tendency of synchronous studies to exaggerate the rate of literature obsolescence by failing to account for growth in literatures. If there are fewer older texts, then fewer will be cited and this finding will say nothing about obsolescence—that is the warning that diachronous studies have helped to deliver.

Many citation studies have attempted to describe differences among fields in the decay rates for use of their literatures. Though the policy implications for library weeding and storage policies are obvious, the goal of most such studies has been to assess the degree to which disciplines have achieved mature "paradigms," as this concept was developed by Thomas Kuhn.[7] The assumption here is that disciplines with highly developed paradigms (in essence, consensus on the appropriate subjects and methods of a discipline) will make progress in a more nearly linear manner that avoids the need constantly to recycle topics of interest.

Derek J. de Solla Price's 1970 contribution to the obsolescence literature exemplified the use of citation data to distinguish among fields.[8] Price found that most journal articles reach their peak of citations a year or more after their appearance and that at this peak articles are cited about six times as frequently as occurs for articles in the nonrecent "archive."

He devised "Price's Index," which measures the percentage of citations by authors in a given field that refer to works published within the previous five years. Journals in physics and biochemistry achieved scores of 60 to 70 percent, while journals in other fields, such as literary criticism, had scores ranging to below 10 percent. It has been pointed out, however, that scores in literary criticism will be higher when references to the original works of literature under analysis are omitted. Price's basic approach has been followed, often with methodological elaborations, by many citation studies of specific disciplines.

The first significant study of obsolescence within the context of library practice was reported by Charles Gosnell in 1944 (Gosnell's study had its predecessors, but it may be noted with a sense of irony that these are now rarely cited). Gosnell did not study library use per se; he examined the age distribution of monographs appearing in three lists of books for college libraries. As with Price's citation study, a few years were required for books to appear in the lists. The largest number of books listed had been published three years previous to their appearance on the lists. Thereafter, "the number of imprints per year [dropped] rapidly at first and then more slowly, approaching the base line of zero asymptotically in the early years."[9]

The curve Gosnell described would be found in a variety of studies in future years. We may compare Gosnell's conclusions to those of Philip Morse. After studying the use of a sample of books from the Science Library at MIT, Morse observed that "on the average, book circulation diminishes as the book ages, rapidly at first then levelling out."[10]

The landmark study of library circulation and especially of the effects of age on use, was Fussler and Simon's *Patterns in the Use of Books in Large Research Libraries*.[11] The data for their analysis of obsolescence effects reflect the circulation of over 16,000 titles from the University of Chicago in the period 1949 to 1958. The date of imprint of each title used was noted. The study team also obtained data on the number of titles held by the library according to their subjects and decades of imprint. By focusing on use in proportion to holdings, Fussler and Simon were able to adjust for the effects of literature growth and so to avoid exaggerating obsolescence. While this precaution avoids the most hazardous source of bias, one should always be cautious in interpreting synchronous data to describe a process which occurs over time.

For their sample as a whole, Fussler and Simon found that use dropped off continuously. This decline was most marked in the earlier years and then slowed—so much so that books over 100 years old were used about as heavily as books 70 to 100 years old. The authors then analyzed their data separately for materials in the broad areas of humanities, natural sciences, and social sciences. The results showed that in all fields the proportion of the collection used is lower for older materials, but—consistent with Price's later citation results—this effect is more pronounced for titles in science.

Broadus concluded from a review of citation studies that scientists rely most heavily on serial titles, humanists prefer monographs, and social scientists' preferences are more evenly split. If it is true that journals and other serials play a disproportionate role in conveying current research findings, Broadus's conclusions from citation studies support Fussler and Simon's findings based on use data.[12]

A study conducted in the Library of Congress in 1977 yielded results highly similar to Fussler and Simon's.[13] Because LC is a closed-stack library, data were available on all 9,605 volumes from the general collections used during a three-day survey. As with Fussler and Simon's study, data were also available on the library's holdings according to subject and date of imprint. Metz's analysis indicated that obsolescence effects were most rapid in the first two decades after publication and thereafter described the slowly declining asymptotic curve noted by Gosnell. Metz divided subjects into four larger categories, leaving it an open question whether use of history materials would more nearly resemble use of social science or humanities books. The results indicated that obsolescence in the natural science and social science literatures was fairly similar, with books from the 1940s having about 15 percent as much probability of use as books from the 1970s. Use of materials in humanities and history resembled one another, but in their case books from the 1940s were about 55 percent as likely to be called as books from the 1970s.

Other Factors Affecting Use

Language

Apart from a book's age, other key "demographic" characteristics include language and subject. For English-language authors and library users, a preference for materials in English has made language a powerful predictor of use, although the strength of this preference varies across disciplines. According to Broadus's summary of book use studies, English-language social scientists use materials in English for all but a tiny fraction of their needs.[14] Because of the international nature of the sciences and the cosmopolitan and far-ranging research style of many humanists, it seems safe to accept Broadus's implication that other disciplines are not so insular about foreign language materials as are the social sciences.

Two book use studies have documented the preference of users for English-language materials in American research libraries. English materials accounted for 91.2 percent of circulation during the 1969 through 1973 period covered by the notable book use study performed by Allen Kent and his associates at the University of Pittsburgh. Materials in Spanish, French, and German accounted for over 6 percent of use, with the remainder being scattered over a variety of other languages. Interestingly, English-language materials accounted for a lower 84.2 percent of all items circulating during the study period. That foreign language materials would account for 16 percent of the books checked out but only 9 percent of circulation suggests a different distribution of use, with few high-use foreign titles, and foreign language use therefore spread more evenly over acquired titles. Even for the Library of Congress study in 1977, English-language materials accounted for 87.7 percent of monographic use and 92.5 percent of serial use. Materials in German, French, Russian, and Spanish each accounted for about 2 percent of use at LC. For various reasons, the Pittsburgh study underestimated use of Oriental materials, while the LC study excluded them altogether.[15]

Subject

It makes little sense to inquire what subject materials are most heavily used unless one can specify the disciplinary or institutional affiliation of the users. Later portions of this chapter examine citation studies of individual disciplines' literature use, as well as studies reporting the use of library materials by researchers in various fields. Here is examined the methods by which library use according to subject has been measured and the various institutional and library characteristics which have been found to influence the subject distribution of library use.

For studies within individual libraries, it has proved useful to determine the subject distribution of library use and of a library's holdings or current investment in acquisitions. These data can be combined to help a library approach equivalent proportional use of materials, or equal "marginal utility" for its investment in various subject literatures. Jenks's study at Bucknell was one of the first to calculate use in proportion to holdings. At the extremes Jenks found that books in call letter BF (psychology) had two and one-half times the circulation per volume as the collection generally, while books in call letter A (general) had only about one-sixth the average chance to circulate. Metz followed Jenks's lead by deriving "proportional use statistics," which have a weighted average of 1.0, for use scores across subjects. By dividing one proportional use statistic by another, one can determine the multiple by which proportional use in one subject exceeds use in another.[16]

Such findings are of course subject to objection or at least careful interpretation on both methodological grounds (call letter "A" contains a disproportion of reference materials likely to be used only within the library) and valid philosophical grounds addressing the library's goals and its need to support research and instruction in all disciplines. The more useful denominator for calculating proportional use is current investment in various subject literatures, but this is often more difficult to obtain than simple shelf list measures of holdings.

Past Use

Both citation and library use studies have shown that use is stable at the level of the individual article or book. Although obsolescence effects will generally depress the overall use of books and articles as they age, the same materials that received disproportionate use in their youth will continue to be more popular than their contemporaries as they age. Price, reviewing longitudinal citation data, proposed that the process of being cited constitutes a "cumulative advantage process."[17]

As Broadus summarizes Price's arguments, "A paper (A) is cited by another author. Those who read the latter then are more likely to look up paper A because of the citation, and in turn to make reference to it in their own writings. Then new readers are led to paper A."[18] For books, Fussler and Simon's analysis showed that a knowledge of past use led to better predictions of future use than such demographic characteristics as age and language, and was the best single predictor of use.[19] Others have attempted to demonstrate that the library use of individual books displays the characteristics of a Markov chain.[20]

At the subject, as opposed to the item level, user preferences have been shown to be remarkably stable. Bulick's comparisons of the rank order of use according to LC classes at Pittsburgh showed only one change in the ordering of the twenty-one classes between 1974-1975 and 1975-1976.[21] Metz and Litchfield calculated four correlations ranging from .958 to .976 to express the stability of circulation across twenty-nine subject categories when circulation data from 1982 and 1987 were compared.[22]

Other Factors

A variety of institutional considerations has proved useful in accounting for differences in the subject distribution of use. For example, the heavier use of materials in science and technology at the expense of humanities materials at Virginia Tech has been attributed to differences between that land grant university and Pittsburgh or Bucknell, where the emphasis is reversed.[23] McGrath was able to account for some of the statistical variation in use across disciplines at the University of Southwestern Louisiana by using master's-level enrollments, credit hours, and more subjective measures of disciplines' likely library dependence as independent variables in a predictive regression analysis model.[24]

The strongest statistical predictor of subject use within academic libraries has proved to be the size of shelf-list holdings within each subject. McGrath, Pierce, and Metz and Litchfield all reported that 65 percent or so of the statistical variation in use may be accounted for by this single variable.[25] It is not clear how useful or surprising this finding should be, or even whether over the long haul the subject distribution of the shelf list is cause or effect of use, but these findings indicate that holdings counts are an important parameter that should at least be used as a control variable in more substantive analyses.

An interesting, if discouraging, effort to identify a factor predicting use was reported by Gunnar Knutson in 1986. When circulation records were analyzed to determine the possible effect of number of access points, and especially of subject headings, the results indicated that the statistical association between the richness of the catalog record and the number of circulations was negligible.[26]

The Scattering of Use

As has happened with the perception of obsolescence effects, both librarians and the public in general understand almost intuitively that library materials and book resources generally are used quite unequally. Once again research bears out, but also refines, the popular conception. As with obsolescence, it is not clear whether this understanding shows that research has merely documented the obvious, or that the lessons of research travel far beyond the immediate readership of reports.

In any event, it is both true and generally recognized that the gulf between the most and least heavily used materials in a library setting, or between the most and least heavily used or cited literatures for any given subject discipline, is vast. Both citation and library use studies have substantiated this point and begun to identify the statistical distributions which describe the spread of use across literatures.

The classic statement of the skewness of subject literatures, that of S. C. Bradford, predicts that articles in a given discipline will be distributed across journals in a highly concentrated manner—a few core journals will contain a large disproportion of articles, and the number of journal titles required to yield the same number of articles in successively less relevant journals will increase at a constant, exponential rate as it progresses outwards from the core.[27] As Bookstein notes in his useful overview of the various common bibliometric distributions, "Thus journal productivity follows a law of diminishing returns, with larger and larger numbers of journals being needed to produce the same number of articles."[28]

Bradford's formulation and later elaborations by Leimkuhler and others have been much misunderstood. It is not always understood that the distribution refers to the simple existence—not use or citations—of relevant articles across journals; or that fields differ in the degree of concentration of their serial literature; or that the predictive power of Bradford's distribution comes not from the mere statement that there will be concentric zones of journals with the same number of articles but that the number of journals in these zones will increase in a uniform and logarithmic way for any given discipline.[29]

The implications of the Bradford distribution for serials collection development may be read optimistically or pessimistically. Optimists may note that a relatively small investment will cover an encouraging percentage of the relevant literature. Pessimists will point out that much desirable literature remains outside the core and that as the library spends more and more to acquire these titles, it achieves fewer and fewer results.

The concentration of subject literatures places a great premium on the library's selection of the most appropriate materials. Here judgments of quality (best articles, not simply most articles) become important. A number of techniques have been proposed for quantifying the notion of quality or usefulness, and not surprisingly these have generated controversy.

The availability of vast stores of citation data has given many librarians an appealing and convenient means of measuring the usefulness of serial publications. Since most libraries do not permit the external circulation of their journals and therefore cannot easily measure their use, citation data have been seen as an especially attractive alternative for measuring client interest in journals.

Garfield's 1972 article in *Science* argued the case for the use of citation data as a sort of consumer's report for individual scientists and editors, as well as librarians. Garfield described the manner in which his staff at the Institute for Scientific Information use highly uniform coding techniques to bring together bibliographically inconsistent references to the same articles, thus making it possible to determine which articles, and by extension which journals, receive the heaviest use. Garfield's techniques allow for the cumulation of raw citation counts per journal or of mean citations per article ("impact factors"), which introduce a rough control for journal size. Extending Bradford's observations, Garfield noted that according to his data, citations are highly concentrated over a small minority of the huge number of extant scientific journals, and commented that "the predominance of cores of journals is ubiquitous."[30]

The use of citation data to evaluate journals rests on arguable and nearly untestable assumptions about the agreement among a number of measures: citation counts; subjective evaluations by subject scholars of the "best" journals; overall frequency of library use; and use in the individual library evaluating a given journal. In debating the usefulness of citation measures for collection development, both sides acknowledge the deficiencies of such data and focus on the issue of whether, given the expense of local studies of journal use, citation data are better than no data at all.

Broadus has emphasized the practicality of citation counts, especially in identifying candidates for deselection review.[31] His arguments win support from studies by Gordon and Baughman showing that citation counts yield rankings highly congruent with reputational assessments by sociologists of the journals in their field.[32] Pan has found a significant correlation of .47 between citation counts and use counts for a group of science journals used in American medical libraries.[33]

Maurice Line of the British Library Lending Division has argued for extreme caution in the use of citation lists, maintaining that there really is no reliable substitute for locally conducted use studies. Line's strongest argument is that outside of the core of journals that all but the smallest libraries will collect in any event, citation counts are simply too low, volatile, and statistically unpredictable to serve as a useful basis for discrimination among marginal titles.[34] Stankus and Rice strike a midground position, arguing that citation counts do vary with use statistics, but can be trusted only for journals receiving enough overall use to yield relatively reliable measures.[35]

Concentration of Use for Books

Much as the use of periodicals has been shown to be concentrated in a core of titles in high demand, empirical studies have shown that the use of monographs is very unequally spread. The availability of circulation data has made it easier to establish patterns in the use of books than is generally the case for serials.

Richard Trueswell, an industrial engineer, adapted the techniques of his discipline to test whether the use of library stock displays a frequently occurring distribution known as the "inventory rule." According to this rule, a minority of the stock in a store or warehouse will account for a large majority of use. The classic statement of this relationship is the 80/20 rule, which predicts that 80 percent of transactions will involve the most heavily used 20 percent of stock.

Trueswell's application of the inventory rule in a library setting requires that the investigator determine the dates of last use for a sample of the collection being studied. A frequency distribution of the entire sample is charted, showing the percentage of books which have had no circulation (y axis) against the amount of time back to last use (x axis). Observations along this curve identify the percentage of books not having circulated within a given period of time. From any point on the curve one may move up the y axis to find the corresponding point on a generally parallel but higher curve describing the percentage of the collection which has been inactive during the time period.

From these two curves Trueswell's technique allows the derivation, for any given time period, of the percentage of book stock which has accounted for a given proportion of circulation. While Trueswell has noted that there is variation among libraries in the curves comparing stock to use, he has consistently reported a degree of concentration of use across titles which many have found disconcerting. Typical of his findings have been reports that at Northwestern's Derring Library, 20 percent of the stack holdings in Dewey class 820s had accounted for 70 percent of use in the prior two years and that at Northwestern's Technological Institute Library, only about 25 percent of the book stock would have been required to satisfy over 99 percent of current (previous eight years) circulation requirements.[36]

While Trueswell's methodology has not escaped criticism, most commentary has focused on how libraries should respond to this knowledge, if at all. To a considerable degree, comments reflect the goals served by differing kinds of academic libraries. From the perspective of the college librarian who knows that his or her collection will never be comprehensive, Daniel Gore has generally spoken for the wisdom of weeding so as to maintain constant, or "zero growth" collections.[37] (Because obsolescence is only one factor accounting for the skewed distribution of use, even the most aggressive weeding programs will always provide for the retention of some older stock and the prompt discarding of some recent materials.) Reflecting the values of a university librarian wishing to meet current demand without sacrificing the utility of his collection to future researchers, Michael Buckland has emphasized duplication and the use of variable loan periods to maximize the availability of high demand titles.[38]

While librarians have not always wanted to hear Trueswell's message, solace has come from the recognition that obsolescence effects account for much of the uneven distribution of use and the belief that most materials receive enough use at some time to justify their acquisition. It was primarily because it challenged this comforting assumption that the 1979 publication by Allen Kent and his associates of *Use of Library Materials: The University of Pittsburgh Study* caused a storm of controversy that spilled far beyond the walls of the academic library.

Kent's study was based on the complete circulation history by the end of calendar year 1975 of the 36,892 books and monographs acquired by Pittsburgh's Hillman Library in 1969. The most surprising and controversial finding was that 48.37 percent of the books had not circulated by the end of the 86-month time period for which data were available. Given what is known about both obsolescence effects and the tendency of the same books to receive recurring use, the study team was able to build a persuasive case that perhaps 40 percent of the books would never yield direct benefits to patrons.[39]

A modest study at a community college in New York representing the opposite end of the spectrum of academic libraries yielded results surprisingly similar to those obtained at Pittsburgh.[40] On the other hand, a study at the libraries of the Associated Colleges of the Midwest showed that the percentage of unused materials was lower than was found at Pittsburgh. The same study, which has not received attention in proportion to its merit, found that while an inventory rule was indeed operative, the percentage of materials required to account for most use was higher than Trueswell had observed in his several studies.[41]

The Pittsburgh study was criticized on many grounds. Many critics argued that the findings were invalid because of sampling problems, because the study excluded stolen books which had presumably also been used, or because not all in-house use had been measured. Other critics argued that the findings, while plausible if exaggerated because of methodological shortcomings, had few implications for policy in research libraries. These commentators focused on the need of research libraries to collect many lightly used materials, and on the obvious point that libraries cannot know until after they have acquired materials whether they will receive use. A representative sampling of criticisms of the Pittsburgh study appeared in the May 1979 issue of the *Journal of Academic Librarianship*.[42] While observers may draw their own conclusions from this debate, few if any criticisms of the Pittsburgh methodology have attempted to put the proportion of disused materials at a level lower than 33 percent or to suggest that collection development activities at Pittsburgh in 1969 had been in any way exceptional or inferior.

Circulation and In-House Use

As noted, one of the criticisms of the Pittsburgh study was that it failed to account for in-house use. Commentators have pointed to the significant amount of recorded in-house use within many libraries and have marshaled anecdotal evidence that many patrons reshelve their own materials despite pleas not to do so, thus generating internal use that cannot be measured.

The issue of in-house use versus external borrowing is important for two reasons. Knowing the ratio of internal to external use is necessary to interpret circulation counts as indexes of all use. Whether individual items or classes of materials are used internally and externally in a fixed proportion, or whether this ratio may differ markedly across materials is also important to know.

Estimates as to the relative proportion of internal use and external circulation vary widely. At the low end, McGrath found half as much inside use as circulation.[43] At the opposite extreme, Harris's study at Newcastle suggested that internal use could exceed circulation by a ratio as high as 20 to 1.[44] Metz and Litchfield's findings at Virginia Tech were that internal use exceeded circulation by over 2 to 1, while Fussler and Simon suggested that the ratio at Chicago was between 3 to 1 and 9 to 1.[45] Ratios between in-house use and circulation are sensitive to circulation policies as well as to differences in measurement techniques. It is probably safe to say that while the ratio varies widely from one academic library to another, in-house use will generally predominate.

Studies of the nature of internal and external use have focused on two separate questions, though on occasion the two have been confused. Asking whether the same items are used internally and externally, Fussler and Simon's study at Chicago led them to conclude that "the recorded circulation use of books is a reasonably reliable index of all use, including the unrecorded, consultative, or browsing use within the library."[46] Bulick and his associates' analysis of use patterns in the Pittsburgh study led them to endorse Fussler and Simon's conclusion, as did Hindle and Buckland's research at the University of Lancaster Library.[47]

If the same physical volumes which circulate tend to receive disproportionate internal use, it is statistically inevitable that the correlations between in-house and external use measured across subject areas will be positive. How high they will be remains an open question however, and one of interest. McGrath's 1971 study at the University of Southwestern Louisiana yielded correlations across his subject categories of .84 and .86, depending on small methodological variations. Even though these correlations explain over 70 percent of the variance, it is worth noting that there was still room for the ratio of external to internal use to vary from 1 to 1 to 4.1 to 1 across McGrath's subjects.[48] Metz and Litchfield's study at Virginia Tech found a correlation of .89 between the subject distributions of in-house and external use. However, the correlation between book circulation and in-house use of current periodicals (which accounted for 30 percent of internal use), was somewhat lower, suggesting the need for greater attention to such use in future studies.[49]

Disciplines and the Relationships among Them

As has been noted, much bibliometric analysis has rested on the key insight that the nature of the literature cited by researchers in a given discipline can tell us much about the intellectual nature of that discipline. Price's examination of the proportion of recent documents among a discipline's cited literature is one example of this use of evidence.[50] Researchers have also looked at the extent to which a discipline cites materials from within its own literature, as opposed to materials from other disciplines. Often the implicit assumption in such studies is that disciplines with mature research paradigms will be more focused in their work and will therefore tend more to cite works from within their own literatures, much as they will also cite more recent works. Other citation evidence, such as the bibliographic format, language, or mix of subject disciplines cited, can reveal much about subject disciplines.

The Disciplinary Level

The number of studies that have examined disciplines in the light of their citation practices is far too large for this review to encompass. Instead, a few good, representative studies in the sciences, social sciences, and humanities are summarized here.

Herman Fussler's 1949 analysis of the literatures of chemistry and physics served in many ways as the prototype for citation studies of individual disciplines. Fussler exhaustively analyzed samples of references drawn from 1899, 1919, and 1939 publications in these fields, investigating the language, country of publication, format, and subject of each referenced document. As examples of his findings, he noted an increase over his time period in the dependence of both disciplines on works published in technology, and an asymmetry of use whereby chemistry was found to be twice as dependent on publications in physics as the reverse. Even though both disciplines relied on publications in their own fields for about two-thirds of their citations, Fussler considered there to be too much interdisciplinary use to justify the existence of branch libraries in the sciences, concluding that "subject classification does not bring together the materials required by research personnel in either chemistry or physics."[51]

Fussler's work was followed in a few years by Charles Harvey Brown's *Scientific Serials*. Also based on citation counts, Brown's study attempted to identify highly cited scientific serials but, more importantly, to use these results to illuminate the characteristics of individual scientific disciplines. His descriptions, field by field, of the variations among these disciplines in terms of their reliance on a compact or widely scattered literature, on recent or more retrospective materials, and on a variety of external literatures are still revealing.[52] Earle and Vickery's 1969 study of a sample of over 45,000 citations from current U.K. scientific publications provides a useful update on the subject distribution of materials used by researchers in a variety of scientific disciplines.[53]

In the social sciences, Baughman's 1974 study of sociology is a good example of a citation study devoted to a single academic discipline. Analyzing the documents cited in a random sampling of sociology publications, Baughman found that serial publications accounted for only 39 percent of use, with citations to books alone accounting for 51 percent. There was a relatively steep obsolescence curve of the familiar shape and a very marked preference for English-language materials. Baughman found the periodical literature of sociology to be highly concentrated, so much so that ten journals accounted for a substantial portion of the significant literature. Noting the intensive use of key journal materials by other key journals, Baughman concluded that "the core is heavily cited by the core."[54]

Studies covering multiple social science disciplines include Earle and Vickery's 1969 analysis, very similar to their study of scientific citations and useful for tracing the subject relationships among the individual social sciences, and Broadus's 1971 review article of bibliometric studies in the social sciences.[55] Broadus's main points are that, apart from economics, the social science literatures are only moderately self-sufficient; that social scientists concentrate greatly on English-language materials; and that social scientists rely less on books and on older materials than do humanists, although they greatly exceed scientists in their use of the monographic and retrospective literatures.

While the humanities have received the least bibliometric attention, there is at least a critical mass of recent studies on literary scholarship. Heinzkill's useful citation study verified, as he put it, aspects of the folklore about humanistic scholarship. He found that books accounted for about 75 percent of materials cited by literary scholars. Of all the disciplines to have received bibliometric attention, Heinzkill found that only in literary scholarship did journals account for less than 20 percent of use. The journals that were used were widely scattered and did not conform to a Bradford-like distribution. Over 70 percent of references were to materials at least ten years old.[56]

Recent studies by Stern and Cullars have refined Heinzkill's results. Both authors found the same heavy predominance of monographic sources. However, Stern distinguished between references to primary sources and the secondary criticism. She found that primary sources could account for as much as 47 percent of citations, especially when an individual literary author (as opposed to a movement) was the subject of study and when the criticism on the author was not yet well developed. Cullars found that when books as opposed to articles are studied, the more in-depth treatment that is possible in the book format leads to a considerable increase in reliance on original manuscript sources.[57]

Although most work defining the dependence of a given discipline on another discipline's literature has relied on citation data, several library researchers beginning with McGrath have used circulation data for a similar purpose. Using aggregated circulation data for students at the University of Southwestern Louisiana, McGrath described patterns of use in terms of the borrower's major field and the book's subject. His emphasis was on the "ethnocentrism" of disciplines (the tendency of practitioners to borrow materials only from within their own fields) and the "supportiveness" of literatures (the proportion of books in a subject loaned to nonmajors).[58]

Bulick's reanalysis of the Pittsburgh data took McGrath's approach a step further by introducing faculty data from a larger research university. Focusing on the social sciences, Bulick noted that economics was the only discipline not widely scattered in its use of subject literatures, suggesting that it was the most mature social science.[59] Metz's 1982 study at Virginia Tech used circulation data from faculty and students in all disciplines to attempt to map some of the topography of interdisciplinary relationships. Many of his findings were compared to the results of citation studies. Data showing that mathematicians are very ethnocentric while geographers draw heavily on other literatures provided one of several instances where Metz's results were similar to those of citation studies. Metz's data in general showed a significantly higher proportion of cross-disciplinary use than citation studies have found, leading him to echo Fussler's warnings about the proliferation of branch libraries.[60]

Megadisciplinary and Subdisciplinary Levels

Citation and library use data have been used to describe larger patterns in the use of subject literatures. Metz's circulation data very closely replicated data from both Fussler and Narin about the one-sided relationship between chemistry and physics and from Narin about the asymmetrical relationship between mathematics and physics.[61] These findings supported in a general sense Campbell's arguments that disciplines are related as fish scales, one overlapping the other in a sequence.[62]

McGrath has experimented with the analysis of data on books charged to individual patrons to support multidimensional scaling of the relationships among disciplines. His results yielded reasonably satisfactory mappings of these relationships when three dimensions were used. Although Metz found a number of moderately high correlations between individual pairs of disciplines, he argued that most correlations between the use of disciplinary literatures were too low to offer much hope for successful efforts to map interdisciplinary relationships by scaling circulation data.[63]

At an even higher level, Garfield has speculated that the social sciences comprise a third culture, bibliometrically distinct from both the humanities and the natural sciences.[64] Metz's circulation data suggested that historians rely more on the social science literatures than on humanities materials. His data also suggested that citation studies have significantly understated the dependence of engineers and others in technology on the literature of the basic sciences.[65]

At the subdisciplinary level, Small and Griffith have pioneered the use of cocitation analysis, which assesses the relationship between two papers by counting the number of subsequent reports that cite them both.[66] Bibliographic coupling, the opposite technique, infers the relationship between two papers from the number of references they make to the same sources.[67] While intriguing, studies at the subdisciplinary level may have limited applications for library practice.

Future Directions for Bibliometric Research

Bibliometric research has proved useful in guiding library practice in many ways. Particularly valuable have been the implications of bibliometric studies for weeding and storage policies, for the grouping of collections and services, and for collection development activities in general. The lessons of these past studies will continue to prove useful to future researchers.

While traditional bibliometric studies will continue to provide new insights, there are also a number of new directions that citation and library use studies could profitably pursue. Some of these represent possibilities opened up by new electronic technologies, while others would simply remedy long-standing needs in traditional bibliometric work. In this author's opinion, the following statements at least begin to describe profitable directions for bibliometric studies to follow:

1. *Traditional book use studies should exploit previously ignored data.* Book use studies have traditionally been just that—studies of the use of monographs. Meanwhile, citation studies have tended to focus heavily on the use of periodicals. Local library use studies should focus more on the use of periodicals and especially on the surprisingly high use accorded current periodicals.

Traditional book use studies should begin more fully to exploit the MARC record. Subject analyses should be complemented by analyses of how language, format, and date parameters interact to affect use. For example, is there an interaction between subject and age of materials such that older materials serve as a means of exchange between disciplines while the use of more recent materials follows disciplinary lines? Fuller use of the potential of the MARC record will make it possible to specify such relationships.

There is an additional need for more use studies that couple information from patron records with bibliographic data to answer the crucial question, "Who uses what?", adding to the contributions of McGrath, Bulick, and Metz in this area.

2. *One-time formal studies should be complemented by ongoing analyses of use.* While a small number of book use studies have made signal contributions to the bibliometric literature, individual libraries often hesitate to apply the results of such studies to their own situations. The potential of integrated local systems to provide ongoing management information to guide collection development and other library policies has been exploited far too little. Prototype studies showing how libraries may integrate collection use information into ongoing patterns of analysis and adjustment would be most useful at this point.

3. *There is a continuing need for citation studies at the disciplinary and interdisciplinary levels.* There has been at best a steady momentum, but no growth, in the library literature investigating individual disciplines and the relationships among them. Since library policy tends to be shaped at the level of disciplines and their literatures, the work of academic bibliometricians in science studies, with its frequent emphasis on the subdisciplinary level, must be complemented by continuing work by librarians. A number of academic fields have still virtually escaped bibliometric attention by librarians.

4. *Use and citation studies should be brought closer to the user.* An unfortunate dichotomy has appeared in the overall literature that studies the flow of information among scholars and scientists. Many sociologists of

science have focused on sociometric studies that seem to assume that personal communication is the only means of scholarly and scientific exchange. Meanwhile, other bibliometricians, including most library researchers, have studied library use or citation patterns as if the printed word were the sole courier of information.

There remains a great need for "grounded" studies—those that begin with intense observation of the individual researcher in the full context of his or her social and bibliographic resources. In research of this nature, it would be possible to determine, for each source a researcher consulted, the original source of reference leading to the use; how and how much the source is read; and its value to the research project. While such studies will be ambitious and difficult to perform, progress in understanding scholarly communications in all its richness may be limited without them.

5. *Bibliometric analyses must begin to exploit the potential of electronic media and to address the unique new questions these media raise.* Library researchers and other bibliometricians must begin to anticipate a day when the use of bibliographic materials may not leave a trail of materials to be reshelved, or checkout slips to be counted. Alternative means must be devised to measure not only the electronic use of more or less traditional materials in new formats, but also user-driven explorations of pictorial or aural materials as users navigate through large databases using hypertext.

It should also be possible to monitor user interactions with electronic media to improve greatly the controlled vocabularies and search languages that indexers, librarians, and systems designers provide to make information intellectually accessible. The analysis of citation and use patterns can usefully complement more traditional methods of improving search procedures and vocabularies, by showing the relatedness of subjects and documents from the user's point of view.

As this chapter should make clear, bibliometric researchers have fairly thoroughly explored certain avenues. Much of their work has elaborated answers to questions laid out over the past twenty to forty years in studies that approach the status of classics. On the surface, the field has settled into what Kuhn has called "normal science," but as most bibliometricians well know, this very settling into comfort and habit may be the first sign that radically new perspectives and questions will soon emerge.[68] However new the challenges that bibliometric researchers will choose to pursue in the age of electronic information, they will be able to build on a solid foundation of past research.[69]

Notes

1. Alan Pritchard, "Statistical Bibliography or Bibliometrics," *Journal of Documentation* 25 (1969): 348–349.

2. Eugene Garfield, "Citation Indexing for Studying Science," *Nature* 227 (August 15, 1970): 669–671.

3. Carolyn O. Frost, "The Use of Citations in Literary Research: A Preliminary Classification of Citation Functions," *Library Quarterly* 49 (October 1979): 399–414.

4. Diana Crane, *Invisible Colleges: Diffusion of Knowledge in Scientific Communiies* (Chicago: University of Chicago, 1972); Jonathan R. Cole and Stephen Cole, "The Ortega Hypothesis," *Science* 178 (October 27, 1972): 368–375; Abraham Bookstein, "The Bibliometric Distributions," *Library Quarterly* 46 (October 1976): 416–423.

5. Herman H. Fussler and Julian L. Simon, *Patterns in the Use of Books in Large Research Libraries* (Chicago: University of Chicago Pr., 1961).

6. Maurice B. Line and A. Sandison, "Progress in Documentation: 'Obsolescence' and Changes in the Use of Literature with Time," *Journal of Documentation* 30 (1974): 283–350.

7. Thomas S. Kuhn, *The Structure of Scientific Revolutions*, 2nd ed., enlarged. *International Encyclopedia of Unified Science*, vol. 1, no. 2 (Chicago: University of Chicago, 1970).

8. Derek J. de Solla Price, "Citation Measures of Hard Science, Soft Science, Technology, and Nonscience," in *Communication among Scientists and Engineers*, ed. Carnot E. Nelson and Donald K. Pollock (Lexington, Mass.: Heath, 1970), pp. 3–22.

9. Charles F. Gosnell, "Obsolescence of Books in Libraries," *College & Research Libraries* 5 (March 1944): 115–125.

10. Philip M. Morse, *Library Effectiveness: A Systems Approach* (Cambridge: Massachusetts Institute of Technology, 1968), p. 89.

11. Fussler and Simon, *Patterns in the Use of Books*, 1969 ed.

12. Robert N. Broadus, "The Literature of the Social Sciences: A Survey of Citation Studies," *International Social Science Journal* 23 (1971): 236–243.

13. Paul Metz, "The Use of the General Collection in the Library of Congress," *Library Quarterly* 49 (October 1979): 415–434.

14. Robert N. Broadus, "Use Studies of Library Collections," *Library Resources & Technical Services* 24 (Fall 1980): 317–324.

15. Stephen Bulick, William N. Sabor, and Roger R. Flynn, "Circulation and In-House Use of Books," in *Use of Library Materials: The University of Pittsburgh Study*, ed. Allen Kent (New York: Marcel Dekker, 1979), pp. 9–56; Metz, "The Use of the General Collection."

16. George A. Jenks, "Circulation and Its Relationship to the Book Collection and Academic Departments," *College & Research Libraries* 37 (March 1976): 145–152; Metz, "The Use of the General Collection."

17. Price, "Citation Measures."

18. Broadus "Use Studies."

19. Fussler and Simon, *Patterns in the Use of Books*, 1969 ed., p. 15.

20. Philip M. Morse and Ching-chih Chen, "Using Circulation Desk Data to Obtain Unbiased Estimates of Book Use," *Library Quarterly* 45 (April 1975): 179–194; R. P.

Coady, "Testing for Markov-Chain Properties in the Circulation of Humanities Monographs," *Collection Management* 5 (Fall/Winter 1983): 37–51.

21. Bulick et al., "Circulation and In-House Use of Books."

22. Paul Metz and Charles Litchfield, "Measuring Collections Use at Virginia Tech," *College & Research Libraries* 49 (November 1988): 501–513.

23. Paul Metz, *The Landscape of Literatures: Use of Subject Collections in a University Library* (Chicago: American Library Assn., 1983).

24. William E. McGrath, "Predicting Book Circulation by Subject in a University Library," *Collection Management* 1 (Fall/Winter 1976–1977): 7–26.

25. Ibid.; Thomas John Pierce, "The Economics of Library Acquisitions: A Book Budget Allocation Model for University Libraries" (Ph.D. diss., University of Notre Dame, 1976), p. 46; Metz and Litchfield, "Measuring Collections Use."

26. Gunnar Knutson, "Does the Catalog Record Make a Difference? Access Points and Book Use," *College & Research Libraries* 47 (September 1986): 460–469.

27. S. C. Bradford, "Sources of Information on Specific Subjects," *British Journal of Engineering* 1934, reprinted in *Collection Management* 1 (Fall/Winter 1976): 95–103.

28. A. Bookstein, "Explanations of the Bibliometric Laws," *Collection Management* 3 (Summer/Fall 1979): 151–162.

29. F. F. Leimkuhler, "The Bradford Distribution," *Journal of Documentation* 23 (1967): 197–207.

30. Eugene Garfield, "Citation Analysis as a Tool in Journal Evaluation," *Science* 178 (November 3, 1972): 471–479.

31. Robert N. Broadus, "A Proposed Method for Eliminating Titles from Periodical Subscription Lists," *College & Research Libraries* 46 (January 1985): 30–35.

32. Michael D. Gordon, "Citation Ranking versus Subjective Evaluation in the Determination of Journal Hierarchies in the Social Sciences," *Journal of the American Society for Information Science* 33 (January 1982): 55–57; James C. Baughman, "A Structural Analysis of the Literature of Sociology," *Library Quarterly* 44 (October 1974): 293–308.

33. Elizabeth Pan, "Journal Citation as a Predictor of Journal Usage in Libraries," *Collection Management* 2 (Spring 1978): 29–38.

34. M. B. Line and R. J. Steemson, "Comparison of Ranked Lists of Journals," *Journal of Documentation* 33 (June 1977): 151–153.

35. Tony Stankus and Barbara Rice, "Handle with Care: Use and Citation Data for Science Journal Management," *Collection Management* 4 (Spring/Summer 1982): 95–110.

36. Richard W. Trueswell, "Growing Libraries: Who Needs Them? A Statistical Basis for the No-Growth Collection," in *Farewell to Alexandria: Solutions to Space, Growth, and Performance Problems in Libraries*, ed. Daniel Gore (Westport, Conn.: Greenwood, 1976), pp. 72–104; Richard W. Trueswell, "User Circulation Satisfaction versus Size of Holdings at Three Academic Libraries," *College & Research Libraries* 30 (May 1969): 204–213.

37. Gore, *Farewell to Alexandria.*

38. Michael K. Buckland, *Book Availability and the Library User* (New York: Pergamon, 1975).

39. Bulick et al., "Circulation and In-House Use of Books."

40. Harold J. Ettelt, "Book Use at a Small (Very) Community College Library," *Library Journal* 103 (November 15, 1978): 2314–2315.

41. Final Report of the Associated Colleges of the Midwest Library Collection User Study, August, 1980, prepared by Mary Kane Trochim and submitted by Arthur E. Miller, Jr. Available from Miller, College Librarian, Lake Forest College, Lake Forest, IL 60045.

42. "Pittsburgh University Studies of Collection Usage: A Symposium," *Journal of Academic Librarianship* 5 (May 1979): 60–70.

43. William E. McGrath, "Correlating the Subjects of Books Taken out of and Books Used within an Open-Stack Library," *College & Research Libraries* 32 (July 1971): 280–285.

44. C. Harris, "A Comparison of Issues and In-Library Use of Books," *ASLIB Proceedings* 29 (March 1977): 118–126.

45. Metz and Litchfield, "Measuring Collections Use"; Fussler and Simon, *Patterns in the Use of Books*, 1969 ed.

46. Ibid., p. 3.

47. Bulick et al., "Circulation and In-House Use of Books"; Anthony Hindle and Michael K. Buckland, "In-Library Book Usage in Relation to Circulation," *Collection Management* 2 (Winter 1978): 265–277.

48. McGrath, "Correlating the Subjects of Books."

49. Metz and Litchfield, "Measuring Collections Use."

50. Price, "Citation Measures."

51. Herman H. Fussler, "Characteristics of the Research Literature Used by Chemists and Physicists in the United States," part 2, *Library Quarterly* 19 (April 1949): 137.

52. Charles Harvey Brown, *Scientific Serials* (Chicago: Assn. of College and Research Libraries, 1956).

53. Penelope Earle and Brian Vickery, "Subject Relations in Science/Technology Literature," *ASLIB Proceedings* 21 (June 1969): 237–243.

54. Baughman, "A Structural Analysis," p. 301.

55. Penelope Earle and Brian Vickery, "Social Science Literature Use in the U.K. as Indicated by Citations," *Journal of Documentation* 25 (June 1969): 123–141; Broadus, "The Literature of the Social Sciences."

56. Richard Heinzkill, "Characteristics of References in Selected Scholarly English Literature Journals," *Library Quarterly* 50 (July 1980): 352–365.

57. Madeleine Stern, "Characteristics of the Literature of Literary Scholarship," *College & Research Libraries* 44 (July 1983): 199–209; John Cullars, "Characteristics of the Monographic Literature of British and American Literary Studies," *College & Research Libraries* 46 (November 1985): 511–524.

58. William E. McGrath, Donald J. Simon, and Evelyn Bullard, "Ethnocentricity

and Cross-Disciplinary Circulation," *College & Research Libraries* 40 (November 1979): 511–518.

59. Stephen Bulick, *Structure and Subject Interaction: Toward a Sociology of Knowledge in the Social Sciences* (New York: Marcel Dekker, 1982).

60. Metz, *The Landscape of Literatures.*

61. Fussler, "Characteristics of the Research Literature," part 1; Francis Narin, Mark Carpenter, and Nancy C. Berlt, "Interrelationships of Scientific Journals," *Journal of the American Society for Information Science* 23 (September-October 1972): 323–331.

62. Donald T. Campbell, "Ethnocentrism of Disciplines and the Fish-Scale Model of Omniscience," in *Interdisciplinary Relationships in the Social Sciences*, ed. Muzafer Sherif and Carolyn Sherif (Chicago: Aldine, 1969), pp. 328–348.

63. William E. McGrath, "Multidimensional Mapping of Book Circulation in a University Library," *College & Research Libraries* 44 (March 1983): 103–115; Metz, *The Landscape of Literatures*, pp. 71–79.

64. Eugene Garfield, "ISI Is Now Helping to Bridge the Three (Not Two) Cultures," in *Essays of an Information Scientist*, vol. 3, ed. Eugene Garfield (Philadelphia: ISI, 1980), pp. 434–439.

65. Metz, *The Landscape of Literatures.*

66. Henry Small, "Co-citation in the Scientific Literature: A New Measure of the Relationship between Two Documents," *Journal of the American Society for Information Science* 24 (July-August 1973): 265–269.

67. Derek J. de Solla Price, "Networks of Scientific Papers," *Science* 149 (July 30, 1965): 510–515.

68. Kuhn, *The Structure of Scientific Revolutions.*

69. For an excellent overview of the bibliometric literature from a slightly different perspective, see Howard D. White and Katherine W. McCain, "Bibliometrics," in *Annual Review of Information Science and Technology*, vol. 24, ed. Martha E. Williams (Amsterdam: Elsevier, 1989), pp. 119–186.

William Gray Potter

Insurmountable Opportunities: Advanced Technology and the Academic Library

A great deal of the work in applying advanced technology to libraries over the past forty years has been energized by a common vision of the future, a unifying image for the use of machines in organizing and delivering information to readers. This vision was conceived as the memex by Vannevar Bush and articulated in his seminal essay "As We May Think," published in the *Atlantic Monthly* in July 1945.[1]

The first director of the Office of Scientific Research and Development and Franklin Roosevelt's chief scientific advisor, Bush was concerned with the vast array of published information that was accumulating, especially in the sciences. He called for society to turn the momentum of research after World War II to the creation of a new means of storing and indexing knowledge. He was most interested in developing ways to connect related items of information.

In his essay, Bush described a machine he called the memex:

> A memex is a device in which an individual stores all his books, records, and communications, and which is mechanized so that it may be consulted with exceeding speed and flexibility. It is an enlarged intimate supplement to his memory.[2]

Bush described the components of the memex, which is essentially a desk at which one works. It offers the following features:

Mass storage of documents such that 5000 pages a day could be added and it would take hundreds of years to fill (Bush proposed microfilm for the medium of storage and, twenty-two years later, changed this format to magnetic tape.[3] However, the medium is not as important as the concept.)

A mechanism to insert published documents already in a format compatible for storage

Use of a scanning device for the entry of photographs, longhand notes, memoranda, and other documents that have to be translated to the medium of storage

Several projection screens to allow the simultaneous viewing of more than one document

Capability to add notes to any document

Ability to generate a copy of any set of documents for distribution to colleagues and insertion into their memexes.

All this, Bush claimed, is "conventional, except for the projection forward of present-day mechanisms and gadgetry." The real value to Bush of the memex lay in a concept he called "associative indexing, the basic idea of which is a provision whereby any item may be caused at will to select immediately and automatically another. This is the essential feature of the memex."[4]

Associative indexing would allow a reader to note that two documents, or pages or paragraphs or sentences within a document, are related in a way that is important to the reader. This relationship would be stored and available for review. Bush envisioned the memex user building a trail among relevant items.

Bush's essay is often cited as seminal in the literature of information science.[5] It has been cited by developers of CD-ROMs and by the progenitor of hypertext as being profoundly important to the use of these technologies.[6] Recently, it has been cited as a model for future library services.[7] It can be argued that Bush's essay can also provide a unifying vision for developers of automated library systems in academic libraries. (To avoid a debate over the taxonomy of library systems and information systems, the concern in this chapter is with the use of advanced technology in libraries.)

Bush described a system that places all relevant knowledge at the fingertips of the reader and provides a means to organize this knowledge in a way that is of particular importance to the research interests of the reader. The general underlying theme of Bush's ideas, though, is that the body of available knowledge must be readily accessible and malleable to those who consult it. While the world is still years away from realizing Bush's vision, the trends are clearly in this direction. Applying advanced technology to academic libraries has made libraries easier and more efficient to use, has gathered more information into one channel for consultation by the reader, and has provided the means to capture information so that the reader can organize it to suit present purposes.

There are many specific applications of advanced technology in libraries, each reported extensively in the literature. These applications, often interrelated and classified in many ways, are grouped and discussed in this chapter under the following eight categories or trends:

Online catalogs, particularly the expansion of these systems to include information beyond the library catalog

Connectivity—attempts to link or connect individual library systems to other library systems or to non-library systems

Bibliographic and information utilities—the status and future of online systems that provide information to libraries for a fee

Workstations—the development of microcomputer-based systems that approach Bush's vision of a memex in terms of storage, display, and indexing

Hypertext—the realization of Bush's concept of associative indexing using microcomputers

Expert systems—the growing power of computers to interpret and apply sets of rules

Electronic publishing—the ability to deliver information through electronic or optical means

Videodisk and CD-ROM—the use of very capacious optical disks to store information.

Each of these trends is described in detail, followed by a discussion of how they are converging to deliver services that approach the characteristics of Bush's memex.

A considerable amount of scientific and technical development work has been done in the years since 1945 to bring Bush's vision closer to reality. The bulk of this work has been done outside the library community. However, the results of this work have been used in libraries, have influenced all other aspects of library service, and have led to some research by librarians, albeit a small amount. For these reasons and because there is a need for future research related to advanced technology and libraries, the present essay is included in this volume.

Literature Consulted

In their recent review of the literature in library automation and network development, Shaw and Culkin classified authors in this area into four types: philosophers, chroniclers, practitioners, and researchers. Philosophers comment upon automation efforts and attempt to relate them to broader, institutional goals. Chroniclers perform surveys and create lists. (Shaw and Culkin found a disproportionate number of authors are one of these first two types.) The third type, practitioners, describes particular experiences. While often disparaged as "how we did it good" articles, these authors' papers provide valuable information on the current state of the art and can also provide a retrospective historical context. Moreover, as Shaw and Culkin point out, taken collectively, the publications of practitioners provide "the building blocks required to create conceptual models." The fourth type of authors is researchers and while their work is scant compared to the other types of publications, it is often solid and valuable. However, their work is seldom research in the classic sense. There is rarely a clear statement of the problem or a detailed description of methodology.[8]

A fifth type of author could be added and that is the synthesizers, those who take the work of the other types of authors and attempt to discern patterns and relationships. In effect, synthesizers build trails among relevant works for the use of others. Shaw and Culkin's paper is an example of such work.

This chapter is also one of synthesis. It discusses a wide range of relevant literature but focuses on the work of practitioners and researchers. It further concentrates on work that deals specifically with the use of advanced technology in academic libraries. Given the volatile nature of developments in this area, the emphasis is on work published in the last five years.

Online Catalogs

Online catalogs are becoming prevalent in academic libraries. While the primary purpose of the online catalog is to provide access to the collection of a library, in essence to replace the card catalog, several libraries are beginning to expand the capabilities of the system to include other databases.

Most online catalogs are very powerful information retrieval systems with impressive searching capabilities. Some catalogs index every word in a bibliographic record, some allow limiting by date or format of material, and some have sophisticated interactive interfaces. Further, because catalogs are used by an audience that may come infrequently to the library, they are relatively easy to use.

Recognizing that the software used by online catalogs might have more general appeal, some libraries have applied this software to databases that go beyond the traditional library catalog. Some of these databases are bibliographic, such as indexes to periodicals or to special collections of materials in a library, while others might contain the full text of a reference book or a statistical database. The experience of four institutions that have expanded their online catalogs illustrate the potential. These institutions are Georgia Institute of Technology, Carnegie Mellon University, the Colorado Alliance of Research Libraries, and Arizona State University.[9]

Georgia Tech was one of the first libraries to mount other bibliographic databases alongside its online catalog. It installed BRS/Search software in 1985 as the basis of its online catalog. Operating on an IBM mainframe, the BRS/Search software provides very sophisticated searching of catalog records as well as other types of files, including the full text of some publications. In 1986, the library mounted several commercial databases of citations to periodicals from Information Access Corporation. *INSPEC*, an index to the technical journals in engineering, *Applied Science Technology Index*, and the full text of the journal *Commerce Business Daily* are also available. Locally produced databases have been mounted, including an index to the architecture library's slide collection.

The library's catalog and these other databases are available to faculty and students at Georgia Tech at no charge. They can use this service at terminals in the library, through terminals or personal computers in their offices or dorm rooms connected to the campus network, or by dial access from home or other off-campus sites. Librarians at Georgia Tech report that success has generated greater demand. "Having seen what is possible, Tech's users want more information in other subject areas and in greater depth."[10]

The Library Information System (LIS) at Carnegie Mellon University is based on a customized version of IBM's STAIRS software. Apart from the library's online catalog, available databases include some of the same files from Information Access Corporation that are available at Georgia Tech. LIS also contains the full text of several reference works, including the Grolier *Academic American Encyclopedia* and the *American Heritage Dictionary*. While all the available files have been well received, the online encyclopedia has proven very popular. One user referred to it as "the greatest thing since the invention of bed sheets."[11]

The public access catalog of the Colorado Alliance of Research Libraries (CARL) supports online catalogs for its eight member libraries: Denver Public Library, University of Colorado at Boulder, University of Denver, University of Northern Colorado, Colorado School of Mines, Auraria Library, Colorado State University, and University of Wyoming. Each library's catalog can be searched as a separate file. The system is based on Tandem computers in Denver that support a network of terminals in the member libraries.

In addition to the catalogs of the member libraries, CARL has also mounted a variety of other databases. As at Carnegie Mellon, the *Academic American Encyclopedia* has proven a popular database. The *Metro Denver Facts* database was taken from a publication by the Denver Chamber of Commerce. It contains economic and business statistics relating to Denver, most comparing Denver to other metropolitan areas. The Auraria Library has compiled a database called *InfoColorado*. Resembling a clipping service, this file contains citations and abstracts culled from newspapers, journals, books, and other publications relating to Colorado's economic development.[12]

CARL's most ambitious project is called UnCover.[13] This is an index that CARL compiles of the tables of contents of about 10,000 journals. Unlike the other databases of CARL, UnCover is marketed to other libraries, library networks, and even to individuals.

Arizona State University (ASU) has licensed and installed the CARL system on a local computer. Unlike the mother installation of CARL in Denver, ASU's installation, called simply the Online Catalog, is oriented to a single campus. In addition to the main catalog for the library's collection, ASU has mounted the *Academic American Encyclopedia.* It has also loaded six periodical indexes from the publisher H. W. Wilson. Several computer-generated printed indexes to the library's special collections have been transferred into the online system, such as the index to the Solar Energy Collection and the index to the Map Collection.[14]

From these examples, it is evident that the capabilities of many online catalogs can be used to support databases beyond the central file of bibliographic records. Perhaps most significantly, some of these systems have moved beyond bibliographic citations to include access to statistical files and to the full text of ready reference works and journal articles. In these cases, the catalogs are evolving into systems that not only lead to information but actually provide direct information that people may use to answer questions. In that sense, the online catalog can be seen as evolving into an online library.

Connectivity

While the online catalog is expanding to include more information locally, no online catalog can contain everything, just as no library can collect every book. Connections are needed that will allow users of an online catalog to access other systems and, conversely, to allow users of those other systems to access the online catalog. These connections facilitate access to systems outside the library and the university, to systems within the university but outside the library, and to other systems within the library.

The Linked Systems Project (LSP) is the most well known effort to link library systems.[15] LSP is a joint effort to link the automated systems of the Library of Congress, RLIN, OCLC, and the Western Library Network with the intention of exchanging MARC authority and bibliographic records and also developing a standard protocol for linking systems that can be used across a variety of automated library systems. This protocol, called the Linked Systems Protocol, is sometimes also referred to as LSP, leading to considerable confusion. The protocol is still in draft form and is formally known as Z39.50: American National Standard—Information Retrieval Service Definition and Protocol Specifications for Library Applications.

Buckland and Lynch have called attention to the distinction between the project and the protocol and discussed the importance of the protocol for all levels of library automation.[16] As they make clear, the linked systems protocol is far more important than the linked systems project. This protocol is one of several within the Open System Interconnection (OSI) suite of protocols, a conceptual model developed by the International Standards Organization.

If properly implemented, the Linked Systems Protocol will allow the connection of library systems at all levels. Thus, from a single workstation, a reader could consult the local library catalog, a CD-ROM based system housed elsewhere in the library, online catalogs of neighboring libraries, a regional union catalog, one or more of the bibliographic utilities, or an online search service. As Buckland and Lynch point out, "It is the library patron, concerned with exploring more of the bibliographic universe, who will be the most empowered by the Linked Systems Protocol." Moreover, efforts to create a National Research and Education Network (NREN) may provide a means to connect online library systems. The beginning of such a system can be seen in Internet.

While the Linked Systems Protocol is some years away from full approval and even further from complete implementation, several libraries have attempted to provide connections without waiting for a true standard protocol. The most obvious way for libraries to connect is to share the same automated library system. OCLC and RLIN illustrate this on a national level. Local and regional examples include LCS in Illinois, the Colorado Alliance of Research Libraries (CARL), and Melvyl in the University of California system.[17] CARL has also linked individual installations of its system in Denver, Colorado Springs, Boulder, and Durango.[18] These systems have demonstrated the benefits of a shared system for interlibrary loan and also for the sharing of periodical indexes and non-bibliographic files.[19] The Irving project has attempted to link disparate systems in the Denver area and, while successful, illustrates the problems involved in linking individual systems that do not adhere to an agreed upon standard for communication between systems.[20]

In addition to dial access, many libraries have connected their online catalogs to campuswide networks that were already in place to provide access to academic and research computing facilities for faculty and students.[21] As mentioned above, the linked systems protocol will allow the connection of CD-ROM or videodisk systems. Thus, a reader could consult the online catalog or one of a number of microcomputer-based CD-ROM products from the same workstation. Connectivity, then, promises to allow the connection of the full range of automated library systems.

Bibliographic and Information Utilities

For this chapter, a bibliographic or information utility is defined as an online service that provides information to libraries or to readers for a fee. OCLC, RLIN, and WLN are most often thought of as bibliographic utilities. However, online search services, such as DIALOG and BRS, are also utilities because they provide information to libraries and readers for a fee. Under this definition, the services supplied by Faxon through its DataLinx network and by EBSCO through EBSCONET to support their efforts in providing journals to libraries are also utilities. CARL, with the introduction of UnCover, a current contents service, verges on becoming a utility.[22]

The cataloging utilities OCLC, RLIN, and WLN have depended upon revenue based upon the number of books cataloged by their member libraries. Since virtually all libraries that will ever join one of these networks have already done so, these utilities are faced with static or declining revenues. Some libraries have purchased LC MARC cataloging on CD-ROM and are using the utilities less and less. This has a detrimental effect because it removes a library's holdings from the resource sharing program of that utility.[23] However, it is an action that may make sense economically to a library.

As these utilities plan for the future, they are looking for new services that will be attractive to libraries and generate additional revenue. Many of the services that have been introduced involve new products separate from the online system, such as CD-ROM subsets of the main database and turnkey local systems such as OCLC's LS/2000. However, what is of most interest here are new services that are offered through the existing network.

RLIN and OCLC both now charge for searching their systems, although libraries that catalog on the system receive a break in pricing. This searching charge indicates a shift away from a reliance on cataloging revenues. OCLC is rewriting its online system with the view of developing a service that will have greater appeal to the end user because of subject searching and other enhancements. RLIN offers several special databases, including the *Avery Index to Architectural Periodicals*, suggesting an interest in mounting scholarly databases.[24]

The ability of readers to search an online search service such as Dialog or BRS without relying upon an intermediary portends expansion for these utilities.[25] Several software packages are available that simplify the procedures for searching these services. Libraries who wish to offer end-user searching are confronted with the problem of controlling costs if they wish to provide some amount of subsidized searching to their patrons. Direct marketing of these services to end-users also concerns some librarians, who fear that readers will bypass libraries completely as these services come to offer full text in addition to more traditional indexes.[26]

The various bibliographic and information utilities are shifting and positioning themselves in an attempt to identify new ways to preserve revenues and as a result are offering a wider range of services. Libraries must be alert to these new offerings and sift through them to identify those that might be used to better serve the reader.

Workstations

The use of personal computers or microcomputers in libraries has mushroomed over the past six years. While much of this use involves generic office software, such as word processors and spreadsheets, many applications have been developed that are specific to libraries. Of particular interest are those applications that turn microcomputers into library workstations for either patrons or staff.

Crawford defines a workstation as "a powerful microcomputer, connected to some network or other system providing access to such resources as the library's online catalog."[27] Two elements are central to this definition. The first element is the microcomputer operating with a program tailored to an application. The second is the connection to another, usually larger computer system but also, in some cases, to other workstations.

The best known examples of workstations are the microcomputer-based terminals used by OCLC, RLIN, and WLN.[28] In each case, a standard microcomputer was configured to serve as a terminal on the network of these bibliographic utilities. Programs were developed that allowed bibliographic records to be transferred from the host system to the local microcomputer for local storage and editing. The display of special characters can also be handled effectively on microcomputers as illustrated by the RLIN and OCLC workstations designed for cataloging publications in Chinese, Japanese, and Korean. Microcomputers have also been established as workstations that communicate with each other to support a wide range of technical activities.[29]

Microcomputers have been configured as workstations for use by readers. The University of Illinois uses IBM PCs to intercede between the patron and the online catalog.[30] This program not only makes the online catalog easier to use, it also offers suggestions for reformulating an unsuccessful search, scans records for relevant subject headings, and provides interactive assistance in using the system. Many programs have been developed to serve as front ends to the online search services as a means of making these services more accessible to the end user, either patrons of a library or individuals who wish to bypass the library and utilize these systems on their own.[31] These programs are available commercially and allow the user to conduct a search without knowing an intricate search language. They also permit the downloading or capture of search results on the local workstation. A series of products from Personal Bibliographic Systems (PBS) facilitates searching of online services, permits the user to create a local database of relevant citations on the workstation, and will even format the citations into one of several accepted styles for bibliographic references and footnotes.[32]

The appeal of workstations is that they put computing power into the hands of the ultimate user. They simplify the host system, capture information, and allow local manipulation of that information. In some cases, as with PBS products, a means is available to transfer the information to a word-processing or database management program, thus allowing the user to incorporate the captured information directly into a document or a personal research database.

As microcomputers become increasingly powerful, their potential as workstations for library systems increases as well. For example, given enough local storage on the workstation and an adequate communications link, a reader could transfer all of the records from an online catalog on a given subject to a workstation and then set up a program that periodically checks the catalog for new titles that are added. The possibilities for capturing and storing full text are also enhanced by the potential of future workstations.

Some writers have foreseen the possibilities for workstations for the users of academic library services. They call these workstations knowledge workstations, scholars' workstations, or simply information workstations.[33] Whatever the term, the future of workstations in libraries augers for the simplification of library systems, increased power in the hands of the user, and a growing emphasis on integrating the library system with other systems used by students, faculty, and researchers in their work. These workstations also are reminiscent of Bush's memex in their ability to organize information to suit the needs of the reader.[34]

Hypertext

Bush's concept of associative indexing inspired Engelbart and Nelson in the 1960s to develop ways of building links between associated items of information that would form a trail through documents. Nelson coined the term "hypertext" to describe "nonsequential writing."[35] Everyone has had the experience of browsing in an encyclopedia, beginning with one article and branching off to other related articles, perhaps using the cross-references provided within the main text. After five or six articles, one may be very far from the subject of the first article, yet there is a definite trail that has been followed. Hypertext systems are designed to allow this type of browsing along predesigned links and also to allow the creation of new links.

While some work was done on hypertext in the 1960s and 1970s, it has taken the arrival of the microcomputer to ignite interest and developments in this area. There are several commercial products available, notably Apple's HyperCard for its machines and Owl International's Guide for Apple's Macintosh and IBM compatible microcomputers. There are also several noncommercial projects, most notably Intermedia developed by the Institute for Research in Information and Scholarship at Brown University.[36]

A hypertext system permits the reader to move quickly and freely from one piece of information to another associated piece. For example, reading a biography of the seventeenth-century English poet Henry Vaughan, one might come across a reference to his brother Thomas and wish to learn more. A few keystrokes or some other simple action, such as moving a mouse, would display a biographical sketch of Thomas Vaughan. Returning to Henry, the reader might begin looking at some of his poetry and notice a distinct similarity between a few lines by Henry Vaughan and a poem by George Herbert. The hypertext system would allow the reader to create a link between the two poems for personal future reference and perhaps for other readers as well.

Sharing the trails one builds among related information is an important feature of hypertext. Bush described how one memex user might copy and transfer a connected set of documents to a colleague for use in his memex.[37] This is happening today with users of Apple's HyperCard who exchange the "stacks" that they develop. Some current hypertext systems are meant to be shared by teams of workers or researchers so that links made by one are immediately available to all.[38]

Hypertext would be very useful in writing articles that attempt to synthesize previous work. In the case of the present essay, this author, as he writes, is surrounded by several heaps of photocopied articles and sections of books with marginal notes and highlighted passages. This essay attempts to boil this accumulated information down, identify and discuss patterns, and discern a direction for the future. A linear, narrative paper is the accepted way to do this. A better way would be to place the full text of all these documents into a storage device along with the chapter. Footnotes would be replaced by a link to the document and to the relevant passage in that document. Even more useful, perhaps, would be connections among the source documents themselves that the author would provide. Indeed, review articles are a pale foreshadowing of hypertext in that they show relationships among previous work. The problem is that it would require significant effort on the part of the reader to track down and assemble the original sources. A hypertext version of this chapter, of any review of the literature, would be much richer.

There are problems with hypertext. One is that as hypertext systems become larger, it is easy for the user to become lost or disoriented. Maps showing the relationships between documents are useful, but users can still get lost.[39] Another problem is breaking information down into segments that can be linked. Obviously, a biography of Henry Vaughan linked to a biography of George Herbert is of limited use. What is needed instead is to link paragraphs, even sentences in one document to paragraphs or sentences in the other. It is not easy to break documents into discrete segments or nodes for linking in a hypertext system, and if it is not done well, the system will not work effectively.[40]

Even with these problems, hypertext shows considerable promise. Online catalog and online databases can become a source of raw material for hypertext systems.[41] With the necessary technology, hypertext can be generalized to hypermedia and include sight and sound illustrations as well as text.[42] Thus, someone interested in Beethoven could read about his life and times, listen to pieces of his music, and view pictures and maps related to his life all from one source.

The application of hypertext in libraries is still at an early stage. There have been a few applications, notably in providing general directional assistance in using a library.[43] The potential, though, for providing improved services through hypertext is significant. Moreover, Bush himself foresaw "a new profession of trail blazers, those who would find delight in the task of establishing useful trails through the enormous mass of the common record."[44] Making the connections among related records as a way of organizing information would be a natural job for librarians to assume with the coming of hypertext.

Expert Systems

Expert systems have been defined as:

> Intelligent computer applications that use data, a knowledge base, and a control mechanism to solve problems of sufficient difficulty that significant human expertise is necessary for their solution.[45]

In this definition, data are the facts about the problem, the knowledge base is a set of rules for solving problems (expressed in "if-then" relationships, but also allowing for some trial and error, or heuristics), and the control mechanism operates the expert system.

Expert systems can best be explained by way of an example. One of the best examples is Answerman, a system developed at the National Agriculture Library.[46] Operating on a microcomputer, Answerman is designed to select a list of likely reference sources to answer a question from a patron. Through a series of menus, Answerman asks the user to select an agricultural subject field, e.g., corn, pigs, politics, or oysters. Once a subject is selected, the user is offered a menu listing the types of information available, such as atlas, bibliography, directory, "how to" books, or statistics. Based upon the selection, the user is given the name of a reference book. For example, if someone asked for a "how to" book on pigs, they would be given the title and location of the *Pork Industry Handbook.*

After a trial period, Answerman was enhanced to connect the user to AGRICOLA or to a CD-ROM bibliographic database. As a further enhancement, it was connected to an online search service offering the full text of journals in chemistry. Thus, the user could not only receive a referral to a reference source but could actually view the full text of an article that might answer his question all from the same source.

Aluri and Riggs have surveyed several other applications of expert systems to libraries. They found uses in reference, government documents, bibliographic instruction, and cataloging. They claim that these systems represent the field in its infancy and that the next ten years will see tremendous refinement. They especially cite the potential for "linking expert systems with external programs/systems."[47]

To date, most expert systems have been stand-alone systems that are not connected to other systems. As Waters, one of the developers of Answerman, has said, "My concern is that this process may produce thousands of building blocks of different sizes and shapes—but never a cathedral of learning."[48] The real promise of expert systems in a library environment, then, is as part of a workstation that guides users to sources and answers questions. Beyond this, expert systems might also become an extension of readers by remembering their interests and bringing relevant items to their attention.

Electronic Publishing

For present purposes, electronic publishing can be defined as a means of disseminating information using telecommunications. A distinction is made between sending information using telecommunications and simply encoding information on optical or magnetic medium and physically shipping it to someone for decoding. For example, an author might prepare a paper on a word processor, send the paper to a reader over an electronic mail network, or could copy the paper to a diskette and mail it. Sending it over electronic mail is closer to electronic publishing than sending the diskette. In another example, a television program can be broadcast or it can be distributed on a videotape. Broadcasting is a higher form of electronic publishing than distributing the physical tape.

As Brownrigg and Lynch point out, "publication is an action, a process, rather than an artifact."[49] In other words, the emphasis in publishing is on the channel through which information is distributed, not the final physical product. In the case of print publishing, the channel consists of the physical paper on which information is printed and the associated systems for delivering the paper to the ultimate reader. These associated systems include the publisher, the mail or other courier system, and the library or bookstore that organizes and offers publications to readers. With electronic publishing, an electronic telecommunications medium replaces paper and the associated delivery systems.

Electronic publishing, then, is not new. Radio and television have been with us for almost seventy years. Only lately has it become possible to publish the stuff of scholarly communication, namely printed words with some illustrations, using computers and telecommunications. Scholarly communication can be boiled down to two essential components—the author and the reader. All the other components—editors, publishers, printers, indexers, booksellers, libraries—are middlemen. They all exist and thrive for the purpose of connecting readers and authors.[50] Electronic publishing may require that the middlemen be juggled and some, perhaps, dropped.

With electronic publishing, it is possible for an author to prepare a work and send it directly to a reader. This happens informally between two colleagues, but the sheer magnitude of formal publication requires that some intermediaries organize the information, establish channels for the delivery, and, if appropriate, ensure that the author is adequately compensated for the work.

Many scenarios have been proposed for the advent of electronic publishing and what it will mean to libraries. Lancaster has predicted that libraries would become museums for books as the paperless society passes them by. Others believe that libraries will continue to have a role.[51]

Building collections of books and journals is only one part of what a library does. An equally important part is organizing information and providing access to these collections and to collections in other libraries. As electronic publishing takes hold, it is reasonable to expect that the functions of organizing and providing access will become more important. What is housed locally will become less important than providing access to electronic publishing based in a national or regional utility.[52]

As mentioned above, some libraries are already involved in electronic publishing. Those libraries that have mounted an online encyclopedia, an online dictionary, statistical files, or other ready reference works as part of their online catalog are already serving as channels for electronic publishing in that information that is of direct value to the user is available, as opposed to bibliographic citations that lead to a print publication.

Bibliographic and information utilities may become an important channel for electronic publishing. OCLC especially has been active in this area.[53]

For electronic publishing to be successful, it is important that the quality of the electronic display be at least as good as the traditional print publication. The reader probably will not be content to simply read the document on the screen, no more than most readers are willing to simply read an article in a journal in their local library. Just as most readers photocopy articles that are of particular value to them, a means should be provided to locally capture information that is disseminated electronically. This could be done on a local storage device or on a printer. In either case, the quality of the display must be preserved.

Brownrigg contends that the technological elements for high quality displays of both text and graphics are available today, but that the means to combine these elements into a useful product are not fully developed:

> Laser printers with very high resolution are readily available at lower and lower costs. High resolution displays, too, are progressing, but more slowly. However, protocols and data formats for transmitting images or mixed text with images to these devices are not well established.[54]

A view of what display technology can provide is available today in the area of desktop publishing.[55]

Optical Storage

Librarians are most familiar with optical storage through the advent of compact disk-read only memory (CD-ROM) devices. CD-ROM–based databases that hold up to 600 million characters of information are becoming ubiquitous in libraries. For publishers, CD-ROM offers a means of distributing works in an electronic format that still allows users to retain a physical artifact much like a book (only shinier and with better indexing!). CD-ROM has been termed "the new papyrus," indicating both the revolutionary potential of this technology but also providing a link to the traditional, physical, and more controllable past.[56] Publishers and many librarians appear to be more comfortable with publications on CD-ROM than they are with electronic publishing.[57] Access to CD-ROMs can be enhanced considerably by placing them on local area or campuswide networks.

Beyond CD-ROMs, the real power of optical storage is that it offers extremely capacious storage on a very small physical item. CD-ROMs presently cannot be erased, edited, or added to. Updating them requires that a new disk be mastered. However, other forms of optical disk are more malleable. Some disks can be installed in a microcomputer-based workstation, and information can be written to them but not erased. Others can be written to and erased much like a magnetic disk. Optical disks that can be erased and rewritten will place tremendous personal storage capacity into a workstation.

Because optical storage can accommodate a large amount of data in a small space, it offers an ideal storage medium for workstations. It can be used to record large volumes of information, including both text and images and, when combined with hypertext techniques, can index this information in a manner that makes the most sense to the reader.[58] As with most of the technology discussed here, optical storage is on the verge of great advances. It is important to keep in mind, however, that Bush originally proposed microfilm as the storage medium for his memex. Technology moves on, and optical storage may well be replaced by something that will make it look like so many reels of microfilm. The point to remember is that optical storage gives us the first practical technology to implement Bush's vision, and we also need to ensure that whatever medium we use will allow us to easily transfer the information to the subsequent medium. Whatever comes next will only increase our capabilities.

Confluence

There are eight areas where the application of new technology has special significance to academic libraries. These areas—online catalogs, connectivity, bibliographic and information utilities, workstations, expert systems, hypertext, electronic publishing, and optical storage of information—are coming together, converging to establish the foundation for a new generation of library services. DeBuse sees a similar set of six technologies combining "to form the basis for what will eventually be a monumental shift in the way that knowledge is recorded and communicated."[59] DeBuse's six technologies are powerful and portable new computers, user interface software, optical storage, hypermedia, artificial intelligence, and authoring systems for the development of hypermedia. In their review of the literature, Shaw and Culkin argue:

> There is clearly some indication in the current literature that there is a convergence of thinking about how these various computer-based capabilities should be packaged for the end user. The components of the package include: 1) traditional automated library systems, 2) PACs, 3) online search services, 4) electronic publishing, 5) electronic delivery, 6) micro-based videodisk services, 7) nonbibliographic databases, and 8) personal computers and scholars' workstations.[60]

Citing the memex as a model, Rice sees online searching services, online catalogs, and microcomputer information management systems combining to offer new opportunities for librarians.[61]

While these earlier articles slice developments in a different way, the argument is essentially the same as this chapter's—technological innovations are converging to offer new systems for library and information services. Each of the individual areas of technological innovation has fostered some application in libraries. However, if we stir these areas together, the following whole begins to take shape.

Online Catalog

The online catalog is crucial. It is becoming the primary avenue for accessing current library services and thus the obvious place to put new services. For those libraries that are expanding their online catalogs to include indexes to the periodical literature, reference works, nonbibliographic databases, and gateways to other systems, the online catalog is bringing increased attention and demand. Providing remote access to the online catalog, so that it can be used from offices, homes, and dormitory rooms, has increased the visibility of library services on many campuses. It makes sense, then, to build upon strengths and use the online catalog as a vehicle to deliver new services that develop in the future. If well designed, the online catalog can provide a familiar avenue for new services, a means to unify and simplify a complex universe for the reader.

Connectivity

No online catalog can contain every available database just as no library can contain every available book. However, properly connected, the online catalog can provide access to services not mounted on the local machine. These would include online search services, bibliographic utilities, and other services available on external computers. Shaw and Culkin see the online catalog as a channel to local resources, to external systems, to nonbibliographic data, and to electronic publishing.[62] Such channels can be opened only through advanced telecommunications, connections to other systems.

These systems might be on computers external to the library and university or they might be local, perhaps even present in the library itself. For example, a microcomputer with a CD-ROM product might be connected to a local network and searchable by other terminals on that network. Providing an online catalog with well-defined, standard connections can greatly increase the number of services available through that catalog.

Evolution of Bibliographic and Information Utilities

Some of the services provided through these connections on the online catalog might come from the bibliographic and information utilities. Currently, it is possible to provide a gateway through the online catalog to online search services and to OCLC, RLIN, or WLN. Few libraries can even consider such an approach to online search services, because turning a campus full of faculty and students loose on these services would be far too costly. The costs of public searching of OCLC, RLIN, and WLN are not insignificant, either. Moreover, the complexity of selecting and searching the many databases presents a critical obstacle to end user searching.

Workstations

The complexity, if not the cost, of searching outside databases can be ameliorated through workstations. Workstations as front ends to the online catalog can simplify and integrate the variety of choices available through an online catalog that provides access to a wide variety of databases. They can also provide a means to capture the results of a search and to manipulate it locally.

Expert Systems

As a component of workstations, expert systems can assist the user in maneuvering through the available choices and in sorting out the results of a search. They can also be used to guide users to sources for basic reference questions and, with a variety of online reference tools available, even answer those questions. Further, as part of an individual's workstation, an expert system could be programmed to remember what was of interest to the reader and learn to evaluate and rank search results.

Hypertext

Once information is captured on the workstation, hypertext programs could be used to provide links between associated items. These links could be built by individual users, and they could also be packaged by librarians acting as "trail blazers," using Bush's term, and provided as a guide to information on a given topic. Hypertext paths may also be established in the databases of the online catalog. For example, the catalog of the central collection of books could use hypertext links to enhance access. A further example would be to mount a hypertext-based encyclopedia alongside the online catalog.

Electronic Publishing

Apart from the economic issues that remain to be resolved, the electronic publication and dissemination of information are certainly possible today. The online catalog can become a conduit for delivering this information to the reader. It seems a natural step that once a reader finds a reference on the online catalog to a given bibliographic item that the item also be made available through the same source. Libraries that have mounted periodical indexes as part of the online catalog have reported that readers are soon clamoring for the delivery of full text through the same terminal or workstation.[63] Some online catalogs are already offering the full text of reference works and of some periodicals and these services will lead to even greater demand for full text.

One element that will hold back the delivery of electronic publishing through the online catalog is the need for the display of information that is at least as good as typeset publications. The technology that supports desktop publishing is evolving rapidly and there are displays available now that rival typeset publications. Moreover, relatively cheap laser printers can provide paper copies for those that need them. One of the benefits of this technology is that the document itself does not need to reside in the library. It could be stored in a regional or national facility and delivered electronically on demand. A further advantage is that more than one reader could have access to the publication simultaneously, unlike the current situation where ownership and access do not always coincide as readers are frustrated to find that the book they want is checked out or that the volume of a journal they want is being used by someone else.

Optical Storage

Some type of mass storage will be required as part of the knowledge workstation so that readers can capture a large volume of material required to support their work. At this time, it appears that some form of optical storage is the best candidate to provide that storage. Currently, readers consult books and journals and make notes or photocopy relevant sections as needed. With a sophisticated workstation, they can instead capture the relevant portion of the work they need, add notes to that work, and insert it into their local storage where they can organize it using hypertext or some other indexing scheme.

Summary

To summarize, a possible scenario illustrates how the technological advances discussed here might be blended. An online catalog in an individual library, or shared by a group of libraries, would offer the catalog of the collection of the library along with periodical indexes and ready reference works that have wide appeal to the campus community. In addition, local resource files such as the college catalog, would be available. Access to the online catalog would be available throughout the campus—in offices, dormitories, and homes.

Databases that would be of moderate appeal to the campus community might be mounted on a server, for example, a microcomputer with a CD-ROM, and made available through the online catalog. Databases of specialized interest or of great cost would be available through gateways from the online catalog. Full text of documents, when available, would be delivered through the online catalog.

A sophisticated and powerful knowledge workstation would simplify and integrate the variety of resources available through the online catalog using expert systems and artificial intelligence. Once information desired by the reader is located through the online catalog, it would be transferred to the workstation. If the information is a full-text document, the workstation would display it in a format equal to or surpassing current typeset quality. The information could be printed on demand or incorporated into the reader's local storage, complete with the indexing from the online catalog that lead the reader to the information. Hypertext programs would allow the user to integrate this new information into the existing bank of documents.

In this scenario, the online catalog becomes an environment that offers a universe of bibliographic information, and eventually the full text of documents, to the reader. In effect, the online catalog evolves into an online library. The workstation approaches Bush's memex in its capabilities, but it also has something Bush did not mention: connection to an organized universe of information through the online library.

Nontechnical Issues

The above scenario is based on what might be possible, given technology that is now or will soon be available. However, there are financial, organizational, and social issues that must be sorted out before this scenario, or one resembling it, can be achieved.

There are several financial issues. The first is how to pay for new services. Assuming that we are currently in a period of transition where more and more documents will be available electronically, how do academic libraries pay for the equipment and the licensing fees for these electronic services while also purchasing an appropriate portion of the print publications that continue to pour forth? The second major financial issue involves publishers. How do they price and control electronic publications? Understandably, publishers wish to at least maintain and possibly increase their profit margins. How will they do this if their publications are loosed upon an electronic network of online catalogs and knowledge workstations? If libraries can provide instant access to any article in a journal without actually owning the journal, why should they subscribe to a paper version? If journal articles are requested and provided one at a time from a national or regional depository, who should be charged and how much?

For the library, there are also social and organizational issues that must be addressed. The major one is, of course, what is the role of the library, if any, as technological advances make electronic storage of information increasingly important and possibly reduce the importance of traditional forms of publication that the library now collects? While some have predicted the demise of libraries or their relegation to museums for books, there seems to be a growing sense that libraries can adapt and are adapting to new technology and that "technology is not making libraries obsolete; rather, it is revitalizing them and expanding their capabilities."[64] Shaw and Culkin see this same revitalization in the development of "systems that inform," that have a direct influence upon learning.[65] They believe that librarians can move beyond providing the passive means for readers to find information to providing new systems that lead, instruct, teach, and inform.

It is easy to envision an online catalog that resembles the systems of today that would provide sophisticated but traditional searching for a collection of catalog records. The difference would be that once the reader finds a book, the system would reveal not where it is physically located in the library but rather how it can be delivered electronically to the reader's workstation. With many libraries now providing periodical indexes as well as the general catalog of the collection, it is also a natural step to envision the delivery of journal articles using the same means. An interim step would be to combine the online catalog with an electronic mail system to allow readers to request physical delivery of books and copies of journal articles.[66]

If libraries are only providing the channel for the delivery of information, why would they even have a role? There are several reasons that argue for the continuation of libraries. First, the transition to electronic publishing will be gradual. An online catalog that now offers access to printed books could begin to offer a few books online as they become available. As time goes by, more and more books would be available electronically, but it would take years before even a 50-50 split is reached.

Second, the current situation is that libraries subsidize readers. Very few individuals can afford to purchase all the books and journals they will ever consult. Instead, libraries gather and organize this information for readers. It is unlikely that with electronic publishing readers will be able to afford all the information that is needed and available. It is more likely that libraries will continue to subsidize the information needs of the community.[67]

Third, libraries provide a valuable service in selecting materials. Simply by making selection decisions, libraries are making judgments for their community about what is important. This role of evaluation will still have to be done by someone, and libraries may simply continue their current role.[68]

Other commentators have stressed the need for librarians to promote their services and to preserve the ideals of equitable and open access to information. Molholt states that "librarians have a role to play if and only if they are prepared to play it."[69] Potter has argued that:

> American librarianship is based upon very populist, democratic ideals of free and open access to information. Our society has funded libraries to provide information freely and without prejudice to anyone in our community who asks for it. I am concerned that if we, as librarians, do not stand up for these ideals, then no one will. Then the only people who will have access to the information they need will be those who are able and willing to pay for it. To paraphrase an old ALA slogan, it is up to us to develop systems that will deliver the best information to the greatest number at the least cost.[70]

Future Research

Based upon the work reviewed for this chapter, the dim outline of new library services can be seen, services that build upon programs that are in place today and that lead us toward an online library. This outline needs further definition so that it can be better understood and appreciated.[71]

As stated earlier, publications in this area can be divided into the work of philosophers, chroniclers, practitioners, researchers, and synthesizers. More work is needed from researchers. Five areas of research need to be explored.

First, applied research that analyzes the potential value of new technology for libraries is required. Librarians recognize that our market does not drive the development of new technology, but we must be open to adapting innovations as they appear. We have a good track record here, as illustrated by the application of CD-ROM. Librarians were quick to see the potential of CD-ROM and were receptive well in advance of other markets.

Second, as libraries expand and extend services, data should be collected and reported on how these services are received and used. For example, many online catalogs can monitor their own use.[72] The systems that evolve from today's online catalogs will certainly retain this capability, and it needs to be exploited fully and completely to enhance our understanding of the use of these systems. Surveys should also be conducted to measure the perception of new services among faculty and students.

Third, as more information products are introduced that veer from the traditional formats of books and journals, work should be done that leads to an analysis of the best way to use available dollars to deliver the most potent mix of products. It is ironic that as new optical and electronic products are introduced, the volume of print material continues to grow. There may be increasing pressure to see the book budget as an information budget and to use the book budget to purchase access to information as well as purchasing physical items. However, this approach must be followed carefully and with a full understanding of the consequences.

Fourth, as new forms of publishing are introduced, the chain that stretches between the author and the reader will be recast. Currently, there is a wide array of middlemen—publishers, indexing services, booksellers, serial agents, bibliographic utilities, libraries—all of whom exist to link readers with authors. There is an economic equation in effect that allows all to thrive. However, new forms of publishing may change this equation. Research is needed to understand the existing economic balance and to project how the situation might change.

Fifth, there is a social balance in effect as well. Libraries exist to serve a function in our society. Some might argue that libraries are unappreciated and poorly funded, but still they exist and show every sign of continuing to exist. New technology may alter this social balance. Bookstore owners accept that libraries compete with them for readers because of the long tradition of libraries in providing books. However, database vendors may not readily accept a library mounting a database itself and offering it free. This may be seen as unfair competition. The more innovative libraries become, the more they move beyond the safe confines of tradition. The implications for libraries of offering new services needs to be examined. Librarians need to be armed with studies that show that the community wants and is willing to support these new services and that libraries are merely extending traditional functions with new techniques.

While more work is needed from researchers, practitioners should also be encouraged to adopt more of a research orientation. Further, those who conduct research should strive to clearly state the problem they are investigating and to describe their methodology. There are many important projects in this field that have never been documented in the literature because those involved were either too busy, not interested, or not encouraged by their superiors to report their findings. Reporting is not enough, however. Rather than simply describe an experience, practitioners should be encouraged to define the problem they were facing, to explain decisions, to describe information that was gathered to support decisions, to list choices that were considered and discarded, to establish measures for gauging success, and to describe any course of action that was tried then abandoned. Most importantly, they should set their applications in the context of similar projects. In other words, they should report their work with a greater orientation toward research.

Conclusion

Libraries are middlemen, just as are publishers, editors, and everyone else in the publishing chain who stand between a reader and an author. It has long been the role of libraries to gather and organize knowledge so that it is possible and, it is hoped, convenient for readers to learn what they need or want to know. Technology allows us to make libraries and our systems less obtrusive, more effective, and more enjoyable to use.

Many of the barriers to developing effective systems are economic and political, not technical. Indications are, however, that once the technical, political, and economic issues are sorted out, libraries will have a significant role in providing new forms of publications to their readers using greatly improved tools. The online catalog can be the precursor of these tools. By extending services through the online catalog, libraries can position themselves to provide services that will grow in sophistication and power. Providing innovative services now will result in increased expectations and escalating demand from our readers. If handled properly, this increased demand can result in the increased funding required to provide improved systems and additional services.

Research on the practical applications of technology, on user reaction to systems, and on the economic, social, and political issues involved in advanced technology can enhance the possibility that librarians will be successful in continuing their historic role of making information available to all. If libraries do not play a role in the development of information technology, there is a real danger that the only people who will have access to knowledge will be those that are able to pay for it. That, and not the disappearance of libraries, would be the real tragedy.

Notes

1. Vannevar Bush, "As We May Think," *Atlantic Monthly* (July 1945): 101–108.
2. Ibid.
3. Vannevar Bush, "Memex Revisited," in his *Science Is Not Enough* (New York: Morrow, 1967), pp. 75–101.
4. Bush, "As We May Think," p. 107.
5. Charles H. Davis and James E. Rush, *Guide to Information Science* (Westport, Conn.: Greenwood, 1979), p. 160; James M. Nyce and Paul Kahn, "Innovation, Pragmatism, and Technological Continuity: Vannevar Bush's Memex," *Journal of the American Society for Information Science* 40 (May 1989): 214–220.
6. *CD-ROM: The Current and Future State of the Art*, ed. Suzanne Ropiequet with John Einberger and Bill Zoellick (Redmond, Wash.: Microsoft, 1986); Theodor H. Nelson, *Computer Lib/Dream Machines*, rev. ed. (Redmond, Wash.: Tempus, 1987).

7. James G. Rice, "The Dream of the Memex," *American Libraries* 19 (January 1988): 14–17.

8. Ward Shaw and Patricia B. Culkin, "Systems That Inform: Emerging Trends in Library Automation and Network Development," in *Annual Review of Information Science and Technology*, vol. 22, ed. Martha E. Williams (Amsterdam: Elsevier, 1987), pp. 266–267.

9. William Gray Potter, "Expanding the Online Catalog," *Information Technology and Libraries* 8 (June 1989): 99–104.

10. Miriam A. Drake, "The Online Information System at Georgia Institute of Technology," *Information Technology and Libraries* 8 (June 1989): 105–109; Miriam A. Drake, "Library 2000—Georgia Tech: A Glimpse of Information Delivery Now and in the Year 2000," *ONLINE* 11 (November 1987): 45–48; Julie Zimmerman, "The Online Information System at Georgia Tech," *Reference Services Review* 15 (Fall 1987): 11–16.

11. Nancy Evans, "Development of the Carnegie Mellon Library Information System," *Information Technology and Libraries* 8 (June 1989): 110–120; Nancy Evans and Thomas Michalak, "Delivering Reference Information through a Campus Network: Carnegie Mellon's Library Information System," *Reference Services Review* 15 (Winter 1987): 7–13.

12. Ted Koppel and Ward Shaw, "What's That Doing Here? Nonbibliographic Data in a Bibliographic Environment," *Reference Services Review* 15 (Winter 1987): 15–19.

13. Gary M. Pitkin, "CARL's Latest Project: Access to Articles through the Online Catalog," *American Libraries* 19 (October 1988): 769–770.

14. George S. Machovec, "Locally Loaded Databases in Arizona State University's Online Catalog Using the CARL System," *Information Technology and Libraries* 8 (June 1989): 161–171.

15. Sally H. McCallum, "Linked Systems Report, Part 1: Authorities Implementation," *Library Hi Tech* 3 (1985): 61–68; Ray Denenberg, "Linked Systems Project, Part 2: Standard Network Interconnection," *Library Hi Tech* 3 (1985): 71–79; Michael A. McGill, Larry L. Learn, and Thomas K. G. Lydon, "A Technical Evaluation of the Linked Systems Project Protocols in the Name Authority Distribution Application," *Information Technology and Libraries* 6 (December 1987): 253–265.

16. Michael K. Buckland and Clifford A. Lynch, "The Linked Systems Protocol and the Future of Bibliographic Networks and Systems," *Information Technology and Libraries* 6 (June 1987): 83–88.

17. Bernard G. Sloan and J. David Stewart, "ILLINET Online: Enhancing and Expanding Access to Library Resources in Illinois," *Library Hi Tech* 6 (Fall 1988): 95–101; Patricia Culkin and Ward Shaw, "The CARL System," *Library Journal* 110 (February 1, 1985): 68–70; In Depth: University of California MELVYL, *Information Technology and Libraries* 1 (December 1982): 350–380 and 2 (March 1983): 58–115.

18. Culkin and Shaw, "The CARL System," 68–70.

19. William Gray Potter, "Creative Automation Boosts Interlibrary Loan Rates," *American Libraries* 17 (April 1986): 244–246; Koppel and Shaw, "What's That Doing Here," 15–19; "MELVYL and MEDLINE," *Information Technology and Libraries* 5 (September 1986): 244.

20. Richard E. Luce, "IRVING: Interfacing Dissimilar Systems at the Local Level," *Library Hi Tech* 2 (1984): 55–61.

21. David A. Anderson and Michael T. Duggan, "A Gateway Approach to Library Networking," *Information Technology and Libraries* 6 (December 1987): 272–277.

22. Jeanetta M. Ireland, "Faxon LINX at Brandeis University Libraries: A User's Appraisal," *Library Hi Tech* 2 (1984): 29–35; Pitkin, "CARL's Latest Project."

23. Pat Molholt, "Libraries and the New Technology: Courting the Cheshire Cat," *Library Journal* 113 (November 15, 1988): 37–41.

24. Janice Woo, "The Online Avery Index End-User Pilot Project: Final Report," *Information Technology and Libraries* 7 (September 1988): 223–229.

25. William H. Mischo and Jounghyoun Lee, "End-User Searching of Bibliographic Databases," in *Annual Review of Information Science and Technology*, vol. 22, ed. Martha E. Williams (Amsterdam: Elsevier, 1987), pp. 227–263.

26. Marydee Ojala, "Views on End-User Searching," *Journal of the American Society for Information Science* 37 (July 1986): 197–203.

27. Walt Crawford, *Patron Access: Issues for Online Catalogs* (Boston: Hall, 1987), p. 111.

28. Debbie Harman and Kate Nevins, "The OCLC M300 Workstation," *Information Technology and Libraries* 3 (March 1984): 47–53; David Andresen, "The WLN PC: Local Processing in a Network Context," *Information Technology and Libraries* 3 (March 1984): 54–58.

29. Edward J. Valauskas, "Library Automation with Workstations: Using Apple Macintoshes in a Special Library," *Information Technology and Libraries* 7 (March 1988): 73–78.

30. Chin-Chuan Cheng, "Microcomputer-Based User Interface," *Information Technology and Libraries* 4 (December 1985): 346–351.

31. Mischo and Lee, "End User Searching."

32. Victor Rosenberg, "Literature Management Software for the Scholar's Workstation," *Library Software Review* (February 1987): 29–30.

33. Richard E. Lucier, Nina Matheson, and Karen A. Butter, "The Knowledge Workstation: An Electronic Environment for Knowledge Management," *Bulletin of the Medical Library Association* 76 (July 1988): 248–255; Barbara Moran, Thomas Surprenant, and Merrily Taylor, "The Electronic Campus: The Impact of the Scholar's Workstation Project on the Libraries at Brown," *College & Research Libraries* 48 (January 1987): 5–16; Victor Rosenberg, "The Scholar's Workstation," *College & Research Libraries News* 10 (November 1985): 546–549; John C. Gale, "The Information Workstation: A Confluence of Technologies Including the CD-ROM," *Information Technology and Libraries* 4 (June 1985): 137–139.

34. Rice, "The Dream of the Memex," 16.

35. Doug Engelbart, "A Conceptual Framework for the Augmentation of Man's Intellect," in P. W. Howerton and D.C. Weeks, eds., *Vistas in Information Handling*, vol. 1 (Washington, D.C.: Spartan, 1963), pp. 1–29; Nelson, *Computer Lib/Dream Machines*. According to Nelson, he first used the term in 1965.

36. Karen E. Smith, "Hypertext: Linking to the Future," *ONLINE* 12 (March 1988): 32–40.

37. Bush, "As We May Think," 107.

38. Michael L. Begeman and Jeff Conklin, "The Right Tool for the Job," *BYTE* 13 (October 1988): 255–266.

39. Smith, "Hypertext," 40.

40. Janet Fiderio, "A Grand Vision," *BYTE* 13 (October 1988): 237–244.

41. Smith, "Hypertext," 40.

42. Raymond DeBuse, "So That's a Book . . . Advancing Technology and the Library," *Information Technology and Libraries* 7 (March 1988): 10.

43. Martin Kesselman, "LSM Infomaster: A Hypercard CAI Program on a Macintosh Network," *College & Research Libraries News* 49 (1988): 437–440.

44. Bush, "As We May Think," 108.

45. N. Shahla Yaghmai and Jacqueline A. Maxin, "Expert Systems: A Tutorial," *Journal of the American Society for Information Science* 35 (September 1984): 297–305.

46. Samuel T. Waters, "Answerman, the Expert Information Specialist: An Expert System for the Retrieval of Information from Library Reference Books," *Information Technology and Libraries* 5 (September 1986): 204–212.

47. Rao Aluri and Donald E. Riggs, "Application of Expert Systems to Libraries," in Joe A Hewitt, ed., *Advances in Library Automation and Networking*, vol. 2 (Greenwich, Conn.: JAI Pr., 1988), pp. 1–44.

48. Waters, "Answerman," 211.

49. Edwin B. Brownrigg and Clifford A. Lynch, "Electrons, Electronic Publishing, and Electronic Display," *Information Technology and Libraries* 4 (September 1985): 201.

50. William Gray Potter, "Readers in Search of Authors: The Changing Face of the Middleman," *Wilson Library Bulletin* 60 (April 1986): 20–23.

51. Wilfred Lancaster, *Libraries and Librarians in the Age of Electronics* (Arlington, Va.: Information Resources, 1982); Richard De Gennaro, "Shifting Gears: Information Technology and the Academic Library," *Library Journal* 109 (June 15, 1984): 1204–1209.

52. Edwin Brownrigg, Clifford Lynch, and Mary Engle, "Technical Services in the Age of Electronic Publishing," *Library Resources and Technical Services* 28 (January/March 1984): 59–67.

53. Thomas B. Hickey and Andrew M. Calabrese, "Electronic Document Delivery: OCLC's Prototype System," *Library Hi Tech* 4 (1986): 65–71.

54. Clifford A. Lynch and Edwin B. Brownrigg, "Library Applications of Electronic Imaging Technology," *Information Technology and Libraries* 5 (June 1986): 103.

55. John A. Barry, *Desktop Publishing* (Homewood, Ill.: Dow Jones-Irwin, 1988).

56. *CD-ROM: The Current and Future State of the Art*, ed. Suzanne Ropiequet with John Einberger and Bill Zoellick (Redmond, Wash.: Microsoft, 1986).

57. Brownrigg and Lynch, "Electrons, Electronic Publishing, and Electronic Display," 204.

58. DeBuse, "So That's a Book," 10.

59. Ibid., 15.

60. Shaw and Culkin, "Systems That Inform," 265.

61. Rice, "The Dream of the Memex," 17.

62. Shaw and Culkin, "Systems That Inform," 275–281.

63. Drake, "Library 2000," 48.

64. De Gennaro, "Shifting Gears," 1204.

65. Shaw and Culkin, "Systems That Inform," 283.

66. Michael K. Buckland, "Combining Electronic Mail with Online Retrieval in a Library Context," *Information Technology and Libraries* 6 (December 1987): 266–271.

67. Brownrigg, Lynch, and Engle, "Technical Services," 67.

68. Ibid.

69. Molholt, "Libraries and the New Technology," 41.

70. William Gray Potter, "Micros, the Online Catalog, and the Online Library," in Nancy Melin, ed., *Connecting with Technology 1988: Microcomputers in Libraries* (Westport, Conn.: Meckler, 1988), p. 79.

71. For another list of research issues, see Pat Molholt, "Research Issues in Information Access," in *Rethinking the Library in the Information Age* (Washington, D.C.: U.S. Department of Education, 1988), pp. 93–114.

72. David W. Lewis, "Research on the Use of Online Catalogs and Its Implications for Library Practice," *Journal of Academic Librarianship* 13 (July 1987): 152–157.

Malcolm Getz

Analysis and Library Management

A library manager with an analytic point of view sees library problems in a special way. An analyst states objectives for the library in terms of benefits gained for costs incurred, decision by decision. The criterion for success is whether a change in library operation has increased the value of library services to the people who pay for them, net of the costs they incur.

In this essay, analysis means the careful examination of cause and effect relationships. When a library makes a specific change in operations, what are the consequences? For example, when a library extends its service by one hour, how do use and other outcomes change? Because many changes in operation result from changes in expenditures, an analyst, with effort, can summarize the cost of the given change in operation in terms of dollars of expenditure. A decision about whether a change in operation is worthwhile, then, requires making a judgment about whether the resulting change in use is worth the change in cost. The act of decision then requires that the decision maker assign a dollar value to the change in use or outcomes. An analyst may be able to infer the values users place on particular changes in outcomes in dollar terms. Such a valuation then might inform the manager's decision.

Most managerial decisions involve incremental changes in library operations. Few managers face a decision about closing the enterprise entirely or creating a new library enterprise from scratch. Rather, most decisions address changes in ongoing operations, for example, acquiring more books in one discipline, cutting back hours of service at one location, or changing the amount of processing of a class of materials. The character of the total library service results from the myriad of individual decisions made about small increments.

To be sure, the manager will likely have a philosophy of the whole, a sense of priorities that derive from fundamental institutional missions. Such a philosophy informs the analysis of individual decisions, helping to define the values and costs associated with a particular choice. Ultimately, one may judge the appropriateness and coherence of the philosophical view by how sharply it defines the costs and values of individual decisions.

Of course, the coherence, appropriateness, and articulation of a philosophy will play an important political role in an organization. This essay addresses the underlying substance and the analytic perspectives that allow a manager to assess individual decisions and so to develop and articulate a coherent philosophy. The selling of the philosophy is also important, but that is beyond the scope of this essay.

A manager faces choices and must make decisions. Typically, information is limited and action is usually required before all conceivable evidence is available. In contrast, a scientist operates under substantially different rules of evidence and should withhold judgment until every competing hypothesis has been set aside. Scientific decisions may be suspended perpetually. The quality of evidence required to move scientific opinion is expensive, samples must be ample and random, hypotheses must be carefully devised and refutable, and procedures must be replicable and replicated. The analysis needed to inform and improve managerial decisions in libraries should involve studies sufficient to influence scientific opinions, that is, with methodologies incorporating refutable hypotheses and appropriate samples.

No manager can afford scientific quality investigations in support of immediate decisions. However, managers can promote the development of scientific quality evidence, that is, encourage the development of a base of research that may inform important choices in the future. Managers can then inform decisions with scientific evidence as a supplement to the traditional source of information, namely, knowledge of standard practice in other similar institutions. As electronic tools create exciting new opportunities, traditional practice is an uncertain guide.

This essay begins with a discussion of efficiency as a standard for measuring library quality. Next, it describes the three parts of an analytic approach to library decisions—measuring outcomes, linking decisions to changes in outcomes, and finally valuing changes in outcomes in dollar terms. Last, it describes a prototype tool that will revolutionize how collections are evaluated and suggests other decisions that may be improved with better analysis. The goal is twofold: first, to promote scientific quality, empirically grounded, inquiries about academic library operations; and second, to encourage managers to consider decisions they make from an analytic point of view. The existing literature on the topics discussed is reviewed in other essays in this volume. The role of this essay is to indicate how good research can be most valuable for managers.

Bigger May Not Be Better

Too frequently, if one asks what is the best library, one will hear about the largest library in whatever set of libraries is under discussion. In contrast, in evaluating automobile companies, publishers, or universities, the largest is not necessarily considered the best—alternative criteria like profits, success rate, and reputation come to mind that are more readily viewed as standards of excellence. These criteria may or may not be correlated with size, and observers are not likely to conclude that the biggest is necessarily the best, at least not without considerable thought.

Vanderbilt University, this author's affiliation, would not want Harvard's libraries. The cost of maintaining them could sink its institution. Vanderbilt would have to increase its tuition sharply to sustain the library budget, and few students would be willing to pay higher tuition for a school with more library staff than undergraduate teaching faculty. Bigger is better only if someone is willing to pay the bill.

Libraries need a criterion of excellence that is independent of size. If the question of better for what is asked, a criterion can be defined that may be useful for any library. The specific criterion used here is: The "better" library yields services that are more valuable than they cost, indeed, as much more valuable as possible. The library that does this best is an *efficient* library.

Efficiency is a more demanding standard than simply effectiveness. An effective library is one that makes a difference. If longer hours attract more users, hours are effective in this regard. To determine whether the extra hours of service increase efficiency, however, the added value of the extra use must be shown to be worth the cost of providing the extra hours. To be efficient, libraries must be effective, but being effective is not sufficient to assure efficiency.[1]

The value of the services a library creates depends on its setting, on its mission. Value here refers to the value defined by those who pay for the library. A library in a small college will generate services of value to its students and faculty. Prospective faculty will make choices about accepting positions at the institution based on the array of opportunities the school provides: the salary offer and the quality of library services being two dimensions of the array. The institution will invest in additional library resources to attract faculty who in turn attract students. Students will elect the school based on the array of attributes the school offers, including tuition, the quality of faculty, and the quality of the library services. An increment in library service can, in this setting, be judged by school budget officers by how the change in the library will likely attract students and faculty, an effect that can be balanced against the extra cost in the library.

In a research university, the same criterion for success applies. Will an increment in expenditure for libraries attract more research funds, better faculty, or more students, than other expenditures that will advance the university? For a public university, the judgment of the legislature and bureaucracy about the value to the institution of a larger library relative to its extra cost plays an important role along with that of students and faculty. In very broad terms, however, the same criterion applies.

In institutions competing in markets, buyers and sellers judge. An academic institution that delivers value that is far in excess of its cost to those who pay for it will thrive, attracting faculty and students easily. An institution that does not deliver value comparable to its competitors will see enrollments dwindle, revenues decline, and ultimately, doors close.

Institutions that compete in competitive markets, then, have a significant incentive to achieve increases in the value of services rendered relative to cost. They will innovate. They will expand libraries in ways that enhance the library's contribution to the institutions' fundamental missions and cut the size of a library operation when resources can be deployed with more effect elsewhere. The market process may create a set of academic libraries of widely differing sizes and character. The most efficient set of academic libraries for today's society, then, will likely include libraries of many different sizes and with different strengths. Size may be an advantage in one setting and a disadvantage in others. Efficiency, then, is a better, but more difficult, standard for measuring library quality.

There are other methods for evaluating libraries. For example, schools often compare their libraries to those at competing institutions. Similarly, library managers may appeal to traditional practice or what has worked in another setting. Convention may define useful rules of thumb, but these methods for evaluating libraries and making decisions are not as robust as the encompassing notion of efficiency. When underlying technologies are changing rapidly, tradition will be a poor guide but the efficiency concept should serve well.

When Libraries Are Not Efficient

To the extent that the values created by library services or even their costs are difficult to judge, how efficiently libraries enhance institutional goals may be uncertain. Where market pressures to yield higher values per dollar of expenditure are weak, a diverse array of libraries may result, but they may not be socially most efficient. Precisely in this instance, when market forces do not exert a strong influence for efficiency, managers may find that careful efforts to measure values and costs may be most beneficial in informing decisions that increase the value of library services per dollar spent.

How much should a library spend to catalog its books? Getz and Phelps's investigation of cataloging costs and Paul Kantor's more extensive study depict considerable diversity in expenditure per volume.[2] They abstract from differences in salary levels and find differences in productivity. Some libraries use professional librarians to copy cataloging from OCLC's database. Others rely exclusively on paraprofessionals to copy cataloging. Some cataloging shops make extensive use of student help; some make little use of students. Even controlling for staffing mix, the libraries achieve very different production rates in cataloging. The studies do not measure the quality of the cataloging, and the accuracy, thoroughness, and attention to detail in cataloging differ significantly across libraries. It is likely, however, that differences in quality explain some of the observed differences in costs, but perhaps not all of them. Some of the cataloging shops might be better managed, have higher expectations for production, and use salary and hiring and firing policies to encourage better performance. A study of cataloging costs of sufficient scope and detail to test this hypothesis would be very interesting.

Systematic investigation of the quality and cost of cataloging has helped libraries discover how their production compares with other libraries. As careful cost and quality comparisons become more common, managers might use the benchmarks in understanding the performance of their own shops, taking due account of differences in mission and local circumstance. Improvements in management and so in performance might then be easier. As a consequence, some libraries might yield more valuable library services per dollar of expenditure.

Measuring Outcomes

To use the efficiency criterion, namely that the value of services be as large as possible given costs, many dimensions of service should be measured. Specifically, each of the causal linkages from the point where a library incurs additional costs through to the effect on institutional outcomes should be measured. Each policy choice may have its own set of linkages, so the notion of comprehensive measurement to encompass all possible policies is unrealistic. Instead, a core set of measurements of important library outcomes, primarily patterns of use, are used. These patterns are likely to be influenced by many different library policies. Once some important core attributes are measured, the causal linkage between a particular policy action and its result in terms of a change in a measured set of library outcomes can be established.[3]

Many libraries measure a set of core outcomes: attendance by entrance turnstiles, circulation of materials outside the library, reshelving of materials used inside the library, and reference questions asked. With electronic systems, the number of electronic transactions can also be known. Each of these categories might be disaggregated by category of library user, and perhaps in other ways.

A few libraries now use Paul Kantor's performance measures.[4] These measures identify some attributes of the quality of library service. One set of measures identifies what tasks users are performing in the library by periodic unobtrusive observation of everyone in the library. Questionnaires administered of library users at entrance or exit turnstiles provide some of the same information at lower cost.

A second measure suggested by Kantor records the amount of time required by users to accomplish particular tasks. For example, how long does it take for a user to find a known item in the catalog, locate it on the shelves, and charge it out? This method can be adapted to a variety of other library tasks.

Using Kantor's third idea, one can record the conditional success rate for finding materials. Among titles sought by users, what proportion are found? Of those items sought and not found, what proportion are not found for particular reasons? Disaggregation by cause of failure allows an investigator to link particular library expenditures to appropriate outcomes. For example, the number of items purchased ought to relate to the number of items sought but not found because they were not purchased. On the other hand, purchasing more titles will not reduce the rate of failure due to users failing to find titles in the catalog that are there.

Kantor does not provide us with a method to measure the success rate or time required for subject searching. In unpublished work, Getz has studied a group of students preparing an open-ended essay assignment for an upper-level political science course. Students spoke into a hand-held dictating machine during their first visit to the Library in preparing the essay. They described their thoughts, strategies, and findings as they proceeded. Getz found that students with a focused topic quickly found relevant material. Those with an unfocused topic took longer and had mediocre results. The instructor in the course reported the grades on the essays, and graded the bibliographies on the essays as well. The students with focused topics had good bibliographies and got good grades on their essays. Students with unfocused topics had weak bibliographies and got poor grades. This study also noted that the students' average grades in other courses were not well correlated with the results on the essay. There were good students (as measured by cumulative grade point average) who did not develop focused assignments, and there were students with lower grade point averages who developed good bibliographies and wrote effective essays.

Mary George's essay in this volume reviews studies of instructional services and considers how investigators have evaluated the success of instructional efforts. The link to subject searching is one such device. In measuring the success of subject searching, an investigator must take account of the searcher's skill level including the degree of focus in the search. Bibliographic instruction may have as one of its goals building such skills. One might then think of measuring the quality of bibliographic instruction, in part, by its success in improving the quality of subject searching.

To measure the quality of subject access, then, seems to require controlling for a specific skill of library users, namely the ability to define a well-focused topic. Such an attribute would seem difficult to measure in the aggregate. Once measured, however, one would expect to be able to look for the linkage between investments in reference materials and electronic reference tools, the nature of subject searching supported in the catalog, and the quality of subject bibliographies generated by typical users. Once the linkage is established, one might then hope to measure the amount of time required to achieve a particular quality level of bibliography. One might then consider the effect of instruction.

Where compact disks are aggressively deployed, they quickly become the tool of choice for subject searching in an article literature. Should OCLC successfully and inexpensively provide online end-user subject access to its full database, subject searching will change in an important way. The quality of bibliography generated by first-pass subject searching would be very little influenced by the local library's collection. Investigation of the change in subject searching brought about by inexpensive compact disks and simple subject searching of a national bibliographic database might cause a significant change in how library decision makers view their collections. The presumption that subject bibliographies are limited by local holdings might fade.

The quality of service to persons asking reference questions can also be measured. To some degree, the reference desk is a part of the process for finding known items and for preparing bibliographies, and for these, quality might be measured as above. However, some reference questions are an end in themselves, namely, those seeking specific facts. For these questions the time required to get an answer and the accuracy of the answer can be measured.

Most academic libraries provide a substantial amount of study space. Users bring their own materials and find a suitable place to study, whether in groups for interactive study or in quiet areas. A survey of library users can reveal the extent of this activity. It would certainly be possible to monitor peak periods to determine the frequency with which users seek study space and do not find it. A library's use as study space is the main impetus for extending academic library hours. Because study makes so little demand on library service, it is hard to think of a quality dimension of this service worth measuring as a general matter. Of course, lighting and temperature control are important and could be measured, but they have a more general impact than simply on study space.

The level of user activities in a library and important dimensions of quality can be measured. Quality relates primarily to success at finding appropriate things and the time required of users to achieve certain outcomes.

Linking Action to Outcome

The decision maker will want to know how a particular decision will affect library outcomes. How will an extra expenditure on library materials improve success rates at known item searching? How will extra staffing at a reference station affect the quantity and quality of outcomes? How does the performance of the reference station differ between a staff of two graduate students versus one librarian? How will an automated catalog affect the time required to find known items? In each case, a decision to be made might be sharpened or made more confidently if the manager had available some systematic information about the link between action and outcomes.

An observed outcome is the result of an interaction between the behavior of the library and the behavior of users. To predict a particular outcome, say the number of searches, the nature of the behavior of both must be understood. This author has reviewed some of these ideas and the theory of search is well developed in the economics literature, especially as it relates to searching for jobs and for consumer goods.[5] In this essay, the same concepts are applied to library searching.

Think of the number of items sought as the measure of searching activity. A library user will want to seek some number of items per interval of time, say a year. For a faculty member, the number of items sought will likely depend on the person's discipline, teaching assignment, activity in publishing new findings in a discipline, and on the time required to do a search in the library and the probability of success. For students, the number of items sought will likely depend on the students' class assignments, on their motivation for success (perhaps measured by grade point average), on their experience in the library, on the time required to do a search in the library, and on the probability of success. The determinants of library searching should be a well-established part of the scientific knowledge about libraries. Possible relationships are sketched here by way of illustration, but much more thought should go into defining the relationship and perhaps in deriving it from a more elaborate description of how individual users behave and of the structure of how faculty produce new knowledge and of how students study. The resulting relationship could be viewed as the demand for searching in an academic library.

The relationship can be shown in a diagram representing the aggregate behavior of users and the library, as in Figure 1. The horizontal axis shows the number of searches per year by a population of users, and the vertical axis represents the probability of not finding an item that is sought, that is, the probability of a search ending in failure. The space defined by these axes describes the search behavior of library users and the search opportunities provided by the library. In the diagram, the downward sloping curve marked "users' behavior" depicts this behavior pattern of users. It holds constant the time required to complete a search and the attributes of users that determine their desire to search.

The lower the probability of a search ending in failure, the larger the number of searches users will undertake, other things being equal. If the probability of failure is 100 percent, there will likely be zero searches. If the probability of a

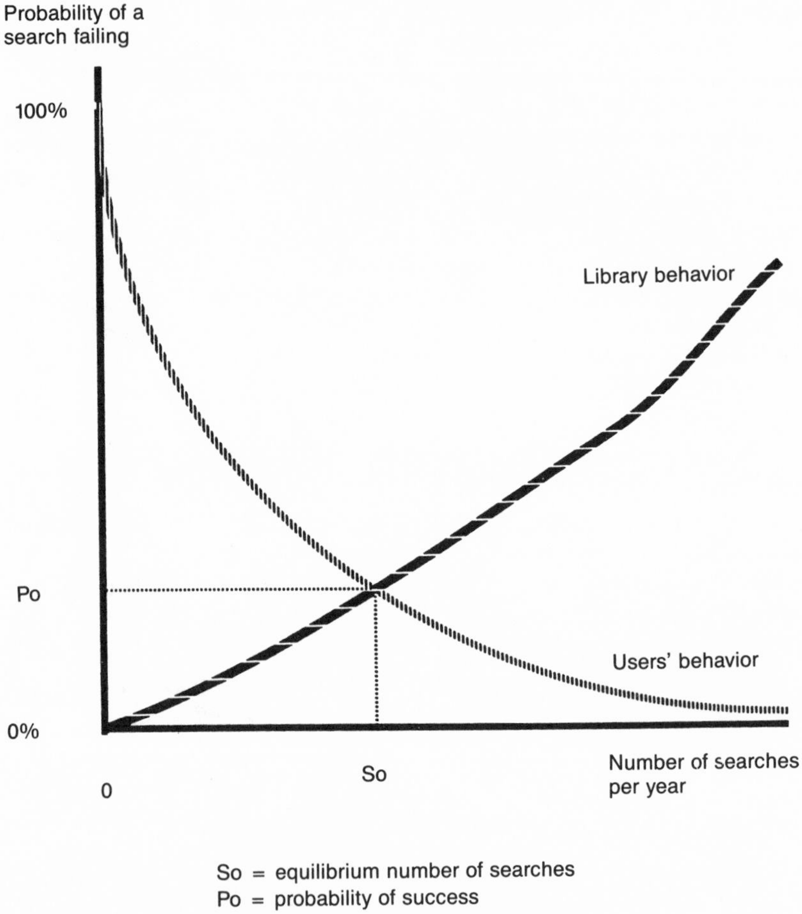

Figure 1. Theory of Search

search ending in failure is zero, then there should be some maximum number of searches, other things being equal.

The upward sloping line marked "library behavior" depicts the search opportunities offered to users by the library. It holds other attributes of the library constant. When there are few searches, the library has a better chance of being able to fulfill the searches, other things being equal, and the probability of a search ending in failure may be low. As the number of searches increases, the library may face progressively higher costs and greater difficulties in sustaining the probability of success. The probability of a search ending in failure may be higher, the larger the number of searches. High rates of use of the library may mean that some materials are unavailable to subsequent searches, and the failure rate may be higher for that reason as well.

The point of intersection of the two lines portrays an equilibrium between users' desires and the opportunities offered by the library. At this point, the probability of a search ending in failure, Po, is such that the quantity of searching users want to undertake, So, is the same as the quantity of searching the library can offer. The equilibrium quantity of searching, So, and the probability of failure in searching, Po, are the only observable quantities. The underlying relationships, that is, the lines, are not directly observable. A very worthwhile object for research would be to observe enough about the quantity of searching, associated probabilities of failure, and the other attributes of libraries and users so as to infer the shapes of the curves depicted schematically in Figure 1.[6]

In drawing the users' behavior line in Figure 1, the time required to complete a search was held constant. Suppose the library adopted an innovation that lowered the time required to complete a search. Such an innovation would lead to an upward shift in the users' behavior line in Figure 1, yielding a situation as shown in Figure 2. If the shapes of the curves drawn schematically are correct, a new equilibrium with a higher quantity of searches and a higher probability of failure on a given search will be seen.

This is exactly the pattern in searching and success rates found in tracking these phenomena at Vanderbilt as it introduced its electronic catalog and circulation system.[7] The investigations at Vanderbilt refer to only one library and they represent at most the observation of three individual points in the space of Figure 1. The position of an individual library at a given point in time is illustrated by a single point in the diagram. The study at three points in time at Vanderbilt is too meager to establish general principles about the nature of user and library behavior sufficient to yield compelling predictions for a class of libraries. However, it does establish that linkages between library action and library outcomes can be observed. As more libraries routinely measure number of searches and failure (or success) rates for searching, more points in the Figure 1 space will appear. In time and with more sophisticated analytic methods, a clearer sense of the nature of user behavior and of library behavior will be gained.

A library might lower its failure rates by increasing the size of its collections or by investing in higher quality cataloging. Such changes would shift the library behavior line down, pivoting on zero as shown in Figure 3. Such a change would be expected to yield a higher number of searches and a lower rate of failure in searching. The decline in the failure rate will not be as dramatic as would be the case had the number of searches not increased.

Studies of how the quantity of searching and the rate of failure of searches

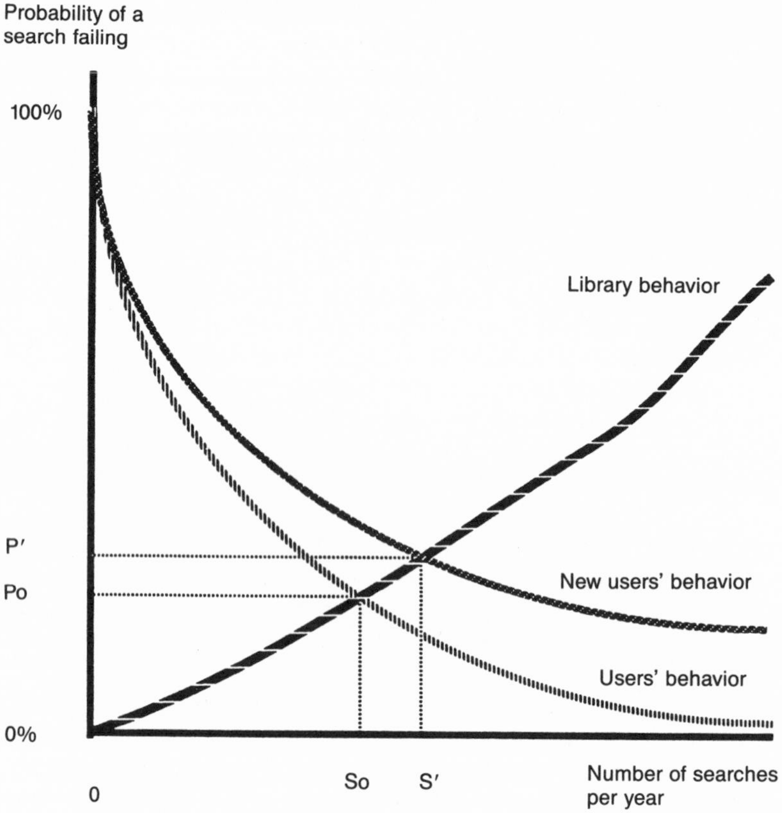

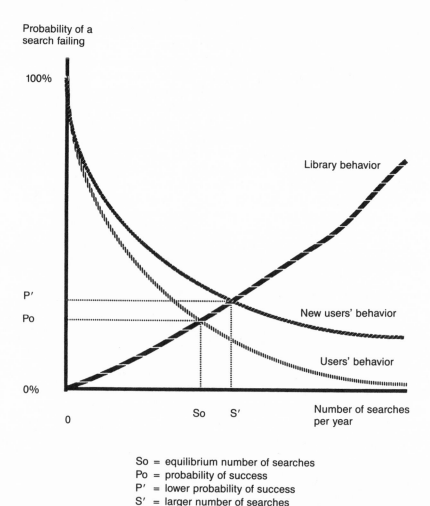

So = equilibrium number of searches
Po = probability of success
P′ = lower probability of success
S′ = larger number of searches

Figure 2. Search with an Innovation

have changed as a consequence of a change in library operations are relatively rare. Saracevic, Shaw, and Kantor measured book availability during a period of a semester loan and then again after a shift to a four-week loan at Case Western Reserve Library, finding that the shorter loan period increased availability.[8] The authors did not comment on the effect of the increase in book availability on the level of use of the library. Their data show a 20 percent increase in successful searches following the change in policy. This change is consistent with a shift of the library behavior line in Figure 1.

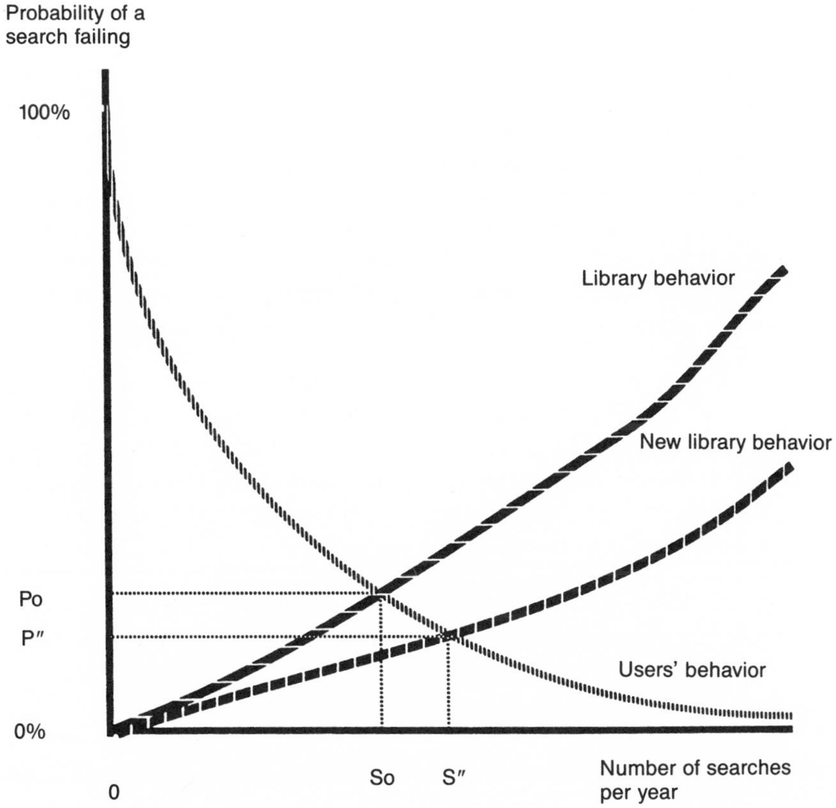

So = equilibrium number of searches
Po = probability of success
P″ = higher probability of success
S″ = larger number of searches

Figure 3. Search with a Larger Collection

Changes in users can also cause changes in the number of searches and the success rate. Suppose a college brings new emphasis to writing by introducing a curricular change that causes students to be assigned to write many more essays. The users' behavior line would shift upward as shown in Figure 2, leading to an increased number of searches and an increased failure rate. No systematic study could be found that relates changes in user attributes and behavior to the quantity of searches and the probability of search failure in academic libraries.

With some thought, behavioral relationships similar to those in Figure 1 might be defined for each library outcome. Changes in library operations can then be seen to cause changes in behavior that lead to changes in observed outcomes. Once the theoretical relationships are defined as in Figure 1, the linkages between library action and library outcomes as libraries make particular changes can be observed. Changes in library operations then become natural experiments that can yield observations about the linkage between a change in library operations and a change in library outcomes. In this way, empirically grounded insights can be made into the linkages between expenditures in libraries and library outcomes.

The boldest effort to estimate causal linkages for libraries makes enough progress that other investigators can refine the techniques so as to establish relationships with enough detail to be useful to managers. Hayes, Pollack and Nordhaus estimated a linkage between library inputs and outputs.[9] This study is a pioneering effort to establish such causal linkages for academic libraries but it is severely limited by its reliance on statistics published by the Association of Research Libraries. The study assumes that libraries deploy capital and labor as inputs to produce a measurable output using the same method that others have used to estimate how much corn a farm might produce with labor, land, and fertilizer as inputs. Over the last decade, farmers have turned to computer-based mathematical models of their farms for support in making managerial decisions. Intuition, tradition, and trial-and-error proved insufficient managerial techniques to satisfy farm lenders. The Hayes study is a first effort to seek a mathematical model for academic libraries to support managerial decisions.

The study falls short of being useful to managers for several reasons. First, it is uncertain about what to measure as the library's output and gives three alternatives. The number of new Ph.D.s awarded by the university might be viewed as one of the outputs of the university but to treat it as simply the output of the library ignores the role of the faculty and of other facilities. A second output might be the number of faculty, but libraries do not produce faculty. The third output might be the number of interlibrary loans, but interlibrary loan transactions are typically less than 5 percent of local circulation transactions and are probably not well correlated with them. Thus, the measures of outputs Hayes uses do not relate well to what most library managers would find central.

Sensing the shortcoming, Hayes goes on to estimate a university production function with number of faculty and size of library collection as inputs and Ph.D.s produced and faculty publications as two alternative measures of output. This latter effort gets closer to a production function for a university in that Ph.D.s and faculty publications are two observable outputs of universities, and faculty and library collections are two important inputs. However, undergraduate degrees and professional school degrees are also important outputs, and the several outputs should be treated as joint products. Many observers would note that quality in a university is very important and so would be wary of a study that considers only quantities of degrees and publications. Moreover, the estimation of a production function for a university leaves library issues largely in the background.

A second problem for Hayes's study may be that the number of units of output may not be determined exclusively by library decisions. Rather, the behavior of library users may be an important determinant, as suggested above. If so, then the estimation method should take account of the simultaneity.

Third, the study does not define input variables that are much subject to control by library managers and so the study proves of little use to managers. Contrast Hayes's method with this author's study of the branches of the New York Public Library, an investigation that takes explicit account of the simultaneity of user and library behavior, that is detailed with respect to individual library branches, and that focuses on elements of library operation that are immediately in the hands of library mangers, namely, hours, books added, and books in stock.[10]

Valuing Changes in Outcomes

Having measured outcomes and established causal linkages between a change in library operation and one or more outcomes, the problem of valuing the outcome is considered. If a library takes an action that increases the number of searches by its users by 100,000 per year, has it made a good decision, that is, a decision that increases the value of library services net of costs? Are the 100,000 added searches worth the extra cost associated with the library's action, for example, in providing dial-up access to an electronic catalog or in introducing keyword searching to an electronic catalog?

The values here are those of the decision makers. The people who decide how much and where to spend funds are making decisions that reflect their valuations in dollar terms. Such decision makers, however, may be acting in behalf of those who use libraries. Often, a decision maker will have in mind how users view the library. Users may reveal how they value particular library services in their behavior. For example, people usually are willing to pay more to save time in achieving a particular outcome; time saving would have an implicit dollar value. The dollar value associated with time saved by library users from a particular change in library operations may be useful in assigning values to changes in library use. The better the information decision makers have about how library users value outcomes, the better the decisions they may make about investments in libraries. Thus, the initial concern for the values of those who pay may translate to the implicit values in dollar terms of those who use libraries.

Dollar values need to be assigned to outcomes and to costs so that they can be compared, even if the valuations are implicit. Most decisions effect incremental changes, whose costs can be identified. Although normal accounting systems give some information useful for determining costs, most accounting systems are designed primarily for financial control and do a relatively poor job of informing managerial decisions about incremental changes in operation. Therefore, some special effort will be required to determine the cost of extra labor, including fringe benefits, training, and supervision costs. The cost of space is often not recorded in accounting systems when buildings are owned. The most appropriate way of valuing the cost of space may be to consider the cost of leasing comparable space or to define the lease value of constructing and operating comparable space. A collection might be valued in aggregate terms by replacement prices plus the cost of processing the materials into the library's collection. The concept of cost as relevant to decision making often requires special care, because the relevant consideration is: How will costs change if a certain action is taken? Because libraries pay for most of the items used, there is at least some market price information available as a starting point for defining costs.

It is difficult to assign dollar values to changes in benefit resulting from changes in outcomes because relevant market prices are seldom near at hand. Newhouse and Alexander developed the value to users for the circulation of a book from a public library by reference to the price of new books in bookstores.[11] They argue that the next best alternative to use of the library's book may be the purchase of a personal copy. Although that notion may have some utility for academic libraries, it seems significantly more relevant to public libraries.

Academic libraries might use the user's implicit valuation of time to define values of changes in library outcomes.[12] When the library outcome itself is measured conveniently by a change in the time required by a user, as with an electronic catalog, then valuation of the outcome in terms of the value of an increment of the user's time seems reasonable. The implicit value of time has played an important role in economic analysis of consumer behavior for many years.[13] Here, read library users as consumers. Getz has suggested an experiment that might be conducted in libraries to determine more directly how library users value their time.[14]

Much less satisfactory is the inference of the value of a library task according to the amount of time required to complete it. One can assume the value of a search from the amount of time required to complete it and argue that the last search a user undertakes must be worth at least as much as the amount of time required to complete it. Using the implicit value of time to estimate the implicit value of a search is much less direct than one would like. Future thought may find new ways to infer the value of specific changes in library outcomes.

Academic library services have a topography, and changes in topography may create changes in travel patterns that give some special opportunities for valuing changes in outcomes. On some campuses, library service is concentrated in a single, large facility. On other campuses, libraries are dispersed, school by school and even department by department. The open or closing of an individual location will cause the rate of library use to change: more convenient locations will tend to be used more. The convenience of a location might be measured by the distances people walk or travel to get to the facility. The economic literature on the value of time spent walking or riding buses or automobiles may then have direct applicability in valuing the convenience of library service. As more library service is delivered to individual user's desks electronically, as with dial-up access to electronic catalogs, the notion of the value of travel time in valuing benefits might be used.

In the three parts of an analytic approach to academic library decisions, the most important is the measurement of outcomes. Without well-defined measures of outcomes, the other parts cannot proceed. Existing library research has had reasonable success in measuring outcomes, but more can be done. The second part is the determination of linkages between decisions and changes in outcomes. Library research has seldom attempted to establish such linkages. The third part is the valuation of changes in outcomes in dollar terms as users or decisions makers see them. Establishing dollar values for products and services that are both complex and not traded in markets is a difficult task in any setting and existing library research is weak. Improvements in all three parts, however, are clearly possible and desirable.

An Illustration: Evaluating Collections

A very important area of research is the evaluation of collections. The analytic techniques for evaluating collections will be revolutionized in the next decade as a consequence of the introduction of new tools. Martin Dillon and David Stephens, both of OCLC, are the leading figures in this movement.[15] This essay concludes with a discussion of these exciting new directions in research on collections as a way of illustrating the themes described above. Collections remain the central determinant of library costs and of the benefit of libraries. More sophisticated methods for evaluating collections decisions may substantially increase the scope and influence of formal analysis in decision making in libraries. Charles Osburn's essay in this volume reviews the existing literature on collection analysis.

The total collection in a library is a stock that may be measured in snapshot form at any instant, often at year end. A library manager can influence the stock of materials only by making adjustments in the flow of materials into and out of the stock over an interval of time. For example, to get a larger stock, the library might increase the flow of materials added to the collection per year, or it might decrease the flow of materials deleted from the collection per year.

Some costs are related to the size of the stock, most notably, the cost of space devoted to storing it. Most library costs, however, are defined by the flow of materials into the collection. The purchase of materials accounts for 30 percent or so of the total operating expenses of many academic libraries. The size of the flow of new material also defines the cost of the staff to select, order, and process the added materials. The increased space required to house the added materials with the flow might be defined as well. Space tends to be added episodically rather than incrementally and the capital costs of added space are not generally included in operating budgets, so the calculation of the increased cost of space to house the material added in a given year may require some interpolation from a longer run perspective. The cost of the flow of materials into a collection probably exceeds 50 percent of the total annual cost of most ongoing library operations. If a library ceased to add materials entirely, its operating budget including materials and staff could probably be cut in half.

The value of a library collection may also be defined by the current flow of materials into the collection as well as by the size of the total stock. Books and periodicals are most valuable when they are new. Philip Morse defines the half life of a book as the number of years from publication within which half the people who will ever read the book will have read it.[16] The half life for scientific materials is under three years. The half life for literature and history may be under five years. Automated acquisition and circulation systems should be able to estimate half lifes in considerable detail.

For most academic libraries, the value of a collection will be greater, the larger the flow of new materials. A library that ceased all current acquisitions would yield sharply reduced benefits within a year or two, perhaps much more than half of its value.

The first principle of the analysis of collections then is that analysis should focus on decisions made about current collecting. Current collecting is the arena where managers can make decisions; prior collecting decisions cannot practically be redone. Current collecting is the most important determinant of costs and current collecting is the single most important determinant of the value of a library's collection.

A second principle is that analysis should be detailed by discipline and subdiscipline. Academic institutions are organized by disciplines, they define programs by disciplines, and they attract faculty and even students with disciplinary interests. Universities, specifically, offer doctoral work in some disciplines and not in others. Within a discipline, most departments emphasize some subdisciplines over others. The benefit of a particular collecting effort can be considered in light of programmatic interests in the institution by being disaggregated to the discipline and subdiscipline level. Similarly, the institution's revenues are often linked to particular disciplines, as for example, via enrollments, research dollars, or even endowments. Analysis of collections at a disaggregated level can allow the analyst to examine the link between collecting effort and programmatic emphasis.

The third principle of the analysis of collections is that decisions about monographs should be analyzed differently than decisions about periodicals and other serials. Although libraries regularly move funds between serials and monograph budgets, the pattern of decision making is usually different enough to justify separate analysis. Decisions about periodical titles, in particular, are made less frequently than decisions about monographs. Once a subscription begins, a positive decision is usually required to terminate the title. Because serials often command two to four times the budget share of monographs, perhaps serials should be the central arena for collections analysis. Because serials offer shorter publication cycles and are more widely read than monographs in many disciplines, the serials are more important on the benefit side as well.

An analysis that follows these three principles would then give primary emphasis to current collecting, it would be detailed by discipline and subdiscipline, and it would differentiate monographs and serials. The analysis should chart the link from dollars of cost to put materials in hand to the value of the materials to the institution's missions.

The OCLC Office of Research has demonstrated a prototype tool for analyzing recent collecting of monographs. This description refers in part to the prototype and in part to the potential offered by tools of this kind. The tool includes a compact disk with brief bibliographic data for all titles in the OCLC database with LC call numbers, perhaps 2 million in number. The CD database includes a count of the number of libraries in individual peer groups that hold each title (as defined by the OCLC holdings symbol). Several peer groups are defined, for example, private universities that are members of ARL and OCLC might be one group, prestigious liberal arts colleges might be another, regional public comprehensive universities might be a third. The tool includes a floppy disk that indicates the titles held by the library that is the target of the analysis. Microcomputer software presents a menu to the analyst to define a discipline or subdiscipline in terms of LC call number range, to compute statistics on holdings that compare the target with any of the various peer groups, and to generate lists of titles on demand.

A person analyzing a collection in a given subdiscipline, such as Latin American anthropology, can:

1. Discover the number of titles in the OCLC universe of recently published titles
2. Compute the proportion of this universe held by the target library

3. Identify the number of titles in this universe held by any given percentage of a particular peer group (thus defining core titles)
4. Identify the proportion of these core titles held by the target library
5. Identify the number of titles purchased by the target that are not in the core.

In this way, the analyst can identify how the recent monographic collecting effort relates to the size of the bibliographic universe in the field, how the target collection relates to the collecting patterns of peer libraries, and how focused the target's purchases have been in core titles.

With an acquisition accounting system that allows mapping dollars of monographic expenditures to LC call number ranges, one can learn how many dollars have been devoted to recent acquisitions in a given range. The system should also reveal an average cost per title in the range. In this way, the analyst can identify the cost of achieving a particular degree of coverage. Next, an analyst can define how many more titles would likely be required to increase coverage to any desired degree, or how coverage would fall with a particular budget cut. With knowledge of programmatic emphases in the school, one would expect a collection budget officer to be able to manage expenditure commitments so as to match coverage to institutional goals.

With annual updates and the ability to narrow the analysis to particular publication years, the analytic tool might allow the collection manager to monitor progress. In year one, the manager commits additional funds to Afro-American history and reduces funds for Latin American anthropology. The analytic tool allows the manager to forecast how the budget shift will affect the coverage in the two disciplines. In year two (or perhaps three or four, given the lags in acquisitions and in the analytic tool itself), the manager can review the coverage in the two disciplines and discover how the budgetary shift actually affected coverage. The analytic tool then allows review of past decisions even as it provides forecasts useful for current decisions.

A circulation system might reveal how many recent titles in a given subdiscipline have been used. (Are circulation systems ever used to register reshelving of books used internally?) One might then compare programmatic emphasis, patterns of use in circulation, and the degree of coverage achieved in collecting with subdiscipline detail. One might think of investigating the link between the collecting coverage in a discipline and the probability of success in known item searching in that discipline.

Finally, one might think of identifying how sources in a particular discipline are used. In economics, this author's native discipline, there is general agreement about the top ten journals. For a recent year, this author examined the bibliographies in a random sample of articles from these journals. The bibliographic citations were sorted by type: journal article, monograph, government document, and the like, and the number of the citations held by the

Vanderbilt library was determined. This analysis gives insight into the mix of serials and monographs, it can reveal the role of English and non-English materials, and it can reveal the role of published and unpublished materials. Such citation analysis might be useful in evaluating the coverage levels for particular disciplines. Paul Metz's essay in this volume reviews studies of library use.

An analytic tool for investigating serials of the same power and sophistication as OCLC's tool for monographs has yet to be developed. Nevertheless, such a tool is likely to come forward soon.

The advent of OCLC's collection analysis system and similar products from others promises to bring analytic tools and perspectives into the kit bag of library managers in a direct way. The linkage between expenditure and result can be understood more clearly. Library collecting can be managed in ways that yield more valuable library services for a given budgetary commitment. When analytic approaches to collecting are routine, analysis in other areas of library service will be easier.

Other Research Frontiers

Analytic support for collection policies is of central importance to improved libraries. Next in importance might be analytic support for decisions about the intensity of cataloging and database maintenance. Do modern electronic catalogs with keyword searching and automatic cross-references substitute for the library's investment in quality cataloging and database maintenance? If the software is so powerful, the university may be better off with lower cost technical services. On the other hand, automatic cross-references and relatively unstructured keyword searching may lead to bizarre hits and a large number of unwanted citations captured in a given search. If the latter effect dominates, then investment in database development and maintenance may complement powerful software. Investigations that would establish the relative costs of database maintenance and the advantages of a high quality database given sophisticated search software have the potential of having very great influence in libraries.

Libraries can deliver more information via networks to offices and dormitory rooms across campus. Online catalogs, article level files in mainframe environments, compact disk-based products connected to a network, full-text reference tools and research databases, all could be made available on a campus network. What information should be maintained locally, what should be left to national services, what information products will individuals buy and maintain personally? The costs of telecommunications, computing, and data storage are changing rapidly enough to make forecasts of relative costs desirable for decision making. What niche should local academic libraries claim in the electronic arena? Jo Bell Whitlatch's essay in this volume reviews the existing literature on library access. Investigations of relative costs and benefits that address this important set of managerial issues may have substantial effect on libraries as well.

Conclusion

Careful measurement of library outcomes, attentive observation of the causal linkages between changes in library operations and the changes in outcomes they cause, and thoughtful investigation of the values library users place on the changes in outcomes can provide fresh insights into library operations. The new insights can be helpful to library managers, sharpening decision making. With such tools, managers may induce a library budget to yield more valuable library services. Indeed, an essentially analytic tool like OCLC's collection analysis prototype may well become a standard feature of collection management in academic libraries.

The introduction to this volume poses three questions about research relevant to academic libraries. First, what has research shown that is relevant to managing libraries? Second, why is past effort of limited interest to managers? Third, what avenues will prove most fruitful for future research? This essay draws attention to the specification and empirical estimation of causal, behavioral relationships that describe the link between actions library managers may take and the changes in outcomes for library users that result. It emphasizes the importance to managers of incremental decisions about library operations and thereby defines a goal for research on academic libraries. Specific research questions are mentioned throughout the essay as well as in the section on other research frontiers. Previous research is of limited value because it does not define and estimate causal, behavioral relationships. Future research will be more helpful when it explores such behavioral linkages. In particular, scientific quality investigations of academic libraries and their users could inform decisions about collections, new technologies, investments in library structures, and staffing. Such research is expensive and difficult. However, such research holds the prospect of changing the academic library from a managerial "black box" to an "open book."

Notes

1. In using these definitions of efficiency and effectiveness, I reflect the tradition of welfare economics, especially as applied in the analysis of the benefits and costs of public services. See Robert Dorfman, ed., *Measuring the Benefits of Government Investments* (Washington, D.C.: Brookings, 1965), or E. J. Mishan, *Cost-Benefit Analysis; an Introduction* (New York: Praeger, 1971). These definitions differ appreciably from those of Peter Drucker, *Management: Tasks, Responsibilities,*

Practices (New York: Harper & Row, 1974), pp. 45–46. Drucker's redefinition of the terms are difficult to quantify and so have less usefulness in analytic research than the conventional definitions.

2. Malcolm Getz and Doug Phelps, "Labor Costs in the Technical Operation of Three Research Libraries," *Journal of Academic Librarianship* 10 (September 1984): 209–219; Paul B. Kantor, "Cost of Monographic Acquisitions and Processing," a study undertaken for the Council on Library Resources, as discussed in Martin M. Cummings, *The Economics of Research Libraries* (Washington, D.C.: Council on Library Resources, 1986), pp. 24–28.

3. In defining causal linkages, we are creating a theory of libraries by deducing relationships from theories of human and organizational behavior. Statistical correlations cannot prove the existence of any causal relationship. They can, however, disprove them. If statistical correlations are consistent with our theoretical expectations about causality, we gain more confidence in our theory. We may also use the specific values of the statistics in defining concrete estimates of the likely magnitudes of the causal linkages. Such estimates may be useful in making forecasts about how a particular decision may affect an outcome. Hypotheses about causal relationships are, then, essential ingredients in the empirical study of libraries, even though statistics themselves can not establish causality.

4. Paul B. Kantor, *Objective Performance Measures for Academic and Research Libraries* (Washington, D.C.: Association of Research Libraries, 1984).

5. Malcolm Getz, "Some Benefits of the Online Catalog," *College & Research Libraries* 48 (May 1987): 224–240; C. J. McKenna, "Theories of Individual Search Behavior," *Bulletin of Economic Research* 38 (Fall 1986): 189–207.

6. The hypotheses about user and library behavior could be stated in the form of implicit functions: User behavior: Searches = f(time to search, probability of success, user attributes). Library time behavior: Time to search = g(Library attributes). Library success behavior: Searches = h(Probability of success, library attributes). Searches, Time to Search, and the Probability of success are simultaneously determined. Library and User attributes are taken as given. In drawing Figure 1, the Time to Search equation is substituted into the first equation, allowing the depiction of two simultaneous equations and an equilibrium.

7. Malcolm Getz, "More Benefits of Automation," *College & Research Libraries* 48 (November 1988): 534–544.

8. T. Saracevic, W. M. Shaw, Jr., and P. B. Kantor, "Causes and Dynamics of User Frustration in an Academic Library," *College & Research Libraries* 38 (January 1977): 7–18.

9. Robert M. Hayes, Ann M. Pollack, and Shirley Nordhaus, "An Application of the Cobb-Douglas Model to the Association Research Libraries," *Library & Information Science Research* 5 (Fall 1983): 291–325.

10. Malcolm Getz, *Public Libraries: An Economic View* (Baltimore: Johns Hopkins Univ. Pr., 1980), Chapter 4.

11. Joseph P. Newhouse and Arthur J. Alexander, *An Economic Analysis of Public Library Services* (Lexington, Mass.: Lexington, 1972).

12. Getz, "Some Benefits of the Online Catalog."

13. Gary S. Becker, "A Theory of the Allocation of Time," *The Economic Journal* 74 (September 1965): 493–517.

14. Malcolm Getz, "Increasing the Value of User Time," *The Bottom Line* 1 (1987): 37–39.

15. Martin Dillon et al., "Design Issues for a Microcomputer-based Collection Analysis System," *Microcomputers for Information Management* 5: 263–273.

16. Philip M. Morse, *Library Effectiveness: A Systems Approach* (Cambridge, Mass.: MIT Pr., 1968).

Beverly P. Lynch

Management Theory and Organizational Structure

Academic libraries have grown in size and complexity over the last fifty years, developing into what now are truly complex organizations. Like managers of other complex organizations, the managers of these libraries have looked to the writings of organizational theorists, based chiefly on studies of large corporations, to find ways of understanding management issues. Textbooks on library management have proliferated. These textbooks, as well as the writings of managers outside the field, have influenced the thinking of many library managers more than has any research in librarianship.

Two schools of thought, reflecting the theoretical base of organizational study since the 1950s, have dominated the textbooks and thus the study of library organization and management. One is the rational model exemplified in the work of the classical management theorists such as Frederick Taylor and Max Weber. The model emphasizes the importance of organizational structure and methods of coordination and control in the attainment of goals. The other model is the human relations approach reflected in the work of theorists such as Abraham Maslow and Douglas McGregor. This model focuses on identifying the needs of the people who work in organizations and tailoring the work to fit those needs. An emerging theme is the political approach, which emphasizes the consideration of organizational conflict and the use of power in the allocation of scarce resources.[1] While most academic libraries operate within highly political environments, it has only been recently that attention has turned to those environments. Most library managers and students of library management still look to the rational model to understand the library organization and to the human relations model to understand why people who work in libraries behave the way they do. The political model has yet to be assimilated into the field; it offers much promise.[2]

The literature on management of academic libraries is large and diverse, and is comprised, by and large, of expert opinion. Little of this literature has a research orientation. The research that does exist is reported, for the most part, in doctoral dissertations and master's theses. These reports, unless revised and published in the journal literature, have little impact on the field as it is practiced. Of the 1848 doctoral dissertations and theses written for degrees granted between 1970 and 1985 that are listed in UMI's catalog, *Library and Information Science*, 370 (20 percent) are listed under the heading "academic and research libraries."[3] Many of these investigations remain locked in the dissertation format, and few of them have been revised for publication and published in the literature of the field, so the impact on the field of research carried out at the doctoral level is less than it might be. Thus, the librarian's understanding of library organization is influenced by textbooks on library management, collections of readings, the journal literature (which is primarily expert opinion), and intuitive judgment.

The topic of job satisfaction provides a useful example of the problem. As of 1987, a total of fourteen studies on job satisfaction in libraries had been published in the journal literature.[4] Job satisfaction is an important issue to many library managers and a relatively easy topic to study since there are valid and reliable measures of job satisfaction that have been widely tested and used and the variables that impact on job satisfaction are easy to measure and to correlate. Five of the published fourteen studies originated in Ph.D. dissertations that were subsequently revised and published as articles. Between 1970 and 1987, however, over a dozen other dissertations on job satisfaction in academic libraries can be easily identified; no doubt, there are more. What impact have these other research investigations on job satisfaction in libraries had on the field? One can only respond, very little. The difficulty for the practitioner is that a dissertation is not in a format that generates any interest. Unless the research is rewritten as a paper for publication in the journal literature, the results of the study are not disseminated into the field; the research is not tested against the practical wisdom of the field; and it does not make much of an impact on librarianship as it is practiced. Because this author believes that research must be reported in the journal literature to be useful, this chapter considers primarily research reported in that format.

Much of the research on libraries as organizations is applied research, that is, investigations that seek to find out what is happening in other libraries or to improve the services provided. The "why" of what is happening is rarely considered. As one author put it, "Library science is an applied field and not a basic branch of knowledge. Society does not care for a better theory of library science per se. The only reason that better theory and greater knowledge of libraries is desirable from society's vantage point is that more effective and/or efficient library service will flow therefrom."[5]

From this viewpoint it is easy to see why many observers suggest that research in librarianship should emanate from practice, that the practitioner should determine the kind of investigations that would be fruitful. Whether such investigations are cumulative or whether they lead to theory construction or the development of models is of less interest to the practitioner than is the answer to practical questions of local interest. Some library researchers are tempted to make their work acceptable to the field as it is practiced by "tacking on" applications to a study that by its nature could not be defined as applied research but would be closer to basic research. The final paragraph in a good study on job satisfaction provides an example:

> It appears, therefore, that there is an integral relationship between a supervisory climate which is conducive to the exercise of individual initiative and professional judgment and the librarian's experience of mastering a job. These two dimensions are, in turn, most strongly related to the degree of job satisfaction reportedly experienced by the librarians in the study. These results tend to indicate that a participatory administrative style, or perhaps even a laissez-faire style, is conducive to job satisfaction among librarians. They also suggest that an assessment of job satisfaction among the personnel of a library would be a useful diagnostic tool for evaluating the performance of library administrators. In order to facilitate the diagnostic review, it would be advisable *to develop standardized instruments for measuring job satisfaction among librarians and for measuring the characteristics operating in the job environments of librarianship. Such standardized instrumentation would lend itself to the development of normative data against which the data generated by local librarians could be compared for diagnostic purposes.* [emphasis added][6]

A fine study is potentially diminished in the eye of the practitioner when an intuitively incorrect application is imposed. In this case, the investigator assumes that instruments can be developed that will measure systematically the job satisfaction among librarians and assumes that individual measures will cumulate into a single score for a given library. He goes further in assuming that a norm can be identified, that local data developed by librarians can be matched against a national norm, and that a library thus can be evaluated as being higher or lower on satisfaction than the national norm. The studies on job satisfaction as well as common sense would probably lead most practitioners to disagree with these assumptions and thus to ignore the proposed application to practice.

The study of libraries as organizations is hampered by the cost of large-scale comparative investigations. A few such studies have been done, but the prevalent method is to survey individuals in many libraries by questionnaire in order to compare individual characteristics, not organizational ones. Most studies on job satisfaction in libraries, for example, have been at the individual level, with the investigator studying librarians as an occupational group. The possible variations in satisfaction by work setting is considered in only four of the fourteen studies reviewed. Longitudinal investigations on organizational structure of libraries are almost nonexistent. Only one such study has been completed, and it is yet unpublished.[7]

Existing research on management issues and on organizational structure in libraries consists of practical problem-solving studies, explanatory studies, and predictive investigations leading to theoretical models. The base of library research in matters pertaining to the complexity of organizations is grounded in the social sciences; most of the theory is derived from other fields. While the base of the research is outside of librarianship, making the task of research more difficult, the task is nonetheless valuable and rewarding. Regrettably, there is not very much research. What the literature of librarianship provides is surveys of practice, speculation about that practice, and recommendations regarding suitable organizational and management strategies. What research there is has been promising. Unfortunately, little of it has been replicated, little of it has been synthesized or popularized for the practitioner, and little of it has made its way into the textbooks on library management.

This chapter reviews the research on management theory and organizational structure of libraries that forms the base of research on libraries as complex organizations for the next decade. Since the research in libraries as organizations is often shaped by research in other fields, that work is also considered where appropriate.

The thesis and dissertation literature on the organizational structure of academic libraries was consulted in the preparation of this chapter chiefly to identify the theoretical perspectives used by the various authors and to determine whether major hypotheses posed by sociologists and organizational theorists were tested in any of the investigations of libraries. The journal literature also was reviewed for research on the questions posed by the Association of Research Libraries (ARL) and the Council on Library Resources (CLR) that are appended to this chapter.

Libraries as Complex Organizations

This chapter reflects the author's interest in the study of complex organizations from the sociological perspective. Issues are discussed that pertain to the goals and the missions of academic libraries, the technology or the nature of the work, the environments of libraries, and innovation in libraries, in addition to the various complex issues of the social structures of organizations.

Organizational structure is a common theme throughout this chapter. Many observers, within and without the profession, assume that libraries are inflexible in their structures and so bureaucratic in their organizational design that organizational change is inhibited. Students of organizations, however, observe that organizations change quite routinely as a function of the basic ways in which they behave, how they respond to their environments, and how they learn.[8] It is this perspective of routine change that guides the discussion.

Sociologists who study organizations define structure somewhat differently than do most managers and librarians. Hage and Aiken, basing their work in the theory of Weber, as have most of the other investigators, define structure in terms of (1) organizational complexity, that is, the level of knowledge and expertise in an organization; (2) centralization, defined as the degree of participation in decision making; (3) formalization, the number of rules and the degree of job codification; and (4) stratification, referring to the distribution of rewards.[9] There is agreement among sociologists that organizational structure is comprised of several dimensions, and the first three definitions by Hage and Aiken are commonly accepted. Measurement issues that flow from structure are not as easily agreed upon.[10]

This approach to organizational structure offers some promise in furthering our understanding of libraries as complex organizations that are constantly changing to meet new challenges. For most library managers, however, structure is not identified as a multiple dimensional variable requiring investigation, but is understood in terms of the library's organization chart.[11] The chart is useful in showing who reports to whom and in suggesting issues pertaining to the communication and coordination within the organization. Sometimes the organization chart is used as a measure of centralization. It does not show what Scott refers to as the peripheral structure and does little to inform the observer about power relationships, about the complexity or the simplicity of the work, and about the centrality of decision making or the location of the decisions in terms of the allocation of scarce resources.[12] Environmental interactions and influences are not displayed. The organization chart places a boundary around the organization that may be incorrect. It suggests that the internal aspects of the organization can be easily separated from the external ones. In terms of today's academic libraries, the boundaries are permeable, and it is not easy to define the organization. The conflict and uncertainty created by ambiguous organizational boundaries are topics yet to be studied systematically.

Hage and Aiken's definitions of structure formed the base of Helen Howard's investigation of four university libraries.[13] Howard's investigation treats structural variables as the independent variables, seeking to find a relationship to the dependent variable, the rate of innovation in libraries. She defines innovation as the mean number of new products or services as distinct from expansion or modification of something already in existence.

Other investigators of structure in libraries explore the relationships of structure as the dependent variable. Sloan, in a dissertation on the organization of collection development in university libraries, finds that the rate of change variable appears to be related to different types of organizational structure.[14] She neither explores nor probes the relationship.

In the course of her work, Sloan describes three basic designs for the organization of collection development common in ARL libraries in the early 1970s. Practitioners, seeking rational models of organization and new organization charts, and influenced by Sloan's work, continue to survey libraries to determine appropriate patterns of organization. Sohn is quite straightforward in her survey, asking, "In what major unit is collection development placed?" and "Has the structure of organizational placement of the collection development unit changed in your library since 1975?" She follows up with other questions relating to decision making in selection and in budget allocation and expenditures.[15] Her survey is a good example of the practitioner systematically seeking answers to practical questions.

Bryant, also seeking a rational model of organization, is motivated by an interest in finding the one best way to organize so as to enhance the power of the collection development function within the library.[16] Her paper, reviewed from the research point of view, offers some hypotheses suitable for investigation. She says that "collection development can account for as much as one–third of a library's total operating budget. One could suppose that this placed the collection development organization of a library in a unique position of power." Stated in a simple hypothesis, Bryant's statement translates into this formulation:

> The larger the budget of collection development, the greater the power of the collection development unit.

Bryant's interest in a more central place for collection development in the library's organization chart could be expressed as a second hypothesis:

> The closer the unit is to the top administration of the library, the greater the perceived power of the unit.

In Bryant's discussion of collection development as a function, she observes, "The larger a library grows in terms of funding and staff size, the more complex its organizational structure becomes, ultimately deemphasizing the basic functions of the library." This observation refers to the size of the library as the independent variable; complexity is the dependent variable; and both these variables then are expected to influence the variable, power (in Bryant's terms, "deemphasizing the basic function of the library"). Bryant thus proposes a research topic that has an established base in the sociological study of organizations. Her article is a good example of observation in the field, stated as fact, by an expert in the field. Although it offers some interesting hypotheses for investigation, it is not research.

Bryant's article illustrates the practitioner's assumption that the organization chart displays organizational power. More sophisticated analyses of organizational power in libraries would help the field understand the myriad of structures the library uses in designing the organization of library work and why one library organizes one way, and another library, in another way.

One early study on libraries as organizations investigates the impact of size on structure. Spence tries to test Weber's theory of the relationship of organizational size to organizational structure by investigating structure as a multidimensional variable.[17] Spence defines eight characteristics of structure: the complexity of responsibilities, the specialization of staff relations, the professionalism of the staff, the percentage of staff in administrative positions, the span of control in the administrative hierarchy, the rules and regulations, the impersonal detachment in decision making, and the career stability of employees. Despite some flaws in the research design and method, the similarity of the results of Spence's study to the findings of two studies by Peter Blau (who also was investigating Weber's theory on the relationship of size to structure) makes Spence's study one of continuing interest.[18] Both Blau and Spence find high correlations between the professionalization of staff and the size of the organization's administrative component. They both find that organizations that hire experts remain organized in a hierarchical fashion. The interesting question "Why is this so?" remains. This similarity of results makes Spence's study of libraries as bureaucracies useful to students of organizational theory and structure. It is this kind of investigation that needs further attention by the field.

Howard's investigation, the work of Sloan, and that of Spence provide good beginnings for further investigations of the organizational structure of libraries. Each acknowledges structure as a multidimensional variable. Each, unfortunately, studies a homogeneous set of libraries so that variations, by definition, could not emerge. Despite that, the contributions of these investigators are of importance to the future investigations of libraries as complex organizations.

In asking the question "Why this structure?" new directions have emerged in the research on libraries as organizations. Size continues to be an important variable in the study of organizational structure. Technology, or the nature of the work, is another.

Lynch's study on technology in libraries asks the question, "What effect does the nature of the work [her definition of technology] have on structure?"[19] Like Spence, who asked the effect of size upon structure, Lynch was interested primarily in the basic research question and less so in the practical application of the results. Her work shows that the nature of the work varies by library department. Analysis of the effect of technology on structural variables was more inconclusive. A replication of Lynch's study shows a continuing variation on the nature of the work by department. Technology, however, does not emerge as a strong predictor of structure, a result similar to the study of technology and structure in other organizational settings.[20]

The interest in the formal structure of organizations on the part of the field is guided by the concept of achieving specific objectives at minimum cost. The study of formal structure of libraries is motivated by the continuing interest in finding ways to organize the library in order to achieve maximum administrative efficiency.

Several applied investigations that seek practical answers to the question

"What way should we organize?" demonstrate the field's interest in cost effectiveness and the most efficent way for libraries to organize.[21] Rationality dominates much of this research stream. Weber's rational view of organizations remains very influential.[22]

The Library and Its Environment

The study of the environmental context of libraries has begun to interest researchers and will become more popular as it is incorporated more fully into the literature of the field. In investigating the library as organization, the first question must be "What is the organizational boundary?" The next question then is "How is that boundary penetrated?" and the next, "Who are the principal actors?" One synthesis of the environmental approach to the study of libraries as organizations has been published.[23] More comprehensive ones are needed to build a base for systematic investigation.

The important study of the MIT libraries by Raffel and Shishko confronts directly the boundary definition of the library.[24] Library managers know intuitively, and Raffel and Shishko demonstrate, that different groups on a campus have different objectives for the library or have different attitudes about the means to achieve objectives. "How does this impact the library?" and "How does the library organize itself to respond?" are among the research questions to be confronted in investigations on library organization. Raffel and Shishko report that some populations in the library's environment are ignored in favor of others. While attempting an economic assessment at the outset of their study, they conclude that a political analysis, not an economic analysis, would improve decision making. Their assessment of the library in its environment is an important contribution to the field and demonstrates the value of the case study in theory and hypothesis development.

Organizational Change

The literature on innovation and change in organizations provides a base for a new series of investigations. Euster, while studying the role of the academic library director, delves into issues of organizational change and environmental concerns.[25] In her study of the role of the academic library director, she investigates organizational change, a concept related to Howard's rate of innovation. Euster says the data from her study and that of Howard are not comparable because of methodological differences. Euster's conceptualizations, however, are clearly of interest to academic librarians as they seek ways to assimilate organizational change.

The innovation variable needs refinement in its definition and in its measurement. The field, as it is practiced, will continue to be interested in innovation as librarians seek rational ways to incorporate and manage change. That change has been accommodated in libraries without extraordinary upheavals has been chronicled in several case studies. Hyatt and Santiago studied four universities and their libraries to determine how these organizations were coping with the information explosion and the incorporation of major change resulting from library automation.[26] The universities studied were Princeton University, the University of Illinois at Urbana–Champaign, New York University, and the University of Georgia. The investigation, an example of practical research, demonstrates that organizations are constantly changing and responding to their external environments.

Lynch and colleagues described change in the various functional units of the University of Illinois at Chicago over the twenty-five–year history of its library.[27] The case studies of that library are the first step in the development of hypotheses for further studies on how the library responds to its changing environment.

The Influence of Political Science and Public Administration

As library managers seek to understand the effect of public policy on library operations, they will turn to the rich literature that forms the political approach to the study of organizations. Questions pertaining to the allocation of resources, disagreement and conflict over organizational goals, investigations of the power of library managers, and studies in the processes of bargaining, negotiating, and coalition building will emerge.

A few dissertations have appeared in the library field that study the variables of power and decision making.[28] But as Raffel has observed, the study of libraries as organizations has been quite apolitical, and the library literature reflects that observation.[29] Future studies of power in libraries will profit from discussions of power and decision making in the public sector.

Those future studies might explain one of the following theories or propositions that have shaped the political approach to the study of organizations:

> The allocation of scarce resources is the most critical decision made in an organization;
>
> Decisions are made through the formation of various organizational coalitions;
>
> Within the organization individuals and groups differ on values, beliefs and perceptions of reality;
>
> Organizational goals are multiple and conflicting. Decisions about them emerge from the ongoing progress of bargaining and negotiating.[30]

The Continuing Quest for Efficiency

Scientific management, particularly the writings of Taylor, dominated much of the early library management literature.[31] Its influence is still felt in terms of time and motion studies and studies of efficiency. Dougherty and Heinritz acknowledge the library manager's interest in reducing the costs of technical services and in finding ways to make the processing of library materials as efficient and as effective as possible.[32] Librarians' interest in scientific management reflects the use made of the management literature with its emphasis on problem solving and the practical approach to management. The emphasis on production systems and the goal of cost effectiveness are well received by library managers who are concerned about technical services, costs, and the efficient organization of staff.

Job and task analysis also remain popular as libraries seek ways to differentiate between professional and nonprofessional tasks. The Ricking and Booth study came about out of concern both for personnel, their education, and utilization, and for the continuing search to find the best way to design jobs that are efficient and can lead to organizational effectiveness.[33] With so many library jobs in the public sector and with civil service a major factor in many libraries, the task analysis approach to jobs and the redesign of jobs will continue to guide the development in this area.

More by chance than by design, the efforts of Ricking and Booth and others led writers on library management to the human relations school. The works of Drucker, Argyris, McGregor, and Maslow were popularized in the library literature.[34] These psychologists had and still have much appeal. Their theories countered much of the influence of scientific management and began to dominate the thinking of the students of library management. Maslow's needs theory particularly seemed relevant for professionals working in organizational settings. His work and that of the others led library investigators into studies of job satisfaction, quality of working life, and the impact of the work setting on the librarian.

Job Satisfaction

The interest in job satisfaction in libraries comes out of the belief that satisfied workers are more productive and thus the library is more effective. The studies of D'Elia, Lynch and Verdin, and others reflect only a little of the complexity in the study of satisfaction.[35] Marchant's work is more ambitious and was designed to develop a predictive model. The model was tested by Bengston and Shields, one of the few tests of prior research in the field.[36] Marchant and these authors make a valuable research contribution. Given the problems of the methodology, it is not surprising that the test corroborates Marchant's findings. Although Marchant's work was critiqued systematically by Lynch, providing another contribution to the research literature in librarianship, the criticism seemingly made little impact upon the research of the field.[37]

The hypothesis used by Marchant, simply put, is the greater the staff member's participation in decision making (the structural variable), the greater the staff member's job satisfaction (the intervening variable), and presumably the greater the library's effectiveness (the dependent variable). Data from hundreds of studies testing this hypothesis in many organizational settings are inconclusive, and the hypothesis itself may have the variables in the wrong order.

Job Enrichment and Quality of Working Life

Studies by Charles Martell have as their base the belief that job redesign and enrichment will meet the psychological needs of workers and ultimately improve worker productivity.[38] The studies of satisfaction of library staff members and the quality of working life investigate the structural variables of the centralization of decision making, the formalization of work rules, and the specialization of tasks as independent variables. The theory is that the structure influences the worker's psychological attitudes regarding the work and the job. Martell proposes change in organizational structures that will lead to possible improvements in the work roles of library staff. Whether libraries respond and why they do so require systematic investigation.

Library Surveys and Consultant Reports

During the 1930s through the 1960s library managers sought help and advice from colleagues outside of their libraries in order to redesign the internal structure of the libraries, to rearrange the administrative control of libraries on the campus, and to acquire justification for the building of new facilities. Library surveys, conducted by nationally recognized authorities in the field, were widely used and shared.[39] The experts conducting these surveys and the institutions commissioning the surveys made the reports available to the profession. The reports constitute an important archive to be used in research on libraries as organizations. They have not yet been used in any systematic way.

Professional library consulting firms began to dominate this type of work in the 1970s. Most of the reports of these commissioned studies have not made their way into the professional collections of library schools or associations, thus diminishing their impact. One consultant's report, commissioned by Columbia University, has been published and is a major contribution to the literature.[40]

The use of surveys and consultants reflects the profession's reliance on the opinion of experts. The consultants often issue reports with recommendations that many top administrators want; that is, the consultants provide external justification for the change the top administration of the library knows it wants, but is reluctant to introduce without the support of others. This observation suggests that the opinion or point of view of a library's top administrator may be an important factor in the internal structural organization and design of reporting relationships. The changes brought about at the University of Illinois at Urbana–Champaign, for example, could be interpreted as coming about not because automation was introduced or because the library's size was such that structural change was important, but because it was the wish of the top administrator to institute change.[41]

The influence of the top administrator upon the library suggests that librarianship would profit from systematic investigation of leadership. It also emphasizes the difficulty of undertaking predictive research in the area of the organization and structure of libraries. There are many variables at play; how to control them or determine systematically which ones explain the most variation are methodological issues of great importance. In order to understand how the leadership of the library will affect library organization and management, studies have to go beyond the use of trait theories or correlations. Again, the case study may be a fruitful beginning for the profession as it seeks rational answers to the questions relating to organizational change. The many published library histories offer a rich base for the beginning of such investigations.[42]

The Research Questions

Many of the research questions posed by ARL and CLR in the documents that appear as Appendix A and B to this chapter are related to the topic of this chapter. The following section comments on some of those questions and cites work related to them.

The thirteen sets of questions posed by the Association of Research Libraries in Appendix A are written from the point of view of librarianship as it is practiced; they are not derived from the research literature of the field. The ARL questions are those on the minds of directors of research libraries as the directors contemplate the future for the collections, services, facilities, and staffing of their libraries, and struggle with the development of the operating and capital budgets for those libraries.

The first set of ARL questions concern the impact of technology on research done by scholars as that work is supported by the research library. The initial question in this set is really three questions. The first is "What is the impact of technology on how scholars do their work?" This question suggests that the behavior of scholars is changing in response to new technologies (an important investigation in its own right). Assuming that behavior is changing, the questions then are, "How will library services be altered?" and "How might the design of library buildings change?"

What must be acknowledged is that the responses of many librarians to questions about user behavior in the past have been based upon untested assumptions. As Metz observes, librarianship has had little empirical data available to answer the questions "Who uses research libraries?" and "What materials are most in demand?"[43] Library administrators have made administrative decisions on assumptions, not on hard data. A response to the question about the impact of technology on the library was proposed by Atkinson in 1974:

> The advent of the new technologies—with their ability of remote query to find out if a book is available, and to charge materials located in the central library from a terminal in a branch library—will affect most profoundly the geographic placement of libraries and the concepts of "main" and "branch" services. The electronics—the cable itself—provides an electronic centralization and the physical centralization no longer has to follow. It makes no difference where a book is located, if the knowledge of and access to a book is possible at any location. If the cable television or computer output is everywhere there is a television set or a remote terminal, there is no particular advantage to having one's reference librarians centrally located if they have access to the necessary devices and materials. The location of the patron, rather than the location of the collection, will no doubt be the primary factor in the organization of most library services.[44]

The assumptions in Atkinson's response have been widely accepted by the field, based as they are on the principle that users, for the most part, seek a known item. Metz's study on the use of research library collections challenges the "known item" assumption. Other work on how scholars do their work also challenges it.[45]

Metz's investigation provides data (in contrast to expert opinion) that suggest solutions to the design of library facilities and the placement of library collections. He concludes that patterns of use depend upon the disciplinary affiliations of the library's users; that specialists and nonspecialists use materials differently; and that branch libraries channel user behavior. Metz urges replication of his study. Data on use are now readily available in machine readable form in many libraries, but these data have yet to be really taken advantage of. They make studies such as Metz's appropriate in assisting research libraries to make the important administrative decisions that influence the use made of the libraries.

The second set of ARL questions, under the heading "Impact of Library Procedures on Research," have their base also in the use scholars make of research libraries. The emphasis in this set is on use of collections, assuming chiefly print collections, in contrast to the first set, which was concerned with the impact on use by the technological aspects of collections and access to them. Again it must be acknowledged how little the field really knows about the way scholars use collections in research libraries.

Two studies, supported by the Council on Library Resources, are investigating scholars' use of libraries. The study being conducted at the University of Illinois at Chicago is finding that humanists make good use of special collections and archival collections, and when barriers to access are encountered, scholars devise ingenious methods of surmounting them. The other study, based at the University of Missouri, is looking at the ways scholars in philosophy use research libraries.[46]

The questions posed by Council on Library Resources (Appendix B) place a high priority on the research on users' requirements. As has just been noted, the Council already has supported some projects related to the question "How do information needs vary by discipline?" Such questions are central to the future of research libraries and the way those libraries organize themselves and their resources.

It may be that the questions posed by ARL and CLR on the use of research libraries by scholars are too narrow to influence the design of collections, services, and facilities of these libraries. In addition to serving scholars, research libraries also must provide for the needs of undergraduates, graduate students, and those faculty members who are at the beginning of their scholarly careers. Studies such as that of Metz and those of Kent and his colleagues at the University of Pittsburgh may be more influential to the future development of research libraries than the narrowly focused studies on the needs of scholars.[47] On the other hand, if one would hypothesize that research libraries respond directly to the demands of the most powerful groups on campus, studies of power in organizations will be very helpful in determining the future of research libraries. Such studies could provide new insights into how decisions are made in libraries and could be as helpful as the rationally designed and articulated investigations being proposed in the ARL questions.

The last question in the second set of questions posed by ARL addresses the matter of the content of the library's catalog, considering the issue of including records for nonbook materials into a single catalog with records describing books and journals. Many research libraries are incorporating bibliographic access to the serials literature into the ubiquitous online catalogs of the book collections. Access to multiple bibliographic files in libraries will be available from the same terminals, and search strategies can be saved and moved from one file to another. Not receiving as much attention as they should are matters pertaining to the vocabularies of different disciplines and how those might be transformed into the language of the library's catalogs. A recent published interview with Velma Veneziano, one of the originators of the NOTIS online integrated library management system, offers some directions for new research in cataloging and classification.

There is so much left that we can do to improve access using the basic structure of the new indexes but applying them in new ways. For example, we need to experiment with providing access by classification numbers. We need to be doing more work with evaluating the logs [of LUIS transactions] and building in means by which we can take a user's terminology and translate it into the term used in cataloging. We need to experiment with 'mapping' the vocabularies of different disciplines into a single unified super vocabulary. We need to be thinking in terms of providing users with an "expert system."...

Keyword–Boolean access is a brute force approach. People think in concepts, not in words.... There are better ways to lead the user to the desired information, using a controlled vocabulary, accessible by concept, with words displayed in context.[48]

The work on medical informatics being supported by the National Library of Medicine and the development of expert systems in certain fields offer opportunities for study and investigation on issues of access to recorded information. While research libraries are concerned about who they can hire to catalog their research collections and who has the necessary language and subject skills to do that work, the more fundamental issues of the vocabularies of scholars, the differences in the bibliographic structures of disciplines, and the approach scholars take to collections, regardless of the formats of those collections, need attention. Some good work has been done on the issues of the vocabularies of scholars.[49] The integration of that research into library operations is an effort yet to be undertaken.

The issues raised in the fourth set of ARL questions, "Assessing Inter-institutional Cooperative Activities," are of major interest to researchers studying complex organizations and to library managers who seek to understand various organizational relationships. The first question seeks to identify the conditions in which interlibrary cooperation will flourish or not. Some work has been done to develop hypotheses on which future studies can be based.[50] Most of Lynch's work in this area has been from the single organization's viewpoint, seeking to identify the influence on the environment on the structure of a library. She proposes several hypotheses related to the place of the library in a network environment:

The lower the autonomy of the library, the greater the library's interest in decision making.

The greater or more complete the participation of the library in a network, the more internal conflict within the library.

The greater the impact on the library by outside forces, the more interest on the part of the library in controlling those forces.[51]

It is not easy for people in librarianship to confront such hypotheses. The field identifies its noble purpose of service to users, with which no one disagrees, and tends to avoid analyses of organizational differences for fear that the outcome may reduce support for the general objective. Thus questions such as "Why do libraries respond differently to cooperative ventures?" are ignored at best or avoided. Yet investigations on organizational variations in terms of technology and size, as well as the influence of the controlling organization, can lead to an understanding of why some interinstitutional agreements are adopted over others, and why some lead to greater internal conflict than do others.

The Council on Library Resources identifies in its research agenda the need for research on multi–institutional operations. It suggests that studies on the relationships between the forms of the organization and the effectiveness of programs would be useful. There are several useful studies on the organization of public library systems that provide models for the study of organizational arrangements among research libraries. Guy Garrison and his colleagues at the University of Illinois at Urbana–Champaign investigated whether the type of organization of a public library made any difference in the service provided by system libraries.[52]

These investigations have their theoretical base in the earlier work of Joeckel, Martin, and their colleagues at the University of Chicago.[53] The Council's agenda looks at network organizations per se instead of the impact of the network on the individual organization within it. Both topics are fruitful areas for research on libraries as organizations.

The tenth set of questions on ARL's list concern "Changing Roles and Contributions of Research Library Staff" and are central to management and organizational structure. The organizational design in many libraries is strongly influenced by the nature of the staff, its various characteristics such as the ratio of professional to nonprofessional staff, and the introduction of more staff specializations. Balbach describes the changes in staffing that occur in a library responding to a turbulent environment.[54] She observes that as jobs change the organizational structure will change and, like March, recognizes that organizations change quite routinely.[55]

The twelfth set of ARL questions seek information on the "Impact of Technology on the Operations of a Research Library." They are related directly to the issues of organizational structure considered in this chapter. Librarianship is practiced within an organizational setting; thus the research agenda is shaped very much by the setting and by the multitude of variables that influence the design of the organization.

The Next Decade of Research on Library Organization

The past being the best predictor of the future, library studies on organizational structure will continue to be influenced by theoretical work and empirical investigations done outside librarianship. The management literature, particularly, will continue to influence much of the applied library research.

Organizational theory is merging the structural model and the behavioral model. Theory will be acknowledged in studies but is unlikely to become very dominant. Investigations into organizational theory will be small and will develop out of the question, "This is the problem; what can I learn about it?" Investigations in librarianship will emphasize the theory of the human relations school. Library managers worry about the well-being of their employees and seek ways to improve job satisfaction, morale, and working life. These interests will drive the research questions of the next decade.

The impact of the variables of size and technology on organizational structure in libraries will interest some researchers. There will be less activity in these areas of investigation, however, for large-scale studies and longitudinal studies are needed in order to make progress and there is little money available to do them. Studies of leadership will continue, for practitioners perceive that the person at the top influences the organization's design (even if it is not true).

A fruitful area of investigation could be applying to libraries the work being done elsewhere on the politics of organizational decision making and on decision making in public policy. Whether researchers in librarianship will be influenced by these areas of investigation remains to be seen.

There is a small research base on which to build good studies of library organization. Librarianship will profit from continuing research in these areas.

Notes

1. Beverly P. Lynch, ed., *Management Strategies for Libraries* (New York: Neal Schuman, 1985), ix–xviii.

2. Jane Robbins–Carter, "Political Science: Utility for Research in Librarianship," *Library Trends* 32 (Spring 1984): 430.

3. *Library & Information Science, A Catalog of Selected Doctoral Dissertation Research* (Ann Arbor, Mich.: University Microfilms, 1985.)

4. Beverly P. Lynch and Jo Ann Verdin, "Job Satisfaction in Libraries," *Library Quarterly,* 53 (October 1983): 434–447; Beverly P. Lynch and Jo Ann Verdin, "Job Satisfaction in Libraries: A Replication," *Library Quarterly* 57 (April 1987): 190–202.

5. Kenneth Shearer, "The Impact of Research On Librarianship," *Journal of Education for Librarianship*" 20 (1979/80): 116.

6. George P. D'Elia, "The Determinants of Job Satisfaction among Beginning Librarians," *Library Quarterly* 49 (July 1979): 283–302.

7. Beverly P. Lynch, "Technology: A Replication," October 1988 (unpublished manuscript).

8. James G. March. "Footnotes to Organizational Change," *Administrative Science Quarterly* 26 (December 1981): 563–577.

9. Jerald Hage and Michael Aiken, "Program Change and Organizational Properties: A Comparative Analysis," *American Journal of Sociology* 72 (March 1967): 503–509; Max Weber, "Bureaucracy," in *From Max Weber: Essays in Sociology* (New York: Oxford Univ. Pr., 1962): 196–244.

10. Richard S. Blackburn, "Dimensions of Structure: Review and Reappraisal," *The Academic of Management Review* 7 (January 1982): 59–66; Eric J. Walton, "The Comparison of Measures of Organizational Structure," *Academy of Management Review* 6 (January 1981): 155–160.

11. Rutherford D. Rogers and David C. Weber, *University Library Administration* (New York: H. W. Wilson, 1971), pp. 61–87; Robert D. Stueart and John Taylor Eastlick, *Library Management* (Littleton, Colo: Libraries Unlimited, 1977), pp. 47–74; Association of Research Libraries, *Spec Kit 129: Organizational Charts* (Washington, D.C.: ARL, 1986).

12. W. Richard Scott, *Organizations* (Englewood Cliffs, N.J.: Prentice-Hall, 1981), p. 15.

13. Helen Howard, "Organization Structure and Innovation in Libraries," *College & Research Libraries* 42 (September 1981): 425–434.

14. Elaine Sloan, "The Organization of Collection Development in Large University Libraries" (Ph.D. diss., University of Maryland, 1973).

15. Jeanne Sohn, "Collection Development Organizational Patterns in ARL Libraries," *Library Resources and Technical Services* 31 (April/June, 1987): 123–134.

16. Bonita Bryant, "The Organizational Structure of Collection Development," *Library Resources and Technical Services* 31 (April/June 1987): 111–122.

17. Paul H. Spence, "A Comparative Study of University Library Organizational Structure" (Ph.D. diss., University of Illinois, 1969).

18. Peter M. Blau, "The Hierarchy of Authority in Organizations," *American Journal of Sociology* 73 (January 1968): 453–467.

19. Beverly P. Lynch, "An Empirical Assessment of Perrow's Technology Construct," *Administrative Science Quarterly* 19 (September 1972): 338–356; Beverly P. Lynch, "A Framework for the Comparative Analysis of Library Work," *College & Research Libraries* 36 (November 1974): 432–443.

20. Lynch, "Technology: A Replication."

21. Booz, Allen & Hamilton, *Organization and Staffing of the Libraries of Columbia University: A Case Study* (Westport, Conn.: Redgrave Information Resources, 1973); Sohn, "Collection Development Organizational Patterns"; Bryant, "The Organizational Structure."

22. Beverly P. Lynch, "Libraries as Bureaucracies," *Library Trends* 27 (Winter 1978): 259–267.

23. Beverly P. Lynch, "The Academic Library and Its Environment," *College & Research Libraries* 35 (March 1974): 126–132.

24. Jeffrey A. Raffel and Robert Shishko, *Systematic Analysis of University Libraries: An Application of Cost Benefit Analysis of the MIT Libraries* (Cambridge, MIT Press, 1969.)

25. Joanne R. Euster, *The Academic Library Director* (New York: Greenwood, 1987.)

26. James A. Hyatt and Aurora S. Santiago, *University Libraries in Transition* (Washington, D.C.: National Association of College and University Business Officers, 1987).

27. Beverly P. Lynch, ed. *The Academic Libraries in Transition: Planning for the 1990s* (New York; Neal–Schuman, 1989).

28. Frank Allen Schmidtlein, "Decision Processes and Their Structural Implications: A Case Study of Library Planning at the University of California" (Ph.D. diss., University of California, Berkeley, 1979); Susan E. McCargar, "The University Library Director in Budgetary Decision Making: A Study of Power, Influence, and Governance" (Ph.D. diss., University of Michigan, 1984); Richard C. Holmes, "The Academic Library Director's Perceived Power and Its Correlates" (Ph.D. diss., University of Minnesota, 1983).

29. Jeffrey A. Raffel, "From Economic to Political Analysis of Library Decision Making," *College & Research Libraries* 35 (November 1974): 412–423.

30. Lynch, *Management Strategies*, xiii.

31. Frederick W. Taylor, *The Principles of Scientific Management* (New York: Harper & Row, 1911).

32. Richard M. Dougherty and Fred. J. Heinritz, *Scientific Management of Library Operations*, 2nd ed. (Metuchen, N.J.: Scarecrow, 1982).

33. Myrl Ricking and Robert E. Booth, *Personnel Utilization in Libraries* (Chicago: American Library Assn., 1974).

34. Peter F. Drucker, *Management* (New York: Harper & Row, 1974); Chris Argyris, *Personality and Organization* (New York: Harper, 1957); Douglas McGregor, *The Human Side of Enterprise* (New York: McGraw–Hill, 1960); Abraham Maslow, *Motivation and Personality* (New York: Harper, 1954).

35. D'Elia, "Determinants"; Lynch and Verdin, "Job Satisfaction."

36. Maurice P. Marchant, *Participative Management in Academic Libraries* (Westport, Conn.: Greenwood, 1976); Dale Susan Bengston and Dorothy M. Shields, "A Test of Marchant's Predictive Formula Involving Job Satisfaction," *Journal of Academic Librarianship* 11 (May 1985): 88–92.

37. Beverly P. Lynch, "Participative Management in Relation to Library Effectiveness," *College & Research Libraries*, 36 (September 1972): 382–390.

38. Charles Martell, "Improving the Effectiveness of Libraries through Improvement in the Quality of Working Life," *College & Research Libraries* 42 (September 1981): 435–446; Charles Martell and Mercedes Untawale, "Work Enrichment for Academic Libraries," *Journal of Academic Librarianship* 8 (1983): 339–343.

39. E. Walfred Erickson, *College and University Library Surveys 1938–1952* (Chicago: American Library Assn., 1961); Maurice F. Tauber and Irlene Roemer Stephens, *Library Surveys* (New York: Columbia Univ. Pr., 1967).

40. Booz, Allen & Hamilton, *Organization and Staffing*.

41. Hugh C. Atkinson, "The Impact of Closing the Catalog in Library Organizations," in D. Kaye Gapen and Bonnie Juergens, *Closing the Catalog* (Phoenix: Oryx, 1980): 123–133.

42. Michael Harris and Donald Davis, Jr. *American Library History: A Bibliography* (Austin: Univ. of Texas Pr., 1978).

43. Paul Metz, *The Landscape of Literature: Use of Subject Collections in a University Library* (Chicago: American Library Assn., 1983).

44. Hugh C. Atkinson, "Extension of New Services and the Role of Technology," *Library Trends* 23 (October 1974): 313–314.

45. Metz, *The Landscape of Literature*; E. Paige Weston and Beverly P. Lynch, "Research Librarianship: Services and Support for Faculty Research in the 1980s," in *Proceedings of the 1989 Conference of the Association of College and Research Libraries* (in press); *Humanists at Work*, ed. Gene W. Ruoff and Beverly P. Lynch (in press).

46. William G. Jones and Stephen E. Wiberley, Jr., "Patterns of Information Seeking in the Humanities" (in press); Donald Sievert and Mary Ellen Sievert, "How Philosophers Seek Information and Use Libraries," a paper presented at the Symposium, "Humanists at Work," Chicago, University of Illinois at Chicago, University Library, April 1989 (in press).

47. Metz, *The Landscape of Literature*; Allen Kent et al., *Use of Library Materials: The University of Pittsburgh Study* (New York: Marcel Dekker, 1979); Jacob Cohen, "Book Cost and Book Use: The Economics of a University Library," in *Library Resource Sharing*, ed. Allen Kent and Thomas J. Galvin (New York: Dekker, 1977), pp. 197–224.

48. Velma Veneziano, "Keep It Simple and Elegant: An Interview with Velma Veneziano," *NOTISes* 35 (October 1988): 4.

49. Stephen E. Wiberley, Jr., "Subject Access in the Humanities and the Precision of the Humanist's Vocabulary," *Library Quarterly* 53 (October 1983): 420–433; Stephen E. Wiberley, Jr., "Names in Space and Time: The Indexing Vocabulary of the Humanities," *Library Quarterly* 58 (January 1988): 1–28.

50. Beverly P. Lynch, "The Academic Library and Its Environment," *College & Research Libraries* 35 (March 1974): 126–32; Beverly P. Lynch, "Comment on the Governance of Library Networks: Purposes and Expectations," in *The Structure and Governance of Library Networks*, ed. Allen Kent and Thomas J. Galvin (New York: Dekker, 1979), pp. 213–219.

51. Lynch, "Comment on the Governance of Library Networks," 214.

52. Guy Garrison et al., *Studies in Public Library Government, Organization, and Support* (Washington, D.C.: U.S. Office of Education, Bureau of Research, 1969).

53. Carleton B. Joeckel, *Government of the American Public Library* (Chicago: University of Chicago Press, 1939); Lowell S. Martin, "The Desirable Minimum Size of Public Library Units" (Ph.D. diss., University of Chicago, 1945).

54. Edith D. Balbach, "Personnel," in Beverly P. Lynch, ed., *Academic Libraries in Transition: Planning for the 1990s* (New York: Neal–Schuman, in press).

55. March, "Footnotes to Organizational Change."

Research Questions of Interest to ARL

1. Impact of Technology on Research
   - 1.1 What is the impact of changing information technology on scholars' behavior and what are the implications for library services and buildings?
   - 1.2 What are the effects of electronic publishing on traditional quality-control mechanisms such as peer review?
   - 1.3 What are appropriate procedures to assess and monitor the quality of commercial databases and the integrity of those who produce and market them?
   - 1.4 To what extent does the existence of databases take graduate students away from libraries and into textual studies? To what extent are limitations of databases imposing limits on research; i.e., do users perceive machine-readable databases as complete?
   - 1.5 How could research libraries best respond to the increase in electronic publishing (acquiring, storing, and providing access to these materials)?
   - 1.6 Is access via a campus LAN (local area network) of sufficient scholarly utility in accessing materials to justify the access

Note: This list was distributed in August 1987 by the ARL president, Herbert Johnson. His cover letter explained that "the attached list represents questions that have evolved from discussions within the Association of Research Libraries and the scope of the list has been defined largely by the recent activities of ARL committees. While it does not represent a comprehensive research agenda, we felt there was some benefit in making it available to people who are in a position to encourage, shape, or direct research activity."

costs from personal workstations? Will selective off-loading to scholars' workstations be a convenient access to publications on optical disk?

2. Impact of Library Procedures on Research
   2.1 How often and under what circumstances do visiting or independent scholars gain access to research library collections? Are there barriers or inhibitions for visiting or independent scholars gaining full access to the material in the collections of research libraries? Are there additional protocols or procedures through which visiting or independent scholars and others might be given improved access to research library collections?
   2.2 How do different physical locations of library resources influence the use of materials? What is the relative cost and impact of using remote locations for housing of library materials? How often and under what conditions do scholars need material on demand as opposed to waiting for delivery from another location? What is the impact of fewer centers for specialized material? What is the impact of multiple remote locations for library materials and speed of availability on collection development decisions?
   2.3 What are the psychological and sociological perceptions of users regarding access to library resources?
   2.4 What is the impact on library users of the inclusion of more and more records for non-book materials into a single catalog with records describing book and journal materials?

3. Impact of Economics and Pricing Policies on Research
   3.1 What are the dimensions and patterns of differential and discriminatory pricing for journal subscriptions, and what has been the effect on research library budgets and the availability of journals?
   3.2 What is the impact on scholarship and library services of restricted access data files (e.g., subscription at low rates but limited in terms of who can use them)?

4. Assessing Inter-institutional Cooperative Activities
   4.1 What conditions in the library or university inhibit or support inter-organizational cooperation? For example, geography? Organization? Staffing? Telecommunication standards? Technology? Proprietary databases? Funding?

4.2 How do you measure changed behavior arising from cooperative resource sharing activities (for example, would it be reflected in collection development statements? Borrowing patterns? Shifting of collections? Shifting of positions? Other?)? Has the behavior of a library changed as a result of another library assuming a cooperative responsibility? Have new technologies made it easier to cooperate with libraries not in geographic proximity? What are the patterns of cooperative agreements now in place in terms of explicitness and subjects covered?

5. Assessing U.S. and Canadian Access to Foreign Publications

5.1 To what extent do the libraries of the United States and Canada provide comprehensive access to research material that is published outside these two countries? What do research libraries spend to acquire journals and other materials published abroad?

5.2 *How* are foreign language materials used? Is the use different from English-language material (patterns of use, categories of users, etc.)?

6. Exploring Costs and Impact of Different Models for Bibliographic Description Practices

6.1 What models could be developed to reflect alternative patterns for distributed cataloging programs (e.g., transfer of books or journeyman catalogers? different roles for LC? investigation of cataloging allocation within the National Coordinated Cataloging Project?); and what would be the cost and impact of each model?

6.2 What are the costs of current methods and standards for creating bibliographic records in relation to the benefits received? How much information in a MARC record is useful in relation to the time lags in cataloging? Can national-standard records be created more cost-effectively than they now are? Are there cataloging practices that can, should, and possibly ought to be refined or eliminated to reduce costs and normalize practices for participation in coordinated cataloging projects?

6.3 How much duplication of expensive original cataloging occurs among the utilities and LC? What languages and specialized materials would best be cataloged by national centers for specialized cataloging and how might such centers operate?

6.4 Does competition among bibliographic utilities benefit research libraries? What are the pitfalls?

6.5 What has been the impact of rising telecommunication costs on shared cataloging, particularly in view of low-cost alternatives such as CD-ROM–based systems? How will optical disk bibliographical access be integrated into the local campuses' databases and into national databases? What are the long-term consequences of state or regional databases that limit the sharing of new cataloging records and holdings information? How will the use of local cataloging systems affect the "national database" and the programs that rely on that database?

6.6 Is it possible to bridge different bibliographic structures used to describe monographic and journal literature, at the article level, to allow a search of both kinds of bibliographic records at once?

6.7 What are the means for providing access to in-process and on-order records in shared cataloging databases?

6.8 What is the impact on cataloging of the AAP Electronic Manuscript Project? What should libraries consider as they decide to implement cataloging of electronic texts?

7. Identification of Material to be Preserved

7.1 What criteria should be considered during the process of identifying materials for preservation? What should be considered when deciding if, in addition to content, the form of the item should be preserved?

7.2 How should priority be assigned given inadequate funds to preserve an entire collection?

7.3 How should materials be preserved in a field for which no library has accepted responsibility?

7.4 How can we stimulate foreign participation in preservation strategies to address this worldwide threat to future scholarship?

8. Assessing New Technologies for Preservation Strategies

8.1 What factors need to be considered when evaluating new technology for application to preservation activities?

8.2 To what extent will libraries use mass deacidification technology when it is readily available, and what are the implications for overall preservation strategies?

8.3 What are the implications of optical disk technological developments for preservation strategies?

8.4 Is it possible to project whether and when optical disk technology might become a viable (preferable) substitute for microform preservation?

9. Impact of U.S. Government Policies on Libraries

9.1 What is the impact on the availability of U.S. government information of the issuance of OMB Circular A-130, Management of Federal Information Resources?

9.2 What is the impact on research library operations and services of budget reductions at the Library of Congress, the National Library of Medicine, the National Agricultural Library, the Government Printing Office, and other library-related programs?

10. Changing Roles and Contributions of Research Library Staff

10.1 What are the patterns of personality characteristics among research library staff and could these patterns assist in designing staff development and recruitment programs?

10.2 What are the implications of multiple role requirements for professional staff?

10.3 What elements should be considered in defining, assessing, and increasing contributions and productivity of staff in research libraries?

10.4 What is the impact of technology on position descriptions and staffing patterns? For example, what new skills are required of public service librarians (e.g., content expertise, ability to retrieve and prepare numeric and full-text data from electronic products, ability to communicate effectively outside the library, etc.)?

10.5 What are the long-term staffing implications for optical disk and other electronic format services?

10.6 What are the effects of unionization and collective bargaining on management practice and philosophy, and on collegial relations and roles within a research library?

11. Measures of Research Libraries

11.1 How do you measure the effectiveness of research libraries?

11.2 Are there measures that would reflect the decreasing importance of ownership and collection size vis-à-vis new technology, telecommunications, and information delivery systems?

11.3 What data elements should be added to the ARL Statistical Program that are more descriptive of research libraries in transition to an access model of service in the "electronic age" of libraries?

11.4 What measurements could be developed to reflect institutional researchness?

12. Impact of Technology on the Operations of a Research Library

12.1 What is the impact of changing technology on library organizational structure? What recasting should take place?

12.2 What is a "wired campus" and what is the place of the library within the university in relation to telecommunications?

12.3 How has the new technological environment (the wired campus) changed relationships among faculty, administrators, and librarians?

12.4 Can libraries promote optical disk standards so commercial competition does not result in a plethora of incompatible services?

12.5 What collection management data (e.g., number of titles in each LC class) is available from machine-readable bibliographic files?

13. Management of Research Library Resources

13.1 What is needed to develop models that might assist in research library management decision making?

13.2 What are the implications of increasing numbers of nontraditional students for library operations and services (e.g., remote locations/campuses and remote students)?

Research Questions of Interest to CLR

An Expanded Research Program

The Introduction to CLR's 1984 Annual Report asserted that a much-expanded research capacity was required to permit fuller exploration of topics related to information and its use in academic and research settings. The projected expansion of the Council's research program to meet that need was only an aspiration a year ago. Now, as the Council's twenty-ninth year comes to an end, the aspiration is about to become a reality.

During the past fall and winter, discussions within the CLR Board, in meetings with faculty and university officers on six campuses, and with many individuals confirmed the need to expand research activity. The discussions also suggested methods and topics for attention and provided some indication of costs, which, even when viewed conservatively, were well beyond existing CLR resources. The spring was devoted to securing financial support, and by the end of the fiscal year, over half of the estimated $4.7 million needed for use over five years had been provided by three foundations: the J. Paul Getty Trust, the Andrew W. Mellon Foundation, and the Pew Memorial Trusts. As our thirtieth year begins, we can turn, in this particular area, from planning to action.

The projected research program has several purposes, including:

Gathering, consolidating, and assessing what is known about the characteristics and use of information in the academic setting;

Encouraging the investigation of questions related to information and its use in teaching, research, and scholarship;

Developing and testing alternative approaches to providing information services and systems;

Note: The text is an excerpt from the twenty-ninth *Annual Report* (1985) of the Council on Library Resources (pages 9–15).

Promoting constructive discussions about the future role and form of libraries, especially in the context of higher education; and

Strengthening professional education for librarianship and the research base on which the educational structure rests.

These specific objectives do not fully convey the underlying reason for the Council's interest in mounting a major research enterprise. *Simply put, the time has come to acknowledge that the capacities of recently developed technologies are such that important aspects of teaching and research now can be fundamentally transformed and improved for the benefit of individual students, scholars, and society. Libraries have a unique and inescapable role to play in this transformation. They need only to find the way.*

The Questions

While the details of the research program will be shaped with the help of advisors and the CLR Board, the initial direction is established. Three general headings seem to cover most of the topics that have been suggested: information characteristics, users' requirements, and the structure of information systems. Examples of questions follow; they may or may not survive further discussion, but they do suggest that the work anticipated will help bridge the gap between specialized basic research in information science and the development and applications work that has characterized past CLR programs. There will be a new emphasis on building the background of facts and conducting the careful analysis required to shape future information services, and on creating the management capacities to provide those services, with special attention to the long-term interests of scholarship, universities, research libraries, and society.

1. Information characteristics

The quantity of recorded information is growing at an unprecedented rate. The fact that information put to use breeds new information is the reality of research. The unprecedented level of information use and the present high rate of information generation are hallmarks of our technology-driven information age. It is imperative that we learn more than we now know about the content and form of information, especially in the context of research and teaching. There are many topics that need exploration. These are examples:

What is the relationship between the characteristics of documents (format, length, language, age, etc.) and their usefulness?

The number of ways in which information can be distributed and stored is increasing. Print on paper has been the primary medium for five hundred years, but in the last two or three decades, photographic and electronic systems with great storage capacities and processing flexibility have been developed. Still, there are many unanswered questions about the utility of each of the new technologies for the needs of scholars. Can the information contained in widely distributed, machine-readable databases be used with the same confidence in validity and consistency that is assured by the availability of multiple copies of the same edition of a printed book? A recent CLR-sponsored study of public records suggests that there are fundamental problems in this area. How can optical disc technology, with its great storage capacity, be efficiently used by research libraries where demand for specific items is unpredictable and service is essentially customized?

If more were known about patterns of use of information and such matters as obsolescence and redundancy (and if these facts were widely understood), the effective application of specific technologies and the process of collection management both would be improved.

Are format requirements fundamentally different for various disciplines or kinds of use?

How does the manner in which information is organized, stored, and presented affect its utility? Do the choices of method reflect only personal preferences, or do research methods typical of individual disciplines pose specific requirements for system performance?

Do large files of machine-readable information and new processing capabilities affect the substance as well as the methodology of research?

Access to large bodies of information in machine-readable form and the ability to organize and analyze data have influenced scientific research and technical development. There is far less experience in humanistic and historical studies, where work has in large part concentrated on various forms of text analysis. Given the prospect of massive text conversion efforts (for preservation purposes, for example), what new avenues of research will be possible? Should these research objectives influence preservation priorities?

Are there useful ways to assess the quality of information and information service?

The sheer quantity of information being generated and distributed and the trend toward viewing information and information service as commodities suggest that quality should be, increasingly, a matter for attention. Which databases, which information services, which sources are most reliable, most important, most useful? Can methods be found to assess information content and system performance in much the same way that books are reviewed?

What is the relationship between knowledge of the existence of information and actual use?

The growing quantity of information, the increasing number of sources, and an expanding body of users require greater precision in identifying and locating recorded information. Are new approaches to the analysis of information needed? Do new computer-based systems open the way to the integration of information on specific topics, regardless of form or source? Can bibliographic systems better meet the needs of users, while still satisfying the operating requirements of libraries?

2. User requirements

Too little is known about the need for recorded information or the influence of information services on the work and life of individuals, whether in universities or in any other sector of society. This lack of understanding, coupled with the cost and complexity of new information systems, opens the prospect that new capabilities will not be fully used or that only the most sophisticated users will benefit. There are many topics to be explored in the context of libraries and higher education:

How do information needs vary by discipline?

Are the needs of historians fundamentally different from those of geologists? Does traditional library operating philosophy (i.e., tending toward "equality" in resources and "uniformity" in services across all academic departments) need revision to accommodate differences in the kinds of services needed and the amount of information required?

How parochial is the information-using community?

Might improved access to information generated abroad improve overall system performance? In which fields? Are new capabilities for direct communication among individuals (outside the established peer review/publishing procedures) likely to curtail wider access? What effect will new informal information subsystems have on libraries?

In the complex information environment that is anticipated, what is the future role of libraries, especially in relationship to teaching?

Finding, assessing, and using information is becoming increasingly complicated and, as a result, it is important that attention be given to the study of information as a discipline at every educational level. Librarians need to understand the information structures supporting major disciplines, the organization of knowledge, the economics of information, direct and indirect forms of censorship and other constraints on access, and the public policy questions concerning information that will, when they are answered, affect our future in fundamental ways. Librarians need to develop better ways to teach not only the techniques but the substance of their calling.

3. The structure of information systems

The once uncomplicated and independent activities of writing, publishing, and managing libraries are all being transformed. The volume of worldwide publishing grows with economic and technical advances and growth in the population itself. Computer, telecommunications, and text storage systems open the way for fragmentation of activity and responsibility. Some information has monetary value, and there is great competition to establish and control markets by commercial and nonprofit organizations alike. But there is no simple correlation between the importance of information and its economic worth, a matter of growing importance that might, if left unattended, provoke serious discontinuities in system performance and unacceptable inequalities in access. This fundamental transformation in the information system is essentially one of providing new capabilities. Changes in the methods of scholarly communication will affect every aspect of society. Libraries have been the keystone of the system in the past, but it is now clear that the shape of that keystone must change if it is to function well. Despite many claims and assertions, the information structure of the future has not yet taken shape, but the pace of change is such that it is imperative that "architects" of great skill, who are concerned with the well-being of universities, scholarship, and libraries, go to work with some sense of coordination before a structure is imposed by default.

Examples of topics for attention include:

The organization of information activities in research universities

The blurring of some aspects of library activity with computer and communication services raises questions of cost control, planning responsibility, and operational overlap. How should universities manage information systems and services? Within libraries, what organizational changes are required as access to information becomes as important as collection ownership?

Collection management

Can libraries develop a collection management strategy that makes full use of such options as storage alternatives, reliance on machine-stored records rather than printed sources, and cooperative collecting ventures, all in ways that control costs without creating unacceptable difficulties for users?

Multi-institutional operations

Formal library cooperatives and library service organizations have increased in number and influence, but there has been little reliable effort to assess the relationships between the forms of the organizations and the effectiveness of their programs. Further, there have been few analyses of the service and economic benefits of such undertakings for individual libraries and their users or, conversely, too little program specification for fully productive cooperative ventures.

Problems of technology

What issues are introduced by information system technology that need attention in the special setting of the research university? (For example, privacy, reliability of databases, limitations on access to information, implications of dependence on commercial data services, etc.)

Opportunities for technology

Are there promising new ways to configure technology for specific purposes? In preservation, for example, can the use of appropriate technology simultaneously protect and expand access to important materials? Can improved management systems be developed for research libraries? What are the realistic prospects for recently developed text and image storage equipment?

The topics and questions in all three categories only hint at the range of subjects being considered for attention. The changes in the composition of library staffs, the future library role in collegiate and university instruction, the prospects for developing international information systems, methods of setting priorities for preservation, exploration of alternate ways to improve planning at the national level, and investigation of funding approaches for national undertakings are equally important matters.

Even this brief summary suggests the magnitude of the task. Methods of selecting participants are not yet established, but to accomplish the work, several approaches will have to be followed. It seems certain that several universities and many individuals from many disciplines will need to take part.

University Research Centers

The preliminary discussions and planning meetings identified a large number of specific topics for investigation. Those same discussions suggested that if there is to be fundamental change in libraries, work must be concentrated on a very few basic matters. By consolidating categories of questions and issues, two broad subjects have been identified for initial attention:

Information characteristics and information use

This general subject includes such issues as the information requirements of various disciplines; the working habits of scholars; the effects on scholarship of alternate ways of organizing, collecting, and distributing information; the influence of technology-based information systems on teaching and learning; and the relationship between the form and utility of information. In short, the intent is to understand better the academic requirements for library service and information systems so that changes might enhance and improve, rather than threaten, what we now have. The research and analytical activity is intended to encourage faculty, university administrators, computer specialists, and librarians to join forces to specify their needs and thus determine their collective future.

The organization and management of information systems and services in universities

The integration of all forms of information, the characteristics of the technologies driving the information revolution, a complex economic and legal setting, and an inescapable set of social obligations and objectives requiring access to information are all powerful forces affecting long-established procedures and institutions. Narrow objectives and constrictive organizations are not compatible with the realities of the developing information structure. New forms for research libraries must be found to meet needs in fiscally responsible ways. The opportunities that technology brings will be realized only if organizational structures reflect the characteristics of scholarly communication itself. Research and reflection in this general area will help clarify the future nature of the information setting in which scholars and institutions will do their work; explore alternate organizational structures within and among universities; and consider the methods, skills, and responsibilities inherent in the systems and structures that will be needed if opportunities are to be realized for individuals and institutions alike.

To consider these matters, it is anticipated that three or four university research centers will be established, thus providing an opportunity for participation by individuals from a variety of disciplines and encouraging both collaboration and productive competition. One component of each participating university (an administrative office, a library, or a library school) would assume administrative responsibility, but emphasis will be on institution-wide participation.

Independent Research

A new grant program will be established and managed by CLR to encourage work by individuals unaffiliated with the university research centers. Guidelines soon to be published will reflect overall objectives and will encourage participation from many disciplines. It is anticipated that the subjects for research and review will complement work undertaken in the university research centers or advance CLR operating programs related to bibliographic service, access, preservation, and management.

Information, evaluation, and promotion

Research, by itself, cannot prescribe action. But, by assembling facts, encouraging participation, and identifying matters for attention, it can help the individuals and institutions that have responsibility for the future. It is most important to stimulate responsible discussion on as many fronts as possible. The methods now projected include encouragement of publication in refereed journals, publication of summary and analytical reports in a new CLR-sponsored series, continuation and substantial expansion of the CLR Forums, and development of and support for a series of seminars on many campuses, where the decisions will be made and the work will be done.

Mary Jo Lynch and Arthur P. Young

Epilogue

The general picture that emerges from these essays is one of a field that has produced a small amount of genuine research despite large gaps in its knowledge base. The view of these experts toward the research that has been done recently on issues of interest to academic librarians and what seems likely to be done in the future can be described in the phrase used by Charles McClure and Ann Bishop to summarize results of their study of the entire corpus of research in library and information science: guarded optimism.[1] None of the chapter authors is under the illusion that the research done to date is good enough or extensive enough to match the need. Nor are they supremely confident that the future will be significantly better than the past. But the optimism is there, and the editors share it.

This epilogue focuses on the future. Some chapter authors described needed research separately at the end of their essays (Metz, Potter, Lynch, and George). Others included such questions within the text and sometimes added additional ideas in the last section (Osburn, Svenonius, and Getz). Whitlatch discusses future research at the end of the two major sections of her paper and makes additional comments in her conclusion. It would be possible to examine the chapters, one by one, and build an agenda for future research on academic libraries. But the library world already has too many research agendas.[2] The editors doubt that another list of researchable questions would be of any value in stimulating more and better research, which is what the field really needs. Therefore, we will leave the questions where they are and encourage the reader to look for them. Instead of listing the questions, then, this epilogue synthesizes the common themes that are sounded in these essays as the authors summarize the past and look to the future.

Tension between Research and Practice

Tension has always existed between the practice of librarianship and research about that practice. It existed in the days of Pierce Butler when research was just beginning to play a role in what was then an emerging profession, and it exists today even though the field has matured considerably and its mission has expanded from a narrow institutional base in libraries to the broader canvas of information creation, organization, and use.[3] Osburn mentions the positive side of this tension when he observes that reflection based on experience stimulated research in the area of collection development and management. But Svenonius points to the darker side when she raises the possibility that there has been little research on catalog code design because such research might show that change was needed and practitioners really don't want change. George mentions a similar dilemma in describing research on the much newer library service—bibliographic instruction. Because much of the research is done by practitioners with a stake in showing that what they do is valuable, it often lacks the objectivity expected in good research.

Lynch points out that most research on management theory and organizational structure dealing with libraries remains locked in doctoral dissertations and does not appear in professional journal literature. Therefore, it is not a factor in library practice. Potter urges practitioners and researchers alike to adopt a research orientation to their work with technology, pointing out that important developmental projects have not been documented in such a way as to be useful to research.

Focus on the User

The importance of the user is a theme sounded in every chapter. Although Svenonius claims that "since the time of Cutter, sensitivity to the user has guided the design of bibliographic tools," librarians have often been criticized for not considering users in the design of bibliographic tools or any other aspect of library management. These chapters, however, describe a considerable amount of research that focuses on the user and the authors recommend more of the same in the future.

Two of the chapters are devoted almost exclusively to studies involving users—the Whitlatch chapter on research that examines how libraries provide access to information, and the George chapter on research about how librarians teach users how to find what they need. In their concluding remarks, both chapter authors mention the need for library researchers to expand their vision beyond libraries and to look at what George calls "the individual's lifelong need to identify, locate, and verify information."

We have already noted that one important feature of computerized catalogs is the record which they can provide of how users behave when interacting with the file. As Metz points out, a similar capability exists with computerized circulation files. They have made possible sophisticated studies of which library materials are borrowed by which users. Both Metz and Lynch call for increased attention by library researchers to the actual use of materials by users.

Osburn observes that such studies are part of the emerging "discipline" of scholarly communication which "rather than librarianship, is our business."

In her conclusion, Whitlatch observes that "as the technology makes innovations in information access possible, innovative studies are needed which examine the impact of these innovations upon access to information." She raises the possibility that the very technology that supposedly increases access may raise new barriers to it. Potter also sees that danger and calls for continuous research on how users adapt to new technology used to manage traditional resources and to new forms of publishing information. He points out the potential importance of research on those topics in providing information that will enable librarians to fulfill their mission of making information available to all.

Technology

Closely related to this focus on the user is the theme of how computer technology is changing both the nature of the questions to be answered and the tools available to study those questions. The most obvious example is the online public access catalog (OPAC). As Svenonius makes clear, the development of OPACs generated a need for considerable research on many aspects of bibliographical control. Automation of catalogs also enabled researchers to study the content of catalog records more precisely and to examine search logs that facilitate the study of user behavior. The Svenonius chapter and the Potter chapter should be read together. Whereas Potter points out that the significant research on advanced technology for use in libraries was done elsewhere, Svenonius describes work done within the library community to answer questions generated by the use of automation to achieve the traditional bibliographical control function of libraries. Such studies are also examined in the Whitlatch chapter on access services.

Technology is also mentioned prominently in other chapters. Lynch notes that research is needed on the impact of technology on the organizational structure of libraries. Getz urges librarians to examine carefully the consequences of specific technological change in library operations in order to determine whether the benefit of a particular change is greater than the cost. He also points out the potential of computers to facilitate the kind of analysis he believes is essential to library management. Early in his chapter, Metz observes that the power of computerized citation databases has been essential to the growth of bibliometrics. He ends the chapter by suggesting that library researchers and other bibliometricians must plan now for how they will analyze user interaction with emerging forms of electronic media.

Final Thoughts

Although the cumulative record of research in academic librarianship reveals gaps in coverage and lack of methodological rigor in some examples, recent trends are encouraging. The best studies tackle a significant problem, identify variables, formulate hypotheses, systematically collect and interpret data, and produce generalizable conclusions. There are outstanding studies in almost every aspect of the field. Encouragement should also be noted in the publishing arena. There are more publishers issuing monographs describing research on academic librarianship than ever before, and several journals frequently publish articles relevant to academic librarianship.

Incremental gains in the quality and impact of academic library research might be achieved through more attention to the research dimension of library education, practice, and publication. Library education at all levels must emphasize the value and conduct of research. Every student should be exposed to research methodology and have some experience in doing or evaluating research. Academic library leaders should require entry-level research competence from new graduates and reinforce the importance of research within their organizations. In the scholarly arena, more doctoral dissertations should be synthesized into periodical articles. A search of *Dissertation Abstracts International* reveals many studies on academic libraries that have not been so transformed. Since librarianship is often influenced by constituencies outside of the profession, nonlibrary journals ought to become regular outlets for our research reports. Finally, library associations, national and local, need to highlight the role and significance of research more systematically through forums, projects, grants, and awards. If these and other concerns are addressed, we remain optimistic that the developing body of research literature will advance the theory and practice of academic librarianship to a new level of maturity.

Notes

1. Charles R. McClure and Ann Bishop, "The Status of Research in Library/ Information Science," *College & Research Libraries* 50 (March 1989): 127–143.

2. Charles C. Curran, ed., "A Symposium on *A Library and Information Science Research Agenda for the 1980s*", *Library Research* 4 (Winter 1982): 385–400; Jane Robbins, "Another! Research Agenda," *Library and Information Science Research* 9 (July-September 1987): 141–142.

3. Pierce Butler, *Introduction to Library Science* (Chicago: Univ. of Chicago Pr., 1933).

Author Index

Subject Index

Contributors

Mary W. George received her A.B. and A.M. degrees both in English, as well as her A.M.L.S., from the University of Michigan and has completed course work for a Ph.D. in information and library studies at Rutgers University. She has been head of the General and Humanities Reference Division of Princeton University's Firestone Library since 1980 and an adjunct Associate Professor at Drexel University's College of Information Studies since 1982, teaching courses in user education and humanities reference. She was co-author of *Learning the Library* (New York: Bowker, 1982) and co-editor of the bibliographic instruction journal *Research Strategies* from 1983 to 1989.

Malcolm Getz received a B.A. from Williams College and a Ph.D. from Yale University, both in economics. He is associate provost for Information Services and Technology and associate professor of economics at Vanderbilt University, Nashville, Tennessee. He is the author of *The Economics of the Urban Fire Department* (Baltimore: Johns Hopkins Univ. Pr., 1979), *Public Libraries: An Economic View* (Baltimore: Johns Hopkins Univ. Pr., 1980), and co-author of *Price Theory and Its Uses* (Boston: Houghton, 1981). He has contributed a column on economic issues in libraries to *The Bottom Line* since its inaugural issue.

Beverly P. Lynch is dean and professor of the Graduate School of Library and Information Science at UCLA, a post she has held since 1989. She was university librarian at the University of Illinois at Chicago from 1977 to 1989. Lynch received her Ph.D. from the University of Wisconsin, Madison, her library degree from the University of Illinois at Urbana–Champaign, and her undergraduate degree from North Dakota State University, which presented her with an honorary degree in 1980. The author of four books and over 100 papers, Lynch is recognized for her work on standards for college and university libraries and for her research and writing on the organization and management of research libraries. She presently is engaged in a research project studying the impact of technology and structure on the organization of university libraries.

The recipient of numerous awards and active in many professional organizations, Beverly Lynch served as president of the American Library Association in 1985–86.

Mary Jo Lynch is director of the ALA Office for Research, a position she has held since 1978. She holds a Ph.D. from Rutgers University, master's degrees from the University of Michigan and the University of Detroit, and a B.A. from Marygrove College. Lynch was a reference librarian at the University of Detroit and the University of Massachusetts and taught at the University of Michigan, Rutgers University, and Wayne State University. She has written extensively on reference service, planning and measurement of library service, and research on libraries and librarianship. Lynch has directed numerous survey research projects for ALA, including the annual *ALA Survey of Librarian Salaries,* and has completed several contracts for the National Center for Education Statistics related to national statistics on libraries.

Paul Metz received his Ph.D. and M.L.S. from the University of Michigan in 1977. He is currently principal bibliographer at the library of Virginia Polytechnic Institute and State University. He is the author of *The Landscape of Literatures: Use of Subject Collections in a University Library* (Chicago: American Library Assn., 1983) and of numerous articles on collection use and collection development.

Charles B. Osburn earned a Ph.D. degree at the University of Michigan and master's degrees at Penn State University and the University of North Carolina. He is dean of libraries and professor of library and information studies at the University of Alabama. He serves on the board of directors of SOLINET, the Association of Research Libraries, and on the Research Libraries Advisory Council to OCLC. Osburn is the author of *Academic Research and Library Resources: Changing Patterns in America* (Westport: Greenwood, 1979), *Research and Reference Guide to French Studies,* 2nd edition (Metuchen: Scarecrow, 1981), and is co-editing *Collection Management: A Treatise* (to be published by JAI Press in 1990).

William Gray Potter holds a Ph.D., a master's in library science, and a master's in English, all from the University of Illinois at Urbana–Champaign. He is currently director of libraries at the University of Georgia and has also held library positions at the University of Illinois at Urbana–Champaign and the University of Wisconsin, Whitewater. From 1984 to 1989, he was editor of *Information Technology and Libraries,* the quarterly journal of the Library and Information Technology Association (LITA), and was president of LITA from 1987–88. Many of his numerous publications emphasize the use of advanced technology to improve and expand library services.

Elaine Svenonius completed her Ph.D. at the Graduate Library School, University of Chicago. She is presently a professor at the Graduate School of Library and Information Science, University of California, Los Angeles and does research and consulting on the design of controlled vocabularies. She has edited several books and written many articles in the areas of cataloging, classification, and indexing. Recent works include "Design of Controlled Vocabularies" (in *The Encyclopedia of Library and Information Science*, vol. 45, 1990), *The Conceptual Foundations of Descriptive Cataloging* (Academic Pr., 1988), and "Unanswered Questions in the Design of Controlled Vocabularies" (*JASIS*, 1986).

Jo Bell Whitlatch completed her Ph.D. at the University of California, Berkeley. Currently, she is associate library director, Access and Bibliographic Services, San Jose State University. She has written articles on document availability, user studies, and innovation in academic libraries. She has served as president of the California Academic and Research Librarians and been active in ALA's Library Administration and Management Association and Reference and Adult Services Division.

Arthur P. Young is dean of libraries, University of South Carolina. He held a similar position at the University of Rhode Island from 1981 to 1989 and prior administrative positions at the University of Alabama and the State University of New York, College at Cortland. Young received a Ph.D. in library science from the University of Illinois, master's degrees from the University of Massachusetts and Syracuse University, and the undergraduate degree in political science from Tufts University. He is the author or compiler of five books, two dozen articles, and 100 book reviews. Young's writings have focused on bibliographic instruction, reference service, and library history. Active in the American Library Association, he served as chair of the Library History Round Table (1985–86) and editor of ACRL Publications in Librarianship (1982–88).